Modern Language Association of America

Options for Teaching

Joseph Gibaldi, Series Editor

Teaching Literature and Other Arts

Edited by

Jean-Pierre Barricelli,
Joseph Gibaldi,
and
Estella Lauter

The Modern Language Association of America
New York   1990

Library of Congress Cataloging-in-Publication Data

Teaching literature and other arts / edited by Jean-Pierre Barricelli,
    Joseph Gibaldi, and Estella Lauter.
       p.   cm. — (Options for teaching; 10)
    Includes bibliographical references.
    ISBN 0-87352-364-4   ISBN 0-87352-365-2 (pbk.)
    1. Arts—Study and teaching.   I. Barricelli, Jean-Pierre.
II. Gibaldi, Joseph, 1942-   . III. Lauter, Estella, 1940-
IV. Series.
NX280.T417   1990   89-13829
700'.7—dc20

Cover illustration of the paperback edition: Raphael, Apollo and Muses, detail from
Parnassus, fresco, Hall of the Segnatura, Vatican. *The Vatican: Its History, Its
Treasures*, ed. Ernesto Begni (New York: Letters and Arts, 1914), 141.

Second printing 1992

Published by The Modern Language Association of America
10 Astor Place, New York, New York 10003-6981

Contents

Introduction

Over the past half-century, the research, study, and teaching of literature in its relations to other arts has evoked an unusual amount of interest. This relatively new discipline is variously and sometimes awkwardly called comparative arts, interdisciplinary arts, interart studies, interrelationships of the arts, and mutual illumination of the arts, in addition to more specific rubrics drawn from particular arts (literature and painting, literature and music). René Wellek's influential 1941 essay "The Parallelism between Literature and the Arts," in many ways the starting point for modern interart scholarship, was followed by such book-length studies, several now considered classic texts in the field, as Calvin Brown's *Music and Literature*, Thomas Munro's *Arts and Their Interrelations*, Jean Hagstrum's *Sister Arts*, John Hollander's *Untuning of the Sky*, Rensselaer Lee's *Ut Pictura Poesis*, Mario Praz's *Mnemosyne: The Parallel between Literature and the Visual Arts*, H. James Jensen's *Muses' Concord*, James Winn's *Unsuspected Eloquence*, Mary Ann Caws's *Eye in the Text*, Wendy Steiner's *Colors of Rhetoric*, Estella Lauter's *Women as Mythmakers: Poetry and Visual Art by Twentieth-Century Women*, John Neubauer's *Emancipation of Music from Language*, W. J. T. Mitchell's *Iconology*, and Jean-Pierre Barricelli's *Melopoiesis: Approaches to the Study of Literature and Music*, to name but a few. At present, books and articles devoted to the subject of the comparative arts are so numerous that researchers in the field must be thoroughly familiar with, among other resources, *Heliconian*, the American Comparative Literature Association's newsletter devoted to literature and other arts, which publishes relevant information as well as abstracts of many scholarly works; and two annual publications—the *Bibliography on the Relations of Literature and the Other Arts* and the *MLA International Bibliography*.

The Modern Language Association of America has consistently reflected this expanding interest through its annual bibliography and the meetings and publications it sponsors. In 1941, the year of the Wellek paper, the association inaugurated the legendary General Topics 9 discussion group, originally entitled Literature and the Arts of Design, with Austin Warren, Wellek's celebrated collaborator, as a member of the founding advisory committee. At the group's first meeting, Ruth C. Wallerstein, chair of the

Committee on a Program of Research, led a discussion on "the problems before the group." Wellek himself first lectured before the group in 1945, on the topic Baroque in Continental European Scholarship. He became the group's secretary in 1947, its chair in 1948, and thereafter a member of its advisory committee through 1953. In 1949, the group officially changed its name to Literature and Other Arts, and when the association reorganized its convention structure in 1976 to reflect more accurately the scholarly and professional concerns of its members, the group evolved into the Division on Literature and Other Arts. It eventually developed into one of the MLA's largest and most active divisions, annually offering its membership scholarly and pedagogically oriented panels on significant and timely topics.

As further recognition of the proliferation and importance of comparative arts scholarship, the MLA's 1967 collection *Relations of Literary Study* (ed. Thorpe) contained the essay "Literature and Music" by Bertrand H. Bronson; its 1982 volume of introductory essays, *Interrelations of Literature* (ed. Barricelli and Gibaldi), offered "Literature and Music" by Steven Paul Scher, "Literature and the Visual Arts" by Ulrich Weisstein, and "Literature and Film" by Gerald Mast. The more recent of these volumes, aimed principally at nonspecialists, including students, presents for each of the thirteen interrelations represented an enunciation of its nature and value; a historical overview, including a history of relevant scholarship; a selection of methodological analyses; discussion of major issues; consideration of prospects for contemporary research; and a basic bibliography.

Other scholarly organizations have similarly recognized the importance of interart scholarship. The American Comparative Literature Association and the International Comparative Literature Association, for example, have sponsored entire conferences and regularly offer panels and papers on the subject. Such papers are also a permanent part of programs at meetings of regional literary associations (such as the Midwest, Northeast, Rocky Mountain, South Atlantic, and South Central Modern Language Associations and the Philological Association of the Pacific Coast) as well as of more specialized professional organizations (e.g., American Society for Eighteenth-Century Studies and the American Institute for Writing Research).

Despite all this activity, comparative arts scholarship and teaching are still very much in an inchoate state; thus there exists a conspicuous need for materials that would help both specialists and generalists to translate interrelational scholarship into the classroom. This volume begins to meet that need.

When we conceived of this project, we expected to address most of the major interrelations of literature and other arts—music, painting, sculpture, architecture, film, dance, theater, photography. But when we began to consider for inclusion in the volume actual interart courses, including those derived from the files of the MLA Division on Literature and Other Arts, which the division generously shared with us, and those submitted in response to our professionwide call in the *MLA Newsletter* for appropriate materials, the number and quality of courses proved overwhelming. We therefore decided, in the light of the page limitation imposed on us and in the hope of presenting a more unified and more useful book, to focus our volume specifically on literary interrelations with music and the visual arts (painting, sculpture, and architecture), although several of our contributors involve dance, theater, film, and so on, in their teaching. This volume, then, represents an initial step in addressing the need for publications devoted to interdisciplinary teaching. We hope that other colleagues will, in due time, create companion volumes concerned with teaching the relations of literature with such disciplines as politics, science, and psychology.

Our present volume focuses primarily on undergraduate teaching and addresses the nonspecialist and graduate student, though specialists will doubtless find much of interest and use within these pages. In addition to serving teachers of literature, the volume can assist the work of art historians, musicologists, and other scholars in related fields who have independently proceeded along parallel courses and who now similarly find meaning in the stimulation provided by the comparative study of the arts.

In selecting the essays and syllabi for a volume devoted to a field still in the early stages of development, we have sought not to present courses as rigid models but rather to reflect the broad variety of interart courses currently available and the vast range of critical orientations and pedagogical methodologies applied in the undergraduate classroom. We have included the experimental as well as the traditional, the theoretical as well as the pragmatic, the more narrowly designed as well as the more broadly focused courses taught in various kinds of institutions in diverse geographical regions. Since our objective is to be informative and descriptive, we have sought out contributions that seem engaging, coherent, representative, and useful and that provide a rich selection of ideas for designing and redesigning courses and curricula. The bibliography is itself an invaluable resource for all teachers of comparative arts.

For the sake of clarity, we have arranged the essays and syllabi into five broad categories, with the awareness that some materials could well appear in more than one category. The first section offers contributions by Jon D. Green, Claus Clüver, Mary Ann Caws, and W. J. T. Mitchell on theoretically oriented courses indicating several of the many directions currently being explored. In the second section are courses that systematically focus on specific interrelations, such as literature and painting (Wendy Steiner), literature and architecture (Jesse J. Easley), and literature and music (Robert Spaethling), while Anthony Mazzella studies adaptations of literature into other media.

Since a great deal of innovation takes place across our educational system, in general education and in introductory courses designed to meet academic requirements, we include in the next section contributions representing radically different approaches to this opportunity. James V. Mirollo's course seeks to clarify the history of Western culture by studying its embodiment in literature and visual art. Linda Dittmar shows how a core interdisciplinary course may be taught effectively by different faculty members to diverse students in an urban university. Jean-Pierre Barricelli uses interart comparisons in conjunction with broad concepts of order and freedom to explore historically significant values of Western and non-Western cultures.

If the essay and syllabus proposals we received are typical of the field at large, period courses remain the most common type of comparative-arts approach, at least in the classroom. Yet the contributions we include here— on the baroque in Europe (Joseph Gibaldi); nineteenth-century fiction, music, and painting (Robert K. Wallace); the arts, not to mention scientific, technological, and other cultural developments, of the single year 1913 (J. Theodore Johnson); and twentieth-century ideas in literature and painting (Betty Jean Craige)—raise significant questions about the concept of "period" even as the authors find fresh ways to continue to make the concept meaningful.

Our final section on themes and topics includes some of the more experimental courses. Marcia Green treats the well-known literary theme of Faust's pact with the devil in music and literature, building the concept of the pact into the course format. Estella Lauter examines the role that women artists play in changing culturally accepted images of women, thus increasing our sensitivity to issues of race, ethnicity, and gender in interart analysis. Sidney H. Bremer describes her course as one in which the city is both a theme to be analyzed and an environment that conditions the creation and reception of literature. All three of these teachers are uncommonly attentive to the changes in the theme or image made by the medium and by the context in which it appears.

Each of the eighteen essays in the book is followed by a syllabus describing the course, setting forth its objectives, and outlining its schedule of classes. The appendix offers six additional syllabi outlining worthy interart courses that we could not treat as full essays simply because we did not have sufficient space. These useful materials include syllabi for Stephen C. Behrendt's theoretically oriented course Literature and the Other Arts; Mildred Meyer Boaz's Literature and Music; Gail Lynn Goldberg's course on the interart relations in illustration; Laura L. Doan's introductory course on literature, music, and the visual arts taught within the limits of a national-literature department; Richard Dellamora's Fantasy in Nineteenth-Century Literature and Art; and Ainslie Armstrong McLees's course on poetry, art, and music from 1850 to 1930.

The Works Cited lists all theoretical, critical, and scholarly works and all anthologies cited as well as all primary texts quoted in the volume. To keep the listing manageable in size, we have omitted well-known primary works that are only casually referred to in the essays and syllabi. An index of names and anonymous works rounds off the book.

In the questions raised and the answers proposed, all the essays and syllabi show the effects of recent theorizing about the interrelations of the arts. Although no evidence of a party line appears, a tendency toward contextual approaches to interpretation is more apparent than we expected, replacing or rather extending mid-century preoccupations with exclusively formal concerns. Thus the framers of these courses are as likely to worry about being truthful to aesthetic or historical experience embodied in the arts as about preserving the integrity of terms or forms.

Throughout the volume, many reasons are given for pursuing interdisciplinary study rather than, or in addition to, the specialized instruction now deeply entrenched and actively promoted by traditional academic departments. Most of us would probably agree that the comparative study of the arts—the study of our verbal experience in relation to our visual and aural experiences—helps us more fully to understand and appreciate the creative process and human artistic achievement as well as human experience itself. And most of our contributors probably share our view that this book contains hopeful signs of a definite pedagogical and perhaps even an epistemological and a cultural reorientation, one far from completed but at least begun.

J-PB, JG, EL

Theoretical Courses

Jon D. Green

Determining Valid Interart Analogies

I begin the course Literature and the Other Arts with an attempt to open the students' thinking to some of the important questions hovering over interart studies. I first ask, How do the arts differ from other humanist disciplines and the sciences? This leads to questions about the definition of art—for example, what is the basis for assembling all these diverse artifacts under one heading? Briefly, I suggest three possible approaches to the ostensible relatedness of the arts: (1) the common-ancient-origins approach, in which we explore the possibility that the separate fine arts evolved from an Ur-gesamtkunstwerk, and that the individual arts then split off from this "ancient unity" like stem languages from some primeval root, or like branches on the family tree; (2) the experiential-psychological approach, where we consider the possibility that the arts are extensions of the senses in time and space; and (3) the structural-semiotic approach, whereby the arts can be viewed as alternative language systems. Discussion of this last point provides a logical transition into the body of the class material: important essays and book excerpts selected from the best scholarship in the field and varying each term according to the most recent scholarship.

To permit diversity and still retain some thread of continuity, I treat the major relations of the arts as they arise chronologically in history, using appropriate variations of a familiar Latin phrase to title the three major units for the course: classical *ut pictura poesis* (comparing literature and the visual arts); romantic *ut musica poesis* (comparing literature to music); and, finally, modern *ut musica pictura* (comparing music and painting). This tripartite division corresponds neatly to Jacques Barzun's famous study *Classic, Romantic, and Modern*; it also lends itself with slight modifications to M. H. Abrams's four critical orientations in *The Mirror and the Lamp*.

Selections from Plato's *Republic* and the *Laws*, as well as Aristotle's *Poetics*, Horace's *Ars Poetica*, and Plutarch's *Moralia*, make clear why the ancients saw literature and the visual arts as sisters, and the opening chapters of Jean Hagstrum's *Sister Arts* (esp. ch. 1) serve as an excellent historical overview of the *ut pictura poesis* tradition. In-class discussion focuses on "The Painting-Literature Analogy," the first chapter of Wendy Steiner's probing *Colors of Rhetoric*, in which she presents a historical and semiotic analysis that dovetails effectively with the structural-semiotic section of the introduction. Working through Steiner's arguments, we encounter the dilemma of trying to "read" a painting linguistically. We conclude that a painting is not dependent on the phoneme-morpheme relation that holds in verbal language because painting offers a much wider latitude for "syntactic deviance" than literature does. In other words, the sound-meaning connections in words are bound more strictly by syntactical conventions than are form-meaning connections in paintings, primarily because we communicate with words, not images. Nevertheless, Steiner's detailed analysis of the semiotic relation between Pieter Brueghel's painting *The Return of the Hunters* and William Carlos Williams's poem "The Hunters in the Snow" reveals hitherto unimagined structural similarities between paintings and poems in terms of structural analogues, framing, color-phoneme correspondences, and the creation of ambiguity.

We also explore other more conventional interrelations, such as Aristotle's comparison of design in painting and plot in literature or the linkage of visual perspective and fictional point of view. We become aware of the limitations of these media as we compare the two arts. For example, painting is more limited than literature is in what it can make known. "Pictures can't say 'ain't'," writes Sol Worth, nor can they depict conditions ("What if?"), express past and future verb tenses, or comment on themselves, as by saying "This is not a painting." They can, however, comment on their own subject matter in cryptic ways, as in René Magritte's surrealist spoof *Ceci n'est pas une pipe* (*This Is Not a Pipe*). With this theory under their belts, the students are prepared to launch into their own comparative efforts to relate painting to literature.

M. H. Abrams charts the next theoretical shift in interart criticism, which occurred at the end of the eighteenth century—a shift in aesthetic focus toward the artist and an expressive view of art. He writes, "The use of painting to illuminate the essential character of poetry—*ut pictura poesis*—so widespread in the eighteenth century, almost disappears in the major criticism of the romantic period" (50). In its place we have a new doctrine—*ut musica poesis.*

After a short introduction to the historical backgrounds relating to music and literature, I follow Steven Paul Scher's schema of the triadic relations between music and literature ("Literature"). First, I introduce the students to literature *in* music, which embraces all aspects of program music. After reading the relevant chapters (18 and 19) from C. S. Brown's pioneering *Music and Literature,* we analyze Claude Debussy's *Prelude to "The Afternoon of a Faun"* on the basis of the Norton Critical Score (which includes the authoritative score, Stéphane Mallarmé's poem, plus background sources, criticism, and analysis).

Regarding literature *and* music, Jack M. Stein (*Poem* 9–27) helps the students think through the difficulty of blending text and tune in the German lied. We then apply Stein's theory to Brown's analysis of Franz

Schubert's *Der Erlkönig* (70–81). Finally, we tackle the most complex and sublime of all forms of music-drama, opera, focusing attention on Wagnerian opera and Wagner's theories concerning the relation of music and word (leitmotiv) and music and drama.

To study the third musical-literary relation, music *in* literature—or "the musicalization of fiction," as Aldous Huxley wrote in *Point Counter Point*—we take three well-known literary works and analyze some musically pregnant parts of them: the verbal evocation of Wagner's prelude to act 2 of *Die Meistersinger von Nürnberg* found in Thomas Mann's *Doktor Faustus*; the polyphonic structure and musicalization of words in the "Sirens" chapter of James Joyce's *Ulysses*; and, an instance Scher overlooks, the insertion of actual musical notation into the body of a fictional work in Arthur Schnitzler's short novel *Fräulein Else*.

We conclude this section by discussing relevant parts of Leonard Bernstein's controversial Norton Lectures, published as *The Unanswered Question*, in which Bernstein makes brilliant although sometimes questionable connections between Chomskian linguistics and the corresponding phonology, syntax, semantics, and "meaning" of music.

If any one thing can characterize the direction the arts have taken until recently in the twentieth century, it is the flight from mimesis, "a zest for dismantlement and devaluation, denial and detachment" (Schmidgall 360). The new art relation of modernism, which I label *ut musica pictura* (as with music, so with painting), is a concept that was most memorably given expression by Walter Pater in his book *The Renaissance*: "All art constantly aspires towards the condition of music" (140). We spend some time discussing the theoretical-mathematical basis for linking music and the visual arts, from Pythagoreanism through Renaissance humanism to modern abstraction. Incidentally, a useful way to help students understand the expressive power of modern abstract art (which is often difficult for them to accept) is to draw analogies to music (whose abstract sound patterns they readily and naturally accept) and then introduce them to the music-based theories and paintings of Wassily Kandinsky.

It is a curious coincidence that, in the history of this new doctrine of *ut musica pictura*, the two artists most responsible for its creative realization, Kandinsky and Paul Klee, were co-workers in the Blue Rider movement of early German expressionism and later teaching colleagues at the Bauhaus. They also represent, respectively, the mystical and mathematical poles of the musicalization of painting in the early twentieth century. Equally coincidental is the close personal and artistic relationship Kandinsky had with Arnold Schönberg, the pioneer of modern atonal music. The students read essays from the *Blue Rider Almanac*, especially those by Kandinsky and Schönberg.

A major challenge for any such course is to generate valid principles for interart comparisons. As recently as 1976, Ulrich Weisstein concluded that the "comparative arts" had come of age as a new sibling of comparative literature. Yet many of the books and articles on the subject are "seriously flawed in their methodological fabric" (6). Thus, I begin this section by showing the students some flawed comparisons of the arts and end by offering a tentatively valid methodology of my own.

Some of the most fertilely flawed studies emerged from the early-twentieth-century practitioners of German *Geistesgeschichte*: Oswald Spengler, for example, speaks of the "visible chamber music of [eighteenth-century] bent furniture," or the *"basso continuo* of [Rembrandt's] costumes" (qtd. in Wellek, "Parallelism" 35–36); more recently, Wylie Sypher considers a Gothic interior a manifestation of the *sic et non* of scholastic thought (*Four Stages* 25) and Mario Praz points to the striking likeness between the typical conical headdress of fifteenth-century ladies and a flamboyant Gothic pinnacle (*Mnemosyne* 28). For Praz, such likenesses verify "beyond all doubt" that *air de famille* that seems to exist between the expressions of the various arts in any historical epoch.

After introducing my students to some of these memorably flawed studies. I have them read several critical essays on art parallels in general: James D. Merriman's "Parallel of the Arts: Some Misgivings and a Faint Affirmation," Susanne K. Langer's candid criticism in her essay "Deceptive Analogies: Specious and Real Relationships among the Arts," and Alastair Fowler's "Periodization and Interart Analogies." From all this reading and our class discussions, we arrive at some basic sources of error in searching out parallels in the arts:

1. *Quellenforschung* tries to ferret out historical sources and cultural influences on art interrelations. A "good" bad example is Helmut Hatzfeld's *Literature through Art*, which seeks to illuminate literature by means of art and art by means of literature, but which provides merely superficial illustration of "the common spirit [*zeitgeist*] in literature and art at a certain epoch" (v).

2. *Geistesgeschichte* assumes that each period has a zeitgeist 'time spirit' that imposes a unifying, stylistic unity on the cultural activities of any given age, a complete parallelism of the arts and sciences. Jean Hagstrum notes, "One can scarcely avoid feeling that such studies serve the purposes of cultural mysticism, not of sober investigation" (xiv).

3. *Inadequate samples* create situations where the resemblances may be only coincidental. One needs to verify causal relations, if possible. An example of this error is James Laver's identification of the Charioteer of Delphi, a Hellenic Greek sculpture, with an Ionic column (see Praz, *Mnemosyne* 29).

4. *Metaphorical transfer of terminology* involves the attempt to compare two elements in different media that seem to be alike but ultimately serve different functions; for example, when Shakespeare's "dramatic perspective" is linked metaphorically (read "loosely") to Renaissance visual perspective.

5. *Subjective responses and free associationism.* Subjective responses are characterized by phrases such as "is reminiscent of" or "calls to mind." Merriman cautions us to avoid letting our subjective responses to art objects "infiltrate our supposedly objective critical and scholarly assertions about art objects" (155).

While I agree generally with these precautionary warnings about loose analogizing among the arts, I find highly problematic, even distressing, the narrow objectivity demanded by most comparative arts criticism. Merriman concludes, "Valid comparison . . . will require the development of sophisticated methods and scales of measurement for the incidence of each kind of individuation, methods of weighting such specific measurements in order to arrive at a composite scoring for each innate form in a given art work" (318). A rigorous application of Merriman's requirements would, it seems to me, amount to the "dissective emasculation" of the aesthetic experience itself, like seeking the secret of a frog's life in its scattered remains. There has to be some middle ground between vacuous admiration and clinical disinterest; complete comparative criticism must yield not only intellectual illumination but also emotional satisfaction. These reciprocally enhancing critical stances both belong in a balanced analytic-synthetic approach, much as Erwin Panofsky connects "intuitive aesthetic re-creation and archaeological research" in his art historical method ("History" 16). But in the real world of comparative arts criticism, such a balanced methodology is almost unknown. Interestingly, the dual nature of art itself parallels this critical dichotomy, for the power of art resides precisely in the suspended tensions of its dual physical-spiritual nature: its material medium (words, stones, sound, pigments, etc.) becomes imbued with spiritual significance by the artist's creative "ministrations" on it. Traditional comparative arts criticism is plagued with the dilemma of an analytic-reductive methodology that is used almost exclusively to comprehend a synthetic-hierarchical medium (using Vitz and Glimcher's terminology from their *Modern Art and Modern Science*).

I therefore conclude by suggesting the following pattern in validating analogies among the major fine arts:

In the first place, we must begin at the end, with the intuited notion of common effects. To a sensitive critic, this stage is invaluable as a guide to later analytical sifting. Intuition provides an indispensable tool with which to begin building bridges between aesthetic criticism and aesthetic experience, for "Intuition is the basic process of all understanding" and is "just as operative in discursive thought as in clear sense perception and immediate judgment" (Langer, *Feeling and Form* 29). In other words, the gut reactions that prompt us occasionally to notice some striking similarity between two seemingly unrelated works of art are often reliable cues to deeper structural and functional similarities.

After mentally cataloging intuited likenesses, we pay careful attention to differences between media. As Joseph Burke admits, "The ultimate justification of comparative studies is the light they throw on differences, and through these on creative originality" ("Hogarth" 173–74). There are certain experimental limitations and potentials germane to each medium, particularly in comparisons of spatial and temporal arts. To provide a graphic demonstration of this, I sometimes use the "penlight analogy," attempting to read a painting as one reads a novel, by illuminating successive portions of a painting with a penlight in a darkened room. Imagine the difficulty of trying to visualize the whole work from such fragmentary exposure. As Jean Laude says, "Absolutely everything distinguishes a literary text from a painting or drawing: its conception, its method of production, its modes of appreciation, its identity as an object irreducible to any other object, and its autonomous functioning" (471). What, then, can one use as a point of comparison? Laude's conclusion echoes virtually every major criticism of specious analogies from Wellek's famous treatise of 1942 to analyses of the present: compare the works themselves, in terms of function and form.

Therefore, the third step is to establish functional relations between comparable elements of any two art mediums. At this stage many comparatists often confuse apples and oranges. Rhythm, for example, is present in the organization of every art, but each medium presents it differently: the rectilinear rhythms of Piet Mondrian's *Broadway Boogie-Woogie* (1942–43), for example, create a static two-dimensional visual analogue of boogie-woogie music, albeit without the perceptual control of heard musical rhythms. The linear arrangement of blocks of color represents the petrified remains of living, moving sound, "diagrams of . . . energy and order," writes Robert Hughes (207). Of course, Mondrian's title helps to clarify the comparison. Indeed, without the specific musical reference in the title, one would be hard-pressed to match the visual design to any particular musical style, although one could probably dismiss rococo and Romanticism as possibilities. Thus, in this case, rectilinear patterns of primary colors in varying cubical sizes are comparable to the simple, syncopated regularity of a boogie-woogie beat, creating analogous effects within the context of each medium (looking at the Mondrian and listening to a jazz piano would obviously be two different experiences) and within the context of the artist's style. E. H. Gombrich points out that, in comparison to Gino Severini's futurist canvases, even Mondrian's painting doesn't seem all that "jazzy," although it certainly does in the context of Mondrian's more characteristically sterile style (*Art and Illusion* 373).

The most critical step may be the fourth one—determining structural similarities. It is the point of comparison that has been seen as the most reliable index of likeness between two different artistic mediums. Form is a more reliable index of aesthetic likeness than influence, zeitgeist, or subjective response is because it satisfies the critical demands of measurable specificity. But, more important, structure governs the *effects* of a work. For Clive Bell, Langer, and others, "significant form" is "the essence of every art" and "stirs our aesthetic emotions" (Langer, *Mind* 24, 33). In other words, it is form that generates feeling in a work of art. For example, the expressive power of music resides in the rise and fall of the melodic line, the harmonic tension and resolution, and the dynamic patterns created by tempo, timbre, dynamics, and so on. But music does more than trace the "morphology of feeling"; it also "reveals the rationale of feelings, the rhythm and pattern of their rise and decline and intertwining, to our minds" (Langer, *Philosophy* 238).

The value of Langer's aesthetics for establishing the structural stage of a comparatist strategy lies in her rigorously reductive methodology, her formalist aesthetics, and her demonstration of the vital connection between feeling and form in art. The traditional method for locating analogies between two arts is to search for the factors common to all the arts. Langer reverses the process by first tracing, as far as possible, the differences among the arts, eventually arriving at the point beyond which no more distinctions can be made. "It is the point where the deeper structural devices— ambivalent images, intersecting forces, great rhythms and their analogues in detail" demonstrate "the principles of dynamic form that we learn from nature" ("Deceptive Analogies" 25). Thus, for Langer, artistic form is organic form because "artistic form is always the form of felt life" (*Mind* 64).

Contrary to virtually all comparative criticism of the arts I have read, my methodology clearly reveals a commitment to individual subjective responses as the foundation for any comparative analysis; otherwise, as Wordsworth warned, "we murder to dissect." Gombrich shares this deep concern. In his brilliant essay *In Search of Cultural History*, he suggests that the humanities, in the process of "aping the sciences," have lost sight of the "holistic view" afforded by the unifying intuitive efforts of the imagination and the emotions (47–48). This bifurcation of perceptual modes has had grave consequences, not only geopolitically and culturally but psychologically and aesthetically.

As comparatists, we ultimately risk becoming afflicted by the twin evils of conceptual myopia and perceptual anesthesia. Therefore, in my view, a class like this must go beyond the teaching of critical skills or bibliographic techniques. The proper pursuit of this discipline places us on the cutting edge of issues that could reshape the whole academic endeavor.

Syllabus

Course   Literature and the Other Arts. Jon D. Green, Humanities, Brigham Young University.

Description   Required course for both undergraduate and graduate majors. Offered every other year, either fall or winter semester. Meets three times a week for one hour in both lecture and student presentation formats. No prerequisites except majors' writing and methods class.

Objectives   To introduce students to interdisciplinary scholarship in the arts; to determine valid and invalid comparisons between selected pairs of fine arts; to develop critical writing and bibliographic skills in individual research; to provide an informed context for the discussion of central humanistic issues.

Schedule

1–2. Introduction to course objectives and definition of terms. Panofsky, "History."

3–5. Comparing and contrasting the arts: common pitfalls. Weisstein et al.; Merriman; Wellek, "Parallelism," or Wellek and Warren 125–35; Langer, "Deceptive Analogies."

6–8. Issues in interrelations: periodization, *Doppelbegabung*, humor, etc. Fowler, "Periodization"; Koestler.

9–11. Literature and the visual arts: historical backgrounds. Plato, *Republic* 1 and 9, excerpts; Aristotle, *Poetics*, chapters 1–8, 25; Horace, *Ars poetica*, excerpts; Plutarch, *Moralia*, excerpts; Lessing, introduction, preface, chapters 1–3, 13, 16–18; Park; Steiner, *Colors* 1–32.

12–14. Bases of comparison and bibliographical overview. Weisstein, "Literature and the Visual Arts"; Steiner, *Colors*, chapter 2; J. Frank.

15–17. Applications. Steiner, *Colors*.

18. Music and literature. Scher, "Literature and Music"; Wallace, *Austen and Mozart* 18–37.

19. Poetry and music: history of relations. Winn 1–29, 287–346; Hollander 3–19.

20. Poetry and music: problems of combining. Stein, *Poem and Music* 9–29; C. S. Brown, *Music and Literature* 70–81.

21. Drama and music: two approaches to opera. Kerman, *Opera* 3–22; Schmidgall 3–28.

22–23. The Wagnerian *Gesamtkunstwerk: Der Ring des Nibelungen.* Stein, *Richard Wagner* 3–9; Cooke.

24. Literature in music: program music. Brown, *Music and Literature* 229–44.

25. Meaning in music. Hospers 78–98; Scher, "How Meaningful"; Bernstein 139–53.

26–28. Music in literature: word music, musical insertions, musical structures, and "verbal music." Joyce, *Ulysses* ("Sirens" ch.); Green; Basilius.

29–31. Musical analysis of Thomas Mann's *Doktor Faustus.* Scher, "Thomas Mann's."

32. Mathematical origins of music-art relations. Haar.

33. Renaissance theories of music-art relations. Wittkower, *Architectural* 103–26.

34. Modern practices: abstraction and mathematics. Lockspeiser 30–36, 145–48.

35. The Blue Rider movement: backgrounds. *The Blue Rider Almanac.* Kandinsky 114–219, 221–26.

36–37. Abstraction and music: Kandinsky.

38. Music and expressionism: Schönberg. Hahl-Koch 133–70.

39. Polyphonic paintings: Klee. Kagan 41–93, 95–143.

40. Operatic paintings: Klee.

41. Review. Preparation for final exam.

Claus Clüver

The Comparative Study of the Arts

Studies of interrelations are based on comparison; therefore, concepts, terms, and methods are needed not only for analyzing individual texts created in different sign systems but also for comparing them, and criteria must be developed by which such comparisons may be judged. These are the primary concerns of the course Modern Literature and Other Arts: An Introduction. Its orientation is consequently more analytical and critical than historical. Chronological relations are emphasized, but the course has not been designed as a study of movements and isms. Comparisons of canonical Western texts are, in fact, also used to suggest that the work of writers, painters, and composers has been governed, during the time span covered (1730–1980), by shared concerns, assumptions, and expectations and that some of these have remained fairly constant while others have undergone profound changes. Some attention is therefore paid to changes in the ways artists and their audiences have thought about what a work of art should be or do. But an introductory course cannot give a coherent historical overview. Students are made aware that the construction of a comparative history of the arts for the past 250 years would require looking at a great many different works as well as examining the social, economic, political, intellectual, and spiritual factors that may have motivated the changes in the ways art was produced and received. Still, considerations of changing conventions and expectations inform the course from the start.

The Arts and the Work of Art

In two initial exercises, students are asked to name all the arts they can think of and to group them according to affinities or shared qualities and properties; they are also presented with a variety of verbal, visual, and aural texts and requested to decide which of these qualify as works of art.

The first exercise makes students realize that the realm of the arts is much broader than what the course will cover and that the boundaries of this realm are difficult to draw. If theater, opera, dance, and mime are arts, what about such other performance arts as vaudeville, clowning, high-wire acts, figure skating, diving, gymnastics, and striptease? At the same time, students are made aware of both the inherent and the conventional criteria that may be used to group the arts and that thus are the basis for possible comparisons (e.g., temporal and spatial dimensions, the senses appealed to, functional considerations). Whereas divisions into simple and complex (multimedia or intermedia) arts or into autographic, allographic, and performance arts may be based on a descriptive approach, classifications into "pure" and "applied" or into "major" and "minor" arts are discovered to be conventional and dependent on societal and cultural values and norms.

The verbal texts offered anonymously in exercise 2 include an advertising couplet, Ezra Pound's "Metro" poem, an obituary and its transformation by Ronald Gross into a "pop poem," and a definition of literature. Pierre Schaeffer's *Railway Study* (an example of early *musique concrète*), a Robert Rauschenberg collage, and one of Josef Albers's *Homage to the Square* pieces are the nonverbal texts held up for consideration as potential artworks. (Most of these will be used again at a later stage.) Students will realize that they have all brought to the course firmly established notions about the nature and function of a work of art; many will find a number of those notions challenged by the discussion of these texts. Whatever the majority decision in each instance, students will recognize that almost none of the texts would have been accessible as art to earlier audiences, which suggests that the status "work of art" is not an inherent property perceived by competent readers but is conferred on a text according to standards and criteria accepted by the readers' interpretive community.

Acquiring Competence as Readers of Artistic Texts

Contemporary discourse may have made the concept of art problematic, but literature, painting, and music all continue to be considered as arts and, as such, related to one another. Before these interrelations can be studied, students must acquire a basic competence in reading verbal, musical, and pictorial texts. We begin with painting, because a visual artwork (or its slide image) can be conveniently placed in front of a class for all to see and point to. Without regard for chronology or historical developments, we proceed from the deceptively simple to the more complex. The first works studied are from the twentieth century, some of them quite recent. Such texts not only challenge conventional notions about the nature and function of art but tend to be self-referential, foregrounding their sign character—the signifying potential of their materials and the ways these materials have been organized. Structural analogies will form the basis of many later comparisons, and, throughout, works are treated as complex signs in the light of some fundamentals of Peircean semiotics, although semiotic terms form only a small part of the terminology to which students are introduced.

Painting   Piet Mondrian's *Composition in Black, White, and Red* (1936) and several of Albers's *Square* paintings illustrate the discussion in the *Basic Text* (Clüver, Solt, et al.) about the properties of the pictorial field and the role of the visual axes, of weight and balance, of visual stasis and dynamics, and of the interaction of colors. Students learn how to describe a painting in terms of its materials and their organization rather than in terms of representation. At the same time, questions are raised about how and what a nonrepresentational painting can be made to mean. This context is enlarged by comparing the Mondrian painting with a 1913 *Composition* by Wassily Kandinsky. Comparison as a tool is thus first introduced to elaborate contrasts within a shared approach—that of nonrepresentation—to image making. Comparison is next used to demonstrate parallels in the ways certain kinds of representational and nonrepresentational painting construct visual images: by withholding all information about its literary program, Jacques-Louis David's *Oath of the Horaces* (1784) is made to appear most accessible if approached with the questions that had been asked about the Mondrian. A side-by-side viewing of the *Oath* and an oil sketch for Eugène Delacroix's *Lion Hunt* (c. 1854) elucidates some contrasts within representational painting that parallel the contrasts discovered earlier in the Mondrian and Kandinsky compositions. Modes and conventions of representation are briefly considered as C. D. Friedrich's *Wreck of the Hope* (c. 1824), a Claude Monet, and an early cubist landscape are added to the repertoire. The introduction to painting culminates in two classes taught in the Indiana University Art Museum and emphasizing those aspects less apparent in slides: texture and the effects of physical media and painting techniques as well as the effect of size on the way viewers position themselves vis-à-vis a painting (we consider works by Morris Louis, Jackson Pollock, Alfred Leslie, and Pablo Picasso). Students are then asked to write a three- to four-page description of a painting in the museum.

Music   A (blank) tape version of John Cage's *4'33"* of 1952 provides the object for our initial discussion of music, raising questions about the possibility of hearing as music random noises occurring in the environment, about the institutional context permitting the piece to be experienced as a musical event, and about the extent to which this offering can be considered a composition. Examples of *musique concrète*—the organization of taped noises as musical material, by Schaeffer and, in more complex and sophisticated ways, by Iannis Xenakis in *Concret P-H II* (1958–68)—lead to considerations of changes in referentiality (transformation of indexical into iconic signs) and of musical structuring in the absence of melody and harmony. The question of such structuring is extended into an analysis of the first instrumental piece heard in the course, Edgard Varèse's *Ionisation* (1933). The concepts of tone color, rhythm, and musical texture are introduced or reinforced; questions are asked about the ways the composer has organized these elements to achieve form and coherence and about the conventions that allow the listener to recognize patterns and their connections and thus to experience more than just a random procession of instrumental noise.

Meanwhile, students have been listening outside class to a special course tape about fundamental conventions of the system of functional tonality. After these conventions have been discussed and clarified in class, we study how they have been applied by J. S. Bach in the construction of a simple minuet. Twentieth-century transformations of or ruptures with those conventions are exemplified by the first movement of Igor Stravinsky's neoclassical Octet for Wind Instruments (1923) and the fourth of Arnold Schönberg's atonal Five Pieces for Orchestra ("Peripetia," 1909). An essay assignment at this point asking for a description of a short musical piece has proved too difficult for most students; instead, the take-home midterm exam contains questions about the music section.

Literature   The discussion of the characteristics of literary texts starts with a sound poem by Ernst Jandl ("Devil Trap," 1970) and the question in what ways it might be considered a musical piece and what if anything makes it a literary text. A piece by Aram Saroyan consisting of a single letter, a four-legged "m" (1968; see Clüver, "From Imagism"), induces reflections about different sign functions of graphic marks and the signifying potential of letter shapes as well as about the arbitrary relations between sound and visual notation and between signifier and signified in verbal signs. These reflections are extended to concrete poems constructed out of single words, notably Robert Indiana's "LOVE" (1966) and Eugen Gomringer's "silencio" (1954), which is also considered in its German version and taken through a number of variations: its "literariness" may be seen in the transformation of the verbal sign from symbol to (visual and phonic) icon through the particular collocation of repeated instances of the word on the page. From there we go on to look at words in combination, both in spatial, nongrammatical arrangements that permit multidirectional readings (Haroldo de Campos, "branco," 1957) and in more traditional structures that use conventional syntax. An analysis of Dylan Thomas's villanelle "Do Not Go Gentle" (1952) introduces considerations of prosody, troping, and lyric voice; and John Keats's sonnet "Bright Star" (1819)—compared on the one hand with Sir Philip Sidney's "With How Sad Steps, Oh Moon" (1582) and William Shakespeare's "Let me not to the Marriage of True Minds" (1609) and on the other with Mary Ellen Solt's wordless "Moonshot Sonnet" (1964)—serves to examine the uses of a popular lyric form in the development of related motifs. Questions of literary language, free-verse techniques, and strategies of interpretation are central to the discussion of William Carlos Williams's "Young Housewife" (1917), which concludes this section of the course. Students are asked to write a three- to four-page analysis of a short lyric according to detailed instructions.

Comparing Pictorial, Musical, and Literary Texts

From comparing texts within each individual art form, we now proceed to systematic and detailed comparisons of a painting, a musical composition, and a literary text on a roughly synchronic basis: the study of three eighteenth-century works is followed by a comparative study of three works from the early nineteenth century. The emphasis is on parallels and analogies and on establishing grounds on which useful comparisons can be made.

Earlier observations about the formal features of David's *Oath* (1784) are linked to its representational and ideological aspects; its form, just as much as the artist's choice of theme and scene, can be read to express the worldview and values of the age. It is with regard to formal features, to the clarity and balance of structural elements and the well-defined hierarchical relations of the works' materials, that striking parallels can be shown to exist between the *Oath* and Wolfgang Amadeus Mozart's *Eine kleine Nachtmusik* (1781), which is studied as a miniature symphony. Though composed fifty years earlier, Alexander Pope's *Essay on Man* (we study the first epistle, 1733) does permit the construction of significant formal and ideological correspondences to David's work. Since the form of the *Nachtmusik* and the musical codes on which it draws exhibit such close parallels to the forms of the other two texts, it may be possible to conclude that musical form has the same signifying power as literary or pictorial form and is similarly susceptible to ideological interpretation.

The effort is repeated with a second series of works created roughly half a century later than their counterparts: Delacroix's *Death of Sardanapalus* (1826–27), Hector Berlioz's *Symphonie fantastique* (1828–30), and Samuel Taylor Coleridge's "Kubla Khan" (1797–98, 1816). Students now see that a new "style" has emerged, signaling that different values, standards, and conventions have come to govern the thinking of artists and their audiences; at the same time, a change can be observed in the artists' attitudes toward reality and in their concepts of the role of art and the artist.

The main purpose of the work in this section is to train students in some of the methods of interart comparison. They also learn to see that it may be possible to use these methods in the study of periods and movements and in the construction of a history of the arts—although they are warned not to consider the results of the comparison of one work by one painter, one poet, and one composer sufficient to draw any conclusions about European Romanticism. The results do, however, undermine commonly held notions about an artist's autonomy and originality: they suggest that every decision made by every artist—concerning choice of theme and subject matter, preference of certain physical media, emphasis on specific materials or qualities of the given material, and even the degree of "objectivity" and "subjectivity" to be communicated—is strongly influenced by the norms and conventions that govern the literary, musical, and pictorial production of the time. These norms and conventions are in their turn to be seen in the context of the experience of the age and of current views of the nature of human existence and of the universe.

The Question of Translation in the Arts

Much closer than the general similarities that can be observed among works created at roughly the same time are the relations established between specific texts by processes of illustration, musical setting, adaptation, and intersemiotic transposition. A detailed comparison of Anne Sexton's poem "The Starry Night" (1962) and Vincent van Gogh's painting by the same title (1889) reveals abundant correspondences, some of which are not immediately obvious. Students frequently resist the suggestion that the poem might be read as a translation of the painting; this notion offers grounds for a fruitful discussion. An analysis of the van Gogh is followed in the next period by a search in the poem for as many parallels and references to the painting as possible and also by an identification of those qualities and properties of Sexton's text that seem to have no parallel in van Gogh's work. Students are then asked to write an exercise (3 to 4 pages) summarizing the results of our classroom discussion and deciding on that basis how they would characterize the relation between the two texts (for a discussion of the van Gogh–Sexton comparison, see Clüver, "Transposition").

The Representation of Reality in the Arts

The "Starry Night" investigation has touched on questions of how late nineteenth-century painting and mid twentieth-century poetry could represent external reality and the subjective experience of that reality. The comparison of eighteenth- and early nineteenth-century works led to the conclusion that "reality" is not the same for every age. Following a chronological agenda, we turn to the representation of reality in the realist tradition, focusing first on painting and literature. A number of questions raised about Gustave Courbet's *Stonebreakers* (1849) are also asked about Gustave Flaubert's "Simple Heart" (1877). These two works are contrasted with the Pope-David and Coleridge-Delacroix pairs. An examination of the means by which Courbet and Flaubert create the image of a whole life (including the issue of how time is represented in the painting) and a sense of objective depiction leads to a discussion of the reader's role and the degree to which these two works remain "closed" texts: ultimately, the reader cannot escape the social criticism achieved by the generalizing anonymity of the workers or the ironic apotheosis of Felicité as a secular saint. Is James Joyce's "Clay" (1905–14), then, a more "open" text? Is the shift in technique from Flaubert to Joyce parallel to the shift from Courbet's depiction of landscape to Monet's? What strikes us as similar, what as different in the conception and representation of reality by Monet and Joyce? Why does Monet produce series of works on the same subject? (Monet's *Rouen Cathedral* series [1894] will later be compared with Albers's squares.)

One way of making sense of the photo-realism of the 1970s is to read it as a dialogue with pictorial impressionism: it is based on images of external reality as received and fixed by the photographic lens, in contrast to images created in rapid translation of visual impressions received by the human eye and mind. After showing one of Richard Estes's photo-realist cityscapes side by side with a Monet *Cathedral*, we explore possible parallels of his *Escalator, Bus Terminal* (1969) and Alain Robbe-Grillet's prose text "Escalator" (1959) from *Snapshots*, especially with regard to the implied observer/narrator (a camera lens?).

Musical representation of external reality, in both its physical aspects and its symbolic significance (Czech nationalism), is examined via Bedřich Smetana's *Moldau* (1874). Here we can show even more clearly than through the pictorial and literary examples that in the arts, all representational signs ultimately turn out to be based less on similarity (which would make them appear "natural") than on convention (which makes them look "artificial" to an audience that is not as familiar with the conventions involved). Smetana's means of musical representation are compared with Arthur Honegger's representation of a machine in *Pacific 2-3-1* (1923), and Honegger's portrait of a locomotive returns us to Schaeffer's use of machine-recorded railway noises for an electronic composition (c. 1948) that undercuts all construction of a musical narrative. Did the tape recorder serve the same function for Schaeffer as the camera lens did for Estes and Robbe-Grillet?

The final paper assigned at this point is a six- to eight-page comparison of a literary text with either a pictorial or a musical text, according to very detailed instructions. These do not, however, include suggestions about the point of the comparison: one of the major tasks is to come up with a worthwhile thesis. Students choose from among five pairings, but they are also permitted to propose their own.

The Twentieth Century: Redefining Conventions

The final section of the course brings back into view some of the twentieth-century works that were analyzed in the introductory sessions. They are now considered in some of the contexts that produced them. What may have appeared strange and difficult to understand in the beginning should now be perceived not as an arbitrary product of a willful individual but as a manifestation of new values and of yet another change in attitude toward reality and in the concept of the role of art and the artist. Consequently, we look at these works not only in the context of the individual artist's career but also as products of the age. Thus, Kandinsky's nonrepresentational "compositions" of 1913 are seen as a stage in a series that includes various modes of representation in the earlier work and leads to greater clarification and geometrization in the Bauhaus years and thereafter. At the same time, some poems from Kandinsky's *Klänge* (1913) are shown to exhibit analogous treatment of verbal and literary material. Schönberg's atonal "Peripetia" is considered as a possible musical counterpart to Kandinsky's early nonrepresentational work, and the composer's development of serialism is seen as having been motivated by the same needs that led to the painter's later formal devices: the institution of new conventions. Interest in the adaptation of received forms is emphasized in Thomas's villanelle and Stravinsky's use of sonata form and fugue in the Octet; Paul Klee's *Fugue in Red* (1921) exemplifies the translation of that musical form into a visual equivalent. An overview of the development of Mondrian's work and of some important phases of Albers's creative engagement with the "discrepancy between physical fact and psychic effect" (Harned and Goodwin 275) sets the stage for a comparison of constructivist, concrete, and op art with concrete poetry, for which these visual efforts served as models. E. E. Cummings's "brIght" and "r-p-o-p-h-e-s-s-a-g-r" (1935) are read as protoconcrete poems; a musical model is provided by an Anton Webern composition. The concrete text is also explored as an example of a characteristic twentieth-century phenomenon: the intermedia text that draws simultaneously on different sign systems. The observation that works reviewed in this last section were among the earliest objects we studied invites a brief assessment of what has been achieved.

Syllabus

Course   Modern Literature and Other Arts: An Introduction. Claus Clüver, Comparative Literature, Indiana University, Bloomington.

Description   Offered every semester, since 1954. On the original conception, see Frenz and Weisstein; on later developments, see Clüver, "Teaching." Each of several sections taught by one faculty member or specially trained graduate instructors. Sophomore level, no prerequisites; fulfills general humanities requirement and part of interart-studies concentration in comparative literature major. Meets for three fifty-minute sessions a week. Two classes held in University art museum. Tapes with musical analyses are on library reserve.

Objectives   To teach students how to read and analyze Western literary, pictorial, and musical texts created during the past 250 years and how to explore ways in which literature, painting, and music may be seen as interrelated; to introduce concepts, terms, and methods used in analyzing such texts and in comparing them; to examine contemporary notions about the nature and function of art. Some emphasis on semiotic approaches, on questions of iconicity and conventionality, and on ideological criticism.

Texts Clüver et al., *Basic Text* (*BT*), specifically designed for the course; Feldman.

Schedule

1. Introduction: The Arts and Their Interrelations.
2-3. What is a work of art? Assorted verbal texts; Schaeffer; Rauschenberg, Mondrian, Albers. *BT* 3–24; Feldman 2–29.
4-8. Introduction to painting. Visual perception and the painter's vocabulary. Mondrian and Kandinsky. David and Delacroix. Friedrich, Monet. Works in university art museum. *BT* 25–52; Feldman 30–61.
9-13. Introduction to music. Sounds and silences: listening to music (Cage, Xenakis). The composer's vocabulary; musical structure; meaning in music (Varèse). The conventions of functional tonality and an eighteenth-century application (Bach). Tradition and innovation (Stravinsky). Atonal music (Schönberg). *BT* 57–114.
14-18. Introduction to literature. The poet's materials: sound, visual shape, semantic charge (Jandl, Saroyan). Spatial syntax in the concrete ideogram (Gomringer, H. de Campos). Patterns of a conventional poem; image, metaphor, symbol (Dylan Thomas). Uses of a poetic form: the sonnet (Sidney, Shakespeare, Keats, Solt). Free verse (W. C. Williams). *BT* 121–59.
19-26. Comparing the arts: the synchronic perspective.
19-22. Three works from the eighteenth century: David, Mozart, Pope. *BT* 167–93; Feldman 196–202.
23-26. Three works from the early nineteenth century: Coleridge, Delacroix, Berlioz. *BT* 194–210; Feldman 202–05.
27. The diachronic perspective. The two groups compared.
28-29. "Translation" in the arts. Sexton and van Gogh. *BT* 212–17.
30-36. Representation in the arts: changing concepts of reality. Realism and impressionism in painting and literature (Courbet, Monet; Flaubert, Joyce). Seeing through the camera lens (Estes, Robbe-Grillet). Conventions of musical representation (Smetana). The machine as object and medium of representation in music (Honegger, Schaeffer). *BT* 221–49; Feldman 205–16.
37-42. The arts in the twentieth century: redefining conventions. Toward nonrepresentational painting and poetry: Kandinsky. From atonality to serialism: Schönberg. Adaptation of received forms (Dylan Thomas, Stravinsky, Klee). Toward constructivist art: Mondrian. Exploration of visual perception: Albers. Concrete poetry and painting. *BT* 262–92; essays by Kandinsky and Mondrian in Herbert.
43. Review and conclusions.

Mary Ann Caws

Perception in Literature and Art

The course I teach entitled Perception in Literature and Art concentrates on how what we see in visual and verbal texts may depend on what we know, or suspect, of the attitudes of their creators or producers, as well as on what we intuit from our previous knowledge, dependent as it is on our frame of vision. Our major presupposition is that the eye of the observer remakes what it is seeing, so that its own vision is as important as the object constructed. Such observation of our observation is necessarily linked to the principle of self-inclusion: the individual perceiving self is included in the scene observed. Choosing examples from various periods, styles, and schools and testing working theories on these examples, we consider the psychology of perception—along with historical, sociological, and philosophical factors—treating issues of context, including those of the course itself, as we proceed.

We raise the following questions to stimulate discussion: How do different schools of thought create different styles and expectations in different epochs? Is it likely that men and women perceive differently? What are the underlying suppositions in various creations? How can they be detected and then described? How does narrative stance correspond to aesthetic perspective? How might certain assumptions about the way the world works control what we are seeing and analyzing? We ask these and other questions not as means of eliciting specifically planned responses but, rather, as ways of opening up our own perception of problems and possible approaches—textual analysis, framing theory, narratology, psychoanalytic perspectives, and so on—and of deepening the ways in which we read. We then discuss the change of perception in relation to various art objects and schools (and their major advocates) insofar as they can illuminate the ways in which reading and perception change over time.

The point at issue in this course is controversial: briefly, it is whether the techniques useful for learning to "read" a text in one field are applicable to another. The course aims to develop perception of nuances and depth in both visual and literary arts. It also introduces the problematics of vision: Does the perception of the *kind* of vocabulary in the written work relate to the perception of the *kind* of brush stroke in the painted one? That is, can seemingly parallel artistic elements be made to mean anything? The interplay of theory and text along these lines can only be instructive, never conclusive. Presumably, the notion of such a course positively values double perceptions and encourages comparisons.

Perception in Literature and Art starts with the premise that learning to read in one field is valuable for the other. Our first few sessions are devoted to the theoretical underpinnings justifying comparison itself and to the various strategies of reading that will be useful for particular visual and verbal texts.

We begin by discussing perception. We look at psychological factors in perception and some philosophical and art-historical disquisitions on the subject before moving on to individual art objects and texts. The reading that accompanies the classroom work is, in general, standard: on the study of iconography and the history of art history (Erwin Panofsky, *Meaning*); on the psychological and theoretical coming to perception (Rudolf Arnheim, *Art*); on the art-historical angle of illusion, ornament, and metaphor (E. H. Gombrich, e.g., Gombrich, Hochberg, and Black); on some correlations and the semiotics of comparison (Wendy Steiner, *Colors*); on looking itself (John Berger, *About Looking*); on looking and painting (Norman Bryson, *Vision*); on the ideas of selection and framing (Jacques Derrida); on the idea of positioning between seer and seen (Michel Foucault, *Order*; a good representative of the poststructuralist mode. We note especially Foucault's interpretation of Velázquez's *Las Meñinas*: Who is present, in the royal couple's positioning in the door of the painting, and who is absent? What presuppositions do we make within the framework of representation or portrait painting? and so forth).

To approach the ways in which different schools of aesthetic thought might create different styles, we trace a figure or an image through its changing aspects as the years and schools go on. For example, the baroque artist Hendrik Goltzius saw Icarus as the hero of the fall, a concentration of twisted and knotted form hurtling backward. The style is dependent on the baroque delight in contortion itself. By contrast, artists who imitate the classics or give them new life emphasize the daring enterprise of challenge embodied in the poet Philippe Desportes's "Icarus, Fallen, Here." Human beings measured against the elements and falling short will be more the point than the falling per se; a lesson is drawn, to be remembered, and the Greek hubris is taken as a warning: Don't try to rise above yourself, or this fate awaits you.

In early modern times, in the context of orphism and cubism, Apollinaire, in a poetry of splendor and glorious occasion, sings of the sun toward which Icarus wanted to rise. The analogous visual works are a circular Robert Delaunay sun of high color in the natural world and, in the cultural one, his Eiffel Tower, akin to poems of Cendrars concerning both sun and tower. The trains of Cendrars and of Boccioni, and their notion of elasticity and simultaneity, bring futurism into our cubist approach. Last, in our own times, to the poets looking back to Pieter Brueghel's *Landscape with the Fall of Icarus*, only Icarus's legs appear; their smallness in relation to the elegance and luxury of a passing ship makes them seem a sadly insignificant human trace around which massive suffering turns. "About suffering," begins W. H. Auden's poem on the subject ("Musée des Beaux Arts"), but that suffering is insignificant by comparison with the rest of human labor (the ploughman under the sky). Or, in William Carlos Williams's poem "Landscape with the Fall of Icarus," on both Icarus and the painting by Brueghel, the drowning is just part of the natural ongoing cyclical movement of humans and seasons (see Caws, *Interference*). In each of these instances, the difference of the focus gives a clue as to the overall design under the rubrics baroque, classical, orphic, futurist, cubist, or modern-day philosophic.

The point of the course, then, is to ensure that students do theoretical reading alongside textual work. Thus, we study Nicolas Poussin's *Arcadian Shepherds* through Panofsky's careful identification and intense scholarly research ("Et in Arcadia Ego"). This work brings up the notions of discourse, address, voice, inscription, and detection. We then read Louis Marin's analysis, which in turn discusses both Panofsky and the issues and leads on to the poet Ian Hamilton Finlay's takeoff on tanks and tombs, on "lyrebirds" and lyres, still in relation to the issues of war and protest (Finlay and Costley). (The course cannot remain entirely free from the political elements deeply involved here.) We also study Arnheim's teaching about balance and imbalance, about the dynamics of form within the paintings, and we look particularly hard at his diagrams of such powerful paintings as Leonardo's *Last Supper*, with the strong line of the table controlling the way we are forced to look (*Art*).

When we study the baroque, we dwell on the ideas of pointing and singling out by arrows and darts within this literature and art (Saint Teresa seen by the poet Richard Crashaw, the painter Hercules Seghers, and the sculptor Gianlorenzo Bernini; see Caws, *Eye in the Text*), and we discuss the wounding and weeping as they strongly bring in the erotic. The students read Jacques Lacan on Saint Teresa and the hysterical and Sigmund Freud on Dora's case ("Fragment").

In subsequent discussions we consider, among others, the work of Susan Suleiman on feminism and the body, Ann Sutherland Harris and Linda Nochlin on feminism and art, Rosalind Krauss on the avant-garde, Fredric Jameson on the political avant-garde, and the mind stretchers Douglas Hofstadter and Daniel Dennett. The last two focus on how psychological issues force our judgment one way or another. Some of their riddles for perception may help with the study of anamorphosis, for example, in Hans Holbein's *Ambassadors*, with its globe, which, seen properly, is also a skull. The whole question of "proper" seeing, how we look *again* at elements of paintings to see what is "there," brings up the problems of control and perspective. We ask how we move from an Albertian mode and Renaissance habits to more flexible ones, in which ambivalence must or can be maintained. Like the issue of the duck/rabbit that Ludwig Wittgenstein would have us consider (can we see both at once or only each successively?), anamorphosis in the visual arts, or the pun in the literary arts, brings with it a whole series of considerations about temporality, successivity, and simultaneity.

At the end of the course, we take up Derrida's analysis (*Truth* 257-382) of Meyer Schapiro's analysis of Martin Heidegger's analysis of a pair of shoes painted by van Gogh (which, in principle, belong to a peasant woman; Derrida wonders whether they are a pair at all) in order to shake up whatever presuppositions and presumptions students may still retain and to encourage them always to think about and question the images they are "given." We tackle the whole notion of *givenness* and conclude by returning to the initial issues about perception.

In the actual process of reading doubled texts lies the crux of the difficulty and the excitement of the course. The objective must never be stability of viewpoint, uniformity of strategic method, or unilinear thinking. Multiple perspectives and optimal flexibility, the principal concerns, can be achieved in a variety of ways: two instructors may lead the discussion and demonstrations; other discussants may be invited in; the instructors may change their own vocabulary over the periods studied and through the diverse objects observed; students work on written papers and present oral reports, individually if the size of the class permits or in groups, with several students sharing a topic and contributing their differing perspectives on it. The course is directed against the blinkered form of a single-minded approach.

Much of the value of the topic lies in the idea of stress. We bring about intensity of vision by the positive confrontation of diverse points of view, whether by reading past critics and viewers or reading against and with other contemporary points of view. I call this "interferences" or "stressed reading" and try to bring out the notion of the vision richly interfering and interfered with, in teaching as in writing (see Caws, *Interference*). The readings are meant, also, to challenge one another, on the principle that interreactions—of the fields observed, of the viewing points, of the instructors and students, of ideologies and interests—can lead only to deeper perceptions.

Syllabus

Course Perception in Literature and Art. Mary Ann Caws, Comparative Literature, City University of New York.

Description Upper-level course. Meets once a week. May be taught with another instructor, often in art history. Occasional guest lecture. Individual projects, individual and collective reports, and discussions.

Objectives To study how we see and what we see in visual and verbal texts, how our perception is influenced by what we know, by what we are looking for, and by the frame of vision in the context of which we are looking; to combine theoretical reading with textual works from different periods; to develop students' perception of nuances and depth in both visual and literary arts.

Schedule

1. What is the course about? Reading texts, visual and verbal; aesthetics and problematics. Panofsky, *Meaning*; Arnheim, *Art*; Gombrich, Hochberg, and Black; Steiner, *Colors*; Berger, *About Looking*; Bryson, *Vision*; Derrida; Foucault, *Order*; Barthes, *Image*; Ehrenzweig; Mitchell, *Iconology*; Suleiman and Crosman; Sypher, *Art History*; Caws, *Art of Interference* and *Eye in the Text*.
2. General concepts of mannerism and baroque: their differences, the critics who write about them, why the two styles make a paradigm case of interart relations. J. R. Martin; d'Ors; Sypher, *Four Stages*; baroque poetry.
3. The religious connection. Architecture, prayer, and the sublime. Red and white sonnets of La Ceppède; Donne. Flesh and language. Martz; Praz, *Flaming Heart*.
4. Issue of control, from above and below. Perspectival play (Borromini et al.). Narrative elements in poetry. Crowding and space. What is the equivalent in poetry? Objects and loving through them.
5. The mannerist impulse. Fountainebleau; Diane de Poitiers in art and text. Toying, playing, erotics (the veiled). The Cavalier poets. Mannerism in Italy (Marino).
6. Saint Teresa and more erotics. Who is looking? Works of Crashaw, Seghers, Bernini; the writing of Saint Teresa. Hysteria and its delights. Freud and Lacan. Pointing and singling out.
7. Icarus in his various forms. Falling and rising. Ideas of figures and heroism. Coutts-Smith. Midterm paper due.
8. The Magdalene and the baroque, on to us. Works of Crashaw, Titian, Correggio, René Char, et al. Issues of cycles, feminist perception, the guilty female, and repentance.
9. Surrealism, from baroque: reversals (flame/fire), the hysterical. The orphic and contemporary poetry. Works of Apollinaire, Breton, Eluard, Robert Desnos. Krauss and Caws et al. on avant-garde and surrealism.
10. Feminist issues: art, language, and the female body. Who, again, is watching? Reading in detail (Schor). Rose on sexuality in the field of vision, on Hamlet and the *Mona Lisa*. Suleiman on female body. N. K. Miller on poetics of gender.
11. Issues of interpretation and concepts: Foucault, *Order*; Derrida. Are these more relevant to us, to the baroque, than iconography? Panofsky, *Meaning*.
12. Puzzles: anamorphosis and the pun—double readings. Where do they go, and how do we read them? Wittgenstein; Hofstadter and Dennett; Arakawa.
13. Psychoanalysis and/in art. Hartman; Kuhns; Stokes.
14. Collective discussion on student papers.

W. J. T. Mitchell

Against Comparison:
Teaching Literature and the Visual Arts

The traditional course in literature and the visual arts is organized around comparisons of (say) paintings and poems linked by historical periods, artistic movements, or shared sensibilities and styles. Baroque or Romantic or neoclassical or modern painting and literature are found to have formal resemblances, and biographical connections (friendships, collaborations, influences) are discovered between artists and writers. Where direct links are unavailable, a prevailing *zeitgeist* or "spirit of the times" is frequently invoked. My approach to the relation of literature and visual art has almost nothing to do with historical resemblances, and it takes up biographical connections only under certain conditions. In my view the traditional course does not address any necessary, unavoidable problems. It may be nice to have students look at cubist painting alongside the poems of Ezra Pound, but is it necessary? Why not have them look at silent movies, listen to Stravinsky, read Einstein, Freud, and Trotsky as well? The real subject of such a course is not literature and the visual arts but modernism, or the twenties, or the history of culture or style. The comparison of the arts is only another part of a broad interdisciplinary survey in what is often a very schematic "history," and there is no particular reason to single out the literature–visual art connection as any special problem. The relation of images and texts is not addressed as a specific theoretical problem demanding any special methodology or encompassing any specific domain of data. Just about any poem can be compared to any painting as long as some link of period style can be made, usually with some highly abstract analogy. Modern painting and poetry, for instance, are often found to be comparable in their tendency to "foreground the medium itself," "spatialize time," or "subvert narrativity." There may be some truth to these analogies, but there is also something unsatisfactory about them. They tend to take students away from the specificity of works, writers, and artists into all too familiar historicist formulas. They always leave me with the question "So what?"

My goal for a course in verbal and visual art has always been to confront this topic only where it is necessary and unavoidable. I began this sort of work with the composite art of William Blake, a poet-painter who seems absolutely to demand a reader capable of moving between verbal and visual literacy. Even with Blake's illuminated books, however, I was always struck by the oddness, the arbitrariness of this demand. Blake's poetry had been (and continues to be) read and taught with only the most cursory attention to his graphic art. I know this because, despite my commitment to critical analysis of Blake's composite art, I still find it important to teach him occasionally just as a writer. For certain purposes it might be more important to read Rousseau's *Emile* next to the *Songs of Innocence and of Experience* than to look at the illustrations. Blake has always served for me, then, as an exemplar of both the necessity and arbitrariness of comparative studies of verbal and visual art. Blake's illuminated books require this sort of comparative analysis, if ever any works of art did; but even they "require" it only for very special purposes involving a confrontation with the materiality and semiotic particularity of Blake's texts.

But the most important lesson we comparatists can learn from Blake's mixed art is that comparison itself is not a necessary procedure in the study of image-text relations. The necessary subject matter is, rather, the whole ensemble of relations among media, and relations can be many things other than analogy, resemblance, formal similarity, and so forth. Difference is just as important as similarity, antagonism as crucial as collaboration, dissonance as interesting as harmony. This fact strikes anyone who pays much attention to Blake's practice as a maker of illustrated books. His illustrations often do not illustrate; they counterpoint, or disrupt, or create a disjunctive alternative, or simply present an independent vision. The relation of poetry and painting that emerges as a material fact in Blake's illuminated books might better be described as a "contrary" or dialectical relation of image and text (see Mitchell, *Blake's Composite Art*).

My basic methodology for studying the relations of verbal and visual arts, then, develops from Blake's illuminated books, though it is not limited to them. The method is dialectical and materialistic (without, however, being orthodox dialectical materialism). It is dialectical in that it treats images and texts as contraries engaged in patterns not just of difference and similarity but of struggles between domination and subversion, of relations of independence, collaboration, and (occasionally) equality. I see texts and images, in other words, as semiotic practices bound together in something like mutual patterns of social otherness or alterity. The difference between texts and images, as articulated in theories about the subject from Plato to modern semiotics (see Mitchell, *Iconology*), is frequently imagined as the difference between races, classes, or sexes, with images generally, but not always, playing the subordinate role. The dialectical relation between texts and images consists, then, in a double movement of affinity and antagonism: the history of aesthetics and critical theory abounds with tropes of affinity based on the wish for texts to become like images, images to become like texts; it is equally abundant in tropes of hostility—debates or, as Leonardo da Vinci's nineteenth-century editors called them, *paragoni* of the arts.

My method is materialistic in that it seeks out the dialectic of image and text, not at the abstract level of formal analogy, but at the concrete level of formal and referential specificity; that is, it asks: What is this work made of? How is it formed, shaped, structured? To what is it directed, addressed, referred? Perhaps it would be simplest to say that I want the relations of visual and verbal art to be treated in the most literal possible fashion, as problems inscribed in the very surface or texture of texts and images. That is why, rather than compare this novel or poem to that painting or statue, I begin with actual conjunctions of words and images in illustrated texts or in mixed media such as film, television, and drama. With these media, one begins with a relatively concrete set of empirical givens: some plays privilege speech over action, dialogue over visual spectacle; the film medium has passed through a technological revolution involving a shift from visual domination (silent films) to verbal (the talkies); television is widely regarded as a predominantly imagistic medium in which language is attenuated and literacy is threatened; illustrated texts have appeared in a wide variety of forms, ranging from the unified field of calligraphy, drawing, and painting in the illuminated manuscript, to the various divisions of labor imposed by letterpress, engraving, lithography, and photography, to the electronic reunification of text and image in the contemporary dot-matrix or laser printer. Any course that takes as its subject the relation of verbal and visual media should, I think, engage at some point with this sort of material. The fact is that we experience the encounter of these media every day, if only in the juxtaposition of news photos with textual stories, and it might be better to begin with these ordinary experiences before moving on to elaborate, refined comparisons between poems and paintings. First let's ask ourselves what the photograph of a president emerging from Air Force One is *doing* next to a story about his sending troops somewhere. Is the photograph there to be seen with any attention? Is it important how the president looked that particular day or how this picture was taken? Or is the picture scarcely seen at all, merely registered the way the presence of a signature or trademark might be noticed, as a sign that the president is alive and well?

From the weave of text and photo in the daily paper we might proceed to more ambitious and self-conscious conjunctions of words and photographs of the sort we find in documentary essays like James Agee and Walker Evans's *Let Us Now Praise Famous Men*. The clear separation of photographs and texts in this book, each with its own space, is clearly a feature of its design, an attempt, in Agee's words, to ensure that photos and text "are coequal, mutually independent and fully collaborative" (xv). But why is it so important for Agee and Evans to maintain their independence of each other? Why not put the photographs next to appropriate passages in the text? If the goal is collaboration and co-equality, why make it difficult for the reader-viewer to correlate image and text? If the goal is independence, why not just print them separately?

It will probably be evident from this example, and from the questions it provokes, that complex, high-tension relations of images and text like those produced by Agee and Evans and Blake are not all that usual. The normal relations of image and word (in the illustrated newspaper or even the cartoon page) follow traditional formulas, usually involving the clear subordination of one medium to the other. In the average book of photojournalism, the text is there only to serve the useful function of identifying the referents of the photographs; sometimes, conversely, the photographs may be there only to illustrate the text, not to be seen as photographic works in their own right. I don't mean to suggest that these normal conjunctions of words and images are unimportant or uninteresting. What they provide is the conventional background or ordinary language of visual-verbal relations, the grammar on which more complex utterances are based. The tendency of mixed forms to array their elements in hierarchies (texts supported by illustrations, images supported by captions) is the normal background against which experiments or deviations take their meaning. Garry Trudeau's deliberately anticinematic, talky cartoon sequences in *Doonesbury* constitute an act of resistance to the normal privileging of the visual on the cartoon page. Perhaps the most familiar symptom of Trudeau's subversion of visual progression in the three-panel strip is his repetition of exactly the same image (a view of the White House, of Uncle Duke's Colorado retreat, of Walden) in every frame, all "movement" displaced onto the bodiless voice indicated by the text.

How do we get from works where visual-verbal relations are unavoidable (films, plays, newspapers, photo essays, and cartoon strips) to the traditional subjects of comparative studies of literature and the visual arts (poems and paintings, novels and statues)? In some ways it should be clear that I hope we never come back to this subject, which I see as a nonsubject without a real method or object of investigation. But in another sense it should be obvious that the subject is just as unavoidable and as necessary with these materials as it is with the mixed, composite forms. Painting, sculpture, architecture, landscape, and other "purely" visual arts never exist, I want to argue, completely independent of language and textuality. The notion of their purity, in fact, is almost always explained by reference to language and cognate or conventionally associated media: words, sounds, time, narrativity, and arbitrary, "allegorical" signification are the "linguistic" or "textual" elements that must be repressed or eliminated in order for the pure visuality of the visual arts to be achieved. This sort of purity, often associated with modernism and abstraction, is, I think, both impossible and utopian, which is not to dismiss it but to identify it as an ideology, a complex of desire and fear, power and interest. There's no need to compare paintings to texts, even if the text happens to be represented in the painting. The point is to see what particular form of textuality is elicited (or repressed) by the painting. What sort of title does it have? Why are so many modern paintings entitled *Untitled*? Why the vigorous, explicit denial of any entitlement of language in painting? What is being resisted in the name of "literature" or "language"? How do words enter into paintings? How do we sort out the differences among the following examples of textuality in painting: a picture that represents, among other things, a text (think of an open book in a Dutch painting); a picture that has words and letters not represented in but inscribed on its surface (like a Chinese calligraphic landscape or an Anselm Kiefer); a picture that depicts an episode from a book (like a still from a movie or a play); a picture in which the words "speak to" or disrupt the image (as in René Magritte's *Key of Dreams*, where verbal labels and pictured objects refuse to cooperate); a picture whose entire composition is designed around a verbal "character"—a hieroglyphic or pictogram, in the style of Paul Klee; a picture that eschews figuration, reference, narrative, allegory, and so on in favor of pure, unreadable visuality. We don't have to look for poems that betray formal analogies with the paintings that interest us: the paintings themselves, and what we can learn about their production and reception, will tell us what texts are relevant to them, what kind of reading they require. For abstract painting, the appropriate texts may well be not literature in the traditional sense but criticism, philosophy, metaphysics—*ut pictura theoria*.

In a similar way, the visual materials appropriate to a literary text need not be fetched from afar with historicist analogies: they are immanent in the text, in the fabric of description, narrative "vision," represented objects and places, metaphor, formal arrangement of parts, even typography, paper, and binding. If it is hard to keep textuality out of painting, it seems equally difficult to keep visuality out of literature (though the impulse to do so is adumbrated in the topos of the blind poet, literature's answer to painting as "mute poesy"). Not that the situation of literature and visual art as mutual "significant others" is purely symmetrical: it seems easier for painting to re-present and incorporate textuality in a quite literal way than for the reverse to happen. Literature becomes "literally" pictorial only when it asserts its material presence as writing, inscription, and typographic space; the more characteristic gesture of literature toward the visual arts is indirect or figurative—the description of paintings, statues, or other visual representa-tions; the resort to that vast miscellany of literary techniques—"images" and verbal "icons," "colors" and "ornaments" of rhetoric. Literature, especially narrative and allegory, has traditionally dominated painting, and the concept of painterly purity is generally regarded as a liberation of the visual from the verbal. Literature, on the other hand, displays the sort of ambivalence toward painting that a master generally has toward a slave: it wants to appropriate the power of the subordinate other, to control and exploit it—even (under special conditions) to identify itself with the other.

This ambivalence about the incorporation of visual into verbal codes is most vividly articulated in ekphrastic poetry, the genre that defines itself as the verbal representation of visual representation. A course in literature and the visual arts should certainly take up this genre, but not with a preconceived notion that the ekphrastic poem is to be *compared* to the painting it describes. For one thing, many of the most interesting ekphrastic poems describe imaginary paintings. Even more important, when the painting actually exists and can be reproduced, comparison is still probably beside the point. The real issue is the relation between text and image established by the text: Does it address the picture or describe it? Does it speak to or for the image? Does the image talk back? In whose voice? Its own or the poet's? As these questions may indicate, the relation of text and image in ekphrasis is frequently a political one, and more specifically a matter of gender. It is remarkable how many ekphrastic images, from Keats's "Urn" to Pater's "Mona Lisa" to William Carlos Williams's "Portrait of a Lady," turn out to be doubled images of the female—feminized (silent, beautiful) images that represent silent, beautiful women.

Characteristically, the male ekphrastic poet finds himself in a state of loquacious ambivalence: To what extent is the "still unravish'd bride" violated by Keats's passion? Is there a touch of envy for the urn as a rival poet who can tell " a flowery tale more sweetly than our rhyme"? A bit of resentment in the characterization of the urn as a "tease," a "cold pastoral" that paralyzes the thought and ultimately the voice of the poet? Keats presents one of the primal scenes of ekphrasis, articulating both his desire as a poet to become the visual graphic other he admires and his fear that the fulfilment of that desire might be muteness, castration, and death. "Ode on a Grecian Urn" also perfectly demonstrates the emptiness of the comparative method. What is gained by bringing a Greek vase, or a photograph of a vase, into the classroom? At best, a sense of the type of thing Keats is referring to, an aid to visualization. The poem and any real or imaginary urn are, strictly speaking, incomparable; the whole point of the text is to place the urn beyond comparison. To understand the relation of literature and visual art in Keats's text, therefore, it is crucial that the urn be absent, that it be imaginary, utopian, absolutely other to the text and the poet's voice.

This insistence on the absence of the image, its presence only as a verbal fiction, not a visual fact, may help us gain some insight into a larger set of questions about the relations of Romantic literature and visual art. Why is so much Romantic poetry and poetic theory so resolutely antivisual, so iconophobic, even to the point where the "visible language" of writing and printing must be consistently displaced by a poetics of voice and invisibility (see Mitchell, "Visible Language")? At this point we may be in a position to see how the study of relations, not comparisons, of literature and visual art may take us back to large historical questions about movements, styles, and periods. We come to these larger matters, however, not directly, not by assuming a similitude or family resemblance to be discovered in poems and paintings of the same era, but by a close examination of the particular dialectics between verbal and visual expression inscribed in specific works of art and literature. The urge to comparative study was always, I suspect, nothing more than an ineffectual way of scratching the itch that is produced by the tantalizing affinity and tension between verbal and visual art. My method won't make this itch go away, but it may offer some local, temporary satisfactions. At the very least, it ought to constrain the urge for comparison by seeing it as only one among a whole ensemble of possible relations between the verbal and visual. These are the relations, as manifested in theories of the image-text difference and in the concrete encounters between words and pictures in a variety of art forms, that constitute the real subject matter of the course in literature and the visual arts.

Syllabus

Course   Literature and the Visual Arts. W. J. T. Mitchell, English, University of Chicago.

Description   Upper-level elective course. Meets once a week.

Objectives   To focus not on comparison of literature and visual art but on relations of the two media in a variety of art forms; to foster both verbal and visual literacy so that students will discover the intimate connections and conflicts between these sorts of literacy; to use texts that address the image-text relation as a theoretical or practical topic or works that seem in themselves to demand some attention to the interplay of visual and verbal codes.

Schedule

1. *Paragoni*: the contest of verbal and visual representation. Basic figures of the difference between image and text: Goodman's semiotics and the icon-symbol-index triad in Peirce and in Eco; nature and convention in Plato's *Cratylus* and Gombrich's *Art and Illusion*; time and space in Lessing's *Laocoön*; eye and ear in Leonardo's *paragoni* (Holt 275–79) and Burke's *Sublime and Beautiful*. Emphasis on the relation between semiotic and social difference and on the inscription of gender, class, and race distinctions in theories of the image. Iconoclasm, iconophobia, and the connection between image theory and image fear.
2. Composite forms 1: cartoons and illustrated books. Main examples: Blake's illuminated books; *Dick Tracy* and Trudeau's *Doonesbury* strip; Saul Steinberg, Gary Larson, and Kliban. Exploration of the conventions of cartoon narration, the graphic representation of speech and thought, framing and montage, pictorial metaphors and puns; the social and aesthetic status of comic strips, cartoons, graffiti, and other forms of mixed graphic and typographic art.
3. Composite forms 2: the ethics of form in the photographic essay. Agee and Evans, *Let Us Now Praise Famous Men*; Barthes, *Camera Lucida*; Alloula, *The Colonial Harem*; Mohr and Said, *After the Last Sky*. Analysis of the special ideological and ethical problems raised by the collaboration of writer (essayist) and photographer. The documentary and the ethics of surveillance, espionage, pornographic

exploitation of damaged subjects. The politics of the camera eye and the journalistic pen.

4. Film text and film image. Examples: Billy Wilder's *Sunset Boulevard* and Hector Babenco's *Kiss of the Spider Woman*; the rivalry between "image" and "text" based on theories of the cinema; visual representation and narrative; sound and sight, voice and gaze. Readings: Panofsky, "Style"; Cavell; Mulvey.

5. Speech and spectacle in the drama. Discussion of the *paragoni* between visual and verbal values in the theater. Readings from Aristotle's *Poetics*; the Inigo Jones–Ben Jonson debate; Brecht and Artaud; essays from *Poetics Today* on the semiotics of drama.

6. *Ut Pictura Theoria*: the repression of language in abstract painting. Introduction to the notion of textuality in painting (Lee, *Ut Pictura Poesis*; Bryson, *Word and Image*). Canonical examples of abstraction discussed in the context of Barr's Museum of Modern Art catalog *Cubism and Abstract Art*. The theory of modernist abstraction in Schapiro, *Modern Art* 185–232; Fried; Greenberg; T. J. Clark, "Greenberg's Theory of Art"; Krauss; Steinberg.

7. Poems on paintings: ekphrasis and the other. Readings from Homer and the Greek Anthology; ekphrastic poems by Shelley, Keats, Browning, Baudelaire, Auden, Stevens, Williams, O'Hara. Focus on the problem of verbal representation of visual representation; the notion of the painter as "rival poet," the painting as image of social or sexual "others" to the poetic voice. Critical texts by Krieger; Riffaterre; Hagstrum; Steiner, *Colors*.

8. The narrator as painter: space and vision in the novel. Main example would be *Jane Eyre*, but discussion might also touch on exemplary texts such as Hawthorne's *Marble Faun*, Conrad's *Under Western Eyes*, Wilde's *Picture of Dorian Gray*, Stendhal's *Red and the Black*, all of which raise the problem of representing visual experience in verbal narrative. Issues such as the visual dimension of reader response, the metaphorics of "perspective" and point of view, the relation between "speaking" and "seeing" in narrative convention. Readings from Genette and the theories of fictional ekphrasis or description by Hamon, Meltzer, and Beaujour.

Interart Courses

Wendy Steiner

Literature and Painting

Wanting students to be able to compare pictorial and literary works is, on the face of it, a rather peculiar pedagogical ambition. Students need to know so many things in order to acquire a grounding in the humanities that to insist they be able to explain what paintings and writings have in common seems eccentric indeed. And yet, anyone who has taught an interart course finds that this peripheral task is the surest way to dramatize the most essential issues in aesthetics, semiotics, and humanistic thought. By seeming indirection, we reach the heart of the matter.

In part, this outcome stems from the nature of comparison itself. To compare two complex entities is inevitably to ask what is actually being compared. When Horace warned painters against combining human heads and animal bodies, as some poets did, he was concerned with different aspects of poems and paintings from those occupying Gotthold Lessing when he cautioned against the confusion of the temporal and spatial arts. Certainly, poems and paintings are both involved with matters of what Horace would think of as decorum and thus with value structures that have an interesting and complex history. Likewise, poems and paintings are both implicated by their media in the spatiotemporal sphere. But what poems or paintings specifically have to do with decorum, time, or space is so difficult a matter to pin down, so variously dealt with at one time or another in intellectual history, and so revelatory of the ideological assumptions underlying any particular approach to the question that these interart *loci classici* may unlock doors to the very structure of cultural thought.

In the introductory class to my course Twentieth-Century Literature and Painting, I lay out the general history of the interart comparison as a periodic alternation between affirmation of and skepticism about the value of the enterprise as a whole. The baroque and neoclassicist *ut pictura poesis* premise gives way to Lessing's formal differentiation of the spatial and temporal arts, to be followed in turn by the extensive interart relations apparent in Romanticism, the Pre-Raphaelite movement, and nineteenth-century notions of period and zeitgeist. Irving Babbitt issued a *New Laokoon* in 1910 arguing against the "confusion" of the arts, and philosophers such as Edmund Husserl investigated more deeply the constitution of temporal and spatial objects. The twentieth century, with its constant violation of the borders between the visual and verbal and its growing body of precise theoretical scholarship, has complicated and enriched the meaning of the interart comparison. Thus, whether students and scholars find themselves proponents or debunkers of the sister-arts argument, the process of formulating a position on it is immensely rewarding.

Since Lessing, the two issues on which the comparison most often rests are the opposition between temporality and spatiality and that between the artificiality and naturalness of signs. The first third of the course is concerned with exploring these notions. I have found that students—already somewhat daunted at the prospect of dealing with painting, literature, and philosophy in a single course—seldom become comfortable with the abstractions of this section unless they see them grounded in a work of art. Accordingly, when I discuss Lessing's *Laocoön*, I show how the strict separation of temporal and spatial media becomes a theme in ekphrastic art and in the ideology of the pregnant moment in painting. In ekphrasis, a literary work mentions or describes a visual one, and the discrepancy between the two efforts is often the crux of the poem. A frequent topos of Romanticism is that poems cannot achieve the immediacy and transcendence of visual art because they are temporal rather than atemporal. Keats's "Ode on a Grecian Urn," the archetypal example of this position, is an ideal tool for dramatizing the issues to a class.

In an even more complicated way, the literary romance has used the presumed stasis of visual artworks to symbolize its own deviations from narrative realism. Sublimity or the ecstasy of love finds analogues—however strained—in the act of regarding a picture; indeed, the association between vision, pictorial perception, and courtly love has a very long history. In Keats's "Eve of St. Agnes," students see how these associations animate a poetic plot; in the "Nausicaa" chapter of *Ulysses*, they learn how a modernist plays on this complex in a delicious parody. Leo Steinberg's article "Picasso's Sleep-Watchers" (*Other Criteria* 92-114) describes the treatment of aesthetic-erotic vision in the visual arts.

I finish the discussion of time and space with the work of modern thinkers—Rudolf Arnheim, Roman Jakobson, and Boris Uspenskij—and with writings by Joyce and Cummings, in which the barriers between space and time are tested, defied, and turned into artistic themes. The three theoreticians refine the discussion of the contrast between temporal and spatial art, providing students with much more precise and focused differentiations than Lessing does. Uspenskij is especially helpful in using examples from fiction, since the general literature on time-space issues concerns poetry much more frequently.

In relating visual perspective to fictive point of view, moreover, Uspenskij provides tools that help students to examine the cognitive structures implied by the two arts. A post-Renaissance painting that organizes a scene in terms of a single fixed perceiver is quite different from a medieval painting whose objects are ordered and scaled in terms of their ideological importance. Literary point of view admits of equally extreme contrasts, depending on whether a narrator is inside a scene or outside it, omniscient or limited, and so forth. Through such ideas, students come to examine the relation between seeing and knowing, perceiver and perceived.

The last week of the theoretical section concerns the naturalness versus the artificiality of signs. The class studies the icon-index-symbol typology of C. S. Peirce; Meyer Schapiro's brilliant discussion of such pictorial properties of painting as right/left or frame/center, which are shown to have not only formal but semantic value ("On Some Problems"); and E. H. Gombrich's treatment of pictorial meaning not as resemblance to reality but as a set of conventions, as well as his later recanting of this position (*Art and Illusion,* "Image and Code"). (I have also used chapters of Goodman's *Languages of Art* in graduate courses, but his book is beyond the reach of most undergraduates.)

These semiotic concerns provide probably the most extreme challenge to students' assumptions about the difference between the visual and verbal arts: that paintings look like reality and that literature is purely "symbolic" or arbitrary. The problematic nature of similarity, the motivation behind literary conventions, and the confusion between the formal and the semantic inevitably arise in this discussion. This relativization of oppositions not only allows students to think more flexibly about the parallelism of painting and literature but also influences any further work in art and philosophy that they may undertake. Semiotics is very useful in structuring and disciplining discussions of meaning, particularly when students must describe the representational capacities of different media.

This background gives students considerable technical and theoretical ammunition for approaching specific works of art. For the remainder of the course, the theoretical issues that have been raised are tested out on various modernist movements, the hypothesis here being that the twentieth century is a period unusually hospitable to interartistic activity.

The seminal exchanges between Gertrude Stein and Pablo Picasso, as well as Wallace Stevens's experiments in fragmentation and multiperspective, are only a few of the examples available for a discussion of literary and pictorial cubism. As the most definitive disruption of the Renaissance pictorial system, cubism is a crucial starting point for understanding modernism. But because the term *cubism* is not often applied to literature, the significance of its break from tradition may seem limited to the visual arts. I believe that much literary experimentation can be seen as a direct or inverse analogue to pictorial cubism, and I raise the possibility—outlined in *The Colors of Rhetoric,* in the chapter called "A Cubist Historiography"—that cubism is the master movement of twentieth-century art *and* literature. The tension between representationality and abstraction, the disruption of the formal and semantic conventions of the two arts, and the programmatically experimental methods of the movement had a determining effect on a vast amount of subsequent writing and painting. Moreover, these developments require a sophisticated treatment of space and time and of sign and function; they lend themselves to the kind of analysis that the earlier section of the course has prepared students to undertake.

Fascinated with the visual arts, many modernist poets have written works based on specific paintings or sculptures. William Carlos Williams sometimes tried for exact structural equivalences between his poems and the paintings on which they were based; indeed, the supply of ekphrastic poetry in this century has grown exponentially. John Ashbery, John Hollander, Richard Howard, and many others have built up this corpus of writing about visual artworks, and students, faced with an indisputable interart connection, must discover on what basis the poem and artwork might be considered equivalent.

The next subject is imagism. This movement aimed to create a perfect correspondence between text and world, a correspondence to reality that Ezra Pound found in Chinese script and in the visual arts. Imagism gives students the opportunity to examine an iconic program for writing—to see how far language can resemble or even embody the meanings it represents. The vorticist sculpture and painting that grew out of imagism employed a similar rhetoric in its manifestos, and students can apply their semiotic and theoretical expertise to test the strength of the interart analogy outlined by Pound and his colleagues.

The next topic is abstraction. We first look at works by Kasimir Malevich, Piet Mondrian, and Wassily Kandinsky and then turn to American abstract expressionism. The aim here is to ask what *abstract* means when applied to an art—painting—that is by definition a semiotic structure. It is useful to consider Jakobson's treatment, in "Linguistics and Poetics," of the various functions of sign systems, since it implies that even if one kind of semiosis in an artwork is disrupted, the work does not thereby become utterly nonsemiotic. Abstraction is inevitably a tendency rather than an absolute state. We then examine the poetry of Ashbery and Frank O'Hara in conjunction with work of the abstract expressionists, whom they associated with, wrote about, and championed. The question is whether there is any connection between these poets and painters beyond common interests and occasional interreferences.

The next week of the course is devoted to concrete poetry and visual art. After contrasting "abstract" and "concrete" to see whether they function as opposites in aesthetic discourse, we discuss the limits of verbal concreteness. How concrete can literature become before it ceases to be literature at all and enters the realm of the visual arts? Moreover, since students are seldom much impressed by the power of concrete art, we may ask how much our notions of aesthetic value in the two arts are conditioned by the limitations imposed by their respective media.

I end the course with two other kinds of semantic disruption, surrealism and nonsense. The class considers why the term *nonsense* is seldom applied to the visual arts, and, through M. C. Escher and Edward Gorey, what would constitute pictorial nonsense. Surrealism, in contrast, even though its representation of the world violates normal assumptions about reality, cannot be equated with nonsense. To explain this, we examine the ideological structure of artistic movements—for example, their use of manifestos and other "intentional" devices to establish the sense of what they are doing. Finally, since both nonsense and surrealism make extensive use of the illustrated book, we discuss this special case of visual-verbal interaction. It is a topic that deserves much more attention, however, than this course gives it. I should add that, whether because of the intrinsic interest of this material or simply because the end of the course is in view, students seem to enjoy the section on nonsense enormously.

By the time the course is over, students have acquired a basic introduction to semiotics, the history of aesthetics, and twentieth-century poetry and painting. They have had semiotics and aesthetics presented, moreover, not as mere subjects to be mastered but as the means for solving certain puzzles about modern art. What do the terms *abstract* and *concrete* mean when they are used in relation to the two arts? How can we describe the peculiar effects of artworks that eschew conventional reference and nevertheless seem to be meaningful? And why were painters and writers so fascinated with each other's experiments at this time? The interart comparison in the twentieth century is a set of problems needing to be solved; thus it dramatizes the importance of a technical vocabulary and a rigorous conceptual system. This merging of subject matter and methodology makes a painting-literature course a highly involving, instructive, and self-reflexive experience.

Syllabus

Course   Twentieth-Century Literature and Painting. Wendy Steiner, English, University of Pennsylvania.

Description   Initially developed for a graduate course. Offered with adjustments in writing assignments to upper-level undergraduates and to an NEH Summer Seminar for College Teachers.

Objectives   To introduce students to the theoretical issues of interart comparison; to sensitize them to the differing demands of the visual and verbal media; to provide a basic semiotic vocabulary for the discussion of representation; to reveal the interpretive richness arising from an interartistic treatment of certain pictorial and literary works.

Schedule
1. Introduction. The history of the painting-literature comparison: Horace; Sidney, "Apology for Poetry"; Lessing; Wölfflin; Peirce; modern semiotics and structur-

alism. The various intellectual and ideological purposes served by the comparison.

2. Spatiality versus temporality. Lee, *Ut Pictura Poesis*; Lessing; Bunn; Mitchell, *Iconology*; Keats, "Ode on a Grecian Urn."

3. The romance and painting. Keats, "The Eve of St. Agnes"; Joyce, "Nausicaa" chapter of *Ulysses*; Steinberg, "Picasso's Sleepwatchers."

4. Twentieth-century views of spatiality versus temporality. Arnheim, "Unity"; Jakobson, "Linguistics" and "On the Relations"; Uspenskij, chapters 3, 5–7; Joyce, "Proteus" chapter of *Ulysses*; Cummings, "these children singing in stone a."

5. Artificiality versus naturalness of signs. Schapiro, "On Some Problems"; Peirce; Gombrich, *Art and Illusion*, "Image and Code".

6. Cubism. E. Fry; Steiner, *Exact Resemblance*, chapter 4; Stein, selections; Stevens, "Thirteen Ways . . ." and "Someone Puts Together . . ."; paintings by Picasso, Braque, Gris.

7. Ekphrasis and interartistic analysis. W. C. Williams, *Pictures from Brueghel.*

8. Imagism, vorticism, futurism. Pound, *A Memoir of Gaudier-Brzeska, The Chinese Written Character as Medium for Poetry*; Jones; Wees.

9. Abstraction. Frank O'Hara; Hobbs and Levin; Steinberg, "Other Criteria" (*Other Criteria* 55-90); paintings by Malevich, Kandinsky, Mondrian.

10. Concreteness. Solt; Steiner, *Colors*, chapter 3.

11. Surrealism. Breton; Worth.

12. Nonsense. Carroll, *Alice in Wonderland*; M. C. Escher (Ernst); Gorey, *Amphigorey.*

13. Conclusion.

Jesse J. Easley

Literature and Architecture:
Spatial Form and Composition

In book 3 of *Gulliver's Travels*, the titular hero and his guide pay a visit to the Grand Academy of Lagado, wherein they encounter a number of the Balnibarbian Projectors who are so preoccupied with their research that "in the mean time, the whole Country lies miserably waste, the Houses in Ruins, and the People without Food or Cloaths. By all which, instead of being discouraged, they are Fifty Times more violently bent upon prosecuting their Schemes, driven equally on by Hope and Despair" (151). Among these various schemes, of course, are the extracting of sunbeams from cucumbers, the softening of marble for the manufacturing of pillows, and the attempted propagation of a breed of naked sheep—all of which, as anyone who has perused the early volumes of the *Transactions of the Royal Society of London* will attest, serve to remind the reader of some of the more enthusiastic endeavors of that institution. Nevertheless, it is with respect to the Academy's "School of Languages" that Swift's satire is the more engaging; for of the efforts of the wisest "three Professors [who] sat in Consultation upon improving . . . their own Country," he writes:

> The first Project was to shorten Discourse by cutting Polysyllables into one, and leaving out Verbs and Participles: because in Reality all things imaginable are but Nouns.
> The other, was a Scheme for entirely abolishing all Words whatsoever: And this was urged as a great Advantage in Point of Health as well as Brevity. For, it is plain, that every Word we speak is in some Degree a Diminution of our Lungs by Corrosion; and consequently contributes to the shortening of our Lives. An Expedient was therefore offered, that since Words are only Names for Things, it would be more convenient for all Men to carry about them, such Things as were necessary to express the particular Business they are to discourse on. (158)

Now, I recall this passage not only because it epitomizes my thrice-weekly journey from my office in the College of Liberal Arts to my classroom in the University of Southern California School of Architecture—where I lecture to forty students armed with triangles and T-squares, models and templates—but because it will serve as our focal point for considering three important divisions of pedagogy related to an interdisciplinary course in architecture and literature: materials, methodology, and meanings. Though these concerns are interdependent in practice, I will treat them in order.

At the most fundamental level, the materials for my course Spatial Form and Composition are buildings and books, the former consisting of photographic reproductions and slides (since neither I nor my students feel at all obliged—as do Swift's philosophers—to haul on our backs the very things themselves). There are fortunately still some academic problems for which one's compromising ignorance is both the convenient and the correct solution, Los Angeles in any case not furnishing us with the requisite number of buildings whose cornerstones are classical, medieval, Renaissance, or pre-Victorian. But as for the latter category of books, my concern here is different, since architects are not especially avid or voracious readers. Rather, when humanities majors are likely to be absorbing at breakfast all sorts of droll and useless information from the back of the cereal box, my design students are likely to be contemplating the shape of that package and its lettering. I was so reminded by a well-meaning colleague: "What good is it going to do if an architect learns how to read or write? He's not going to parade around in front of his buildings and explain them to the public. He's not going to distribute fliers." I would have had great pleasure in ridiculing this latter-day Lagadocian (and such a sexist one at that!) were it not for the annoying reality that his point was essentially valid. Professional architects are in fact restricted in their careers to expressing their ideas through things and not through words, making it extremely difficult for instructors of literature to converse with them about the subtleties and the beauties of our language. Such ephemeral interests are a veritable anathema to architects' logical, scientific, mathematical, and tangible way of thinking. In discussing a student's problems with organizing his term paper, for example, I made little progress until I actually ripped the pages out of his portfolio and then displayed them in their entirety on his drafting table, forcing him at that point to spatialize before my very eyes his essay's confusing order, its apparent lack of symmetry in the argumentation, and its ungainly proportions. Herein, I realized some minutes later, was a clue for selecting the proper reading materials for my course in literature.

The ideal work, whether primary or secondary, should teach students of architecture about the larger intellectual and aesthetic context residing outside those very buildings that they will have been sketching for nearly four semesters in their theory and design sections; it should delight them with its shapely, pictorial descriptions rather than its complicated, amorphous dialogue; and when it moves them, it should do so kinetically—up, around, backward and through, forward, and in between definitive textual loci. At the obvious risk of philistinism, one may say that *The Canterbury Tales* is a marvelous work of poetry, but its narrative-dramatic form, its linear pageantry, and its sophisticated interplay of genres will create only so many more verbal impediments in the minds of these students, who will be extremely interested in knowing where Chaucer's pilgrims are going and not interested at all in what his characters are saying. Rather, for the purposes of this course, Chaucer's unfinished *House of Fame* is the superior "architext" because of its attractive title and because it poses no similar conceptual barriers. Instead, by thus extrapolating from their knowledge of the anthropomorphic and Christocentric plan of the medieval cathedral, my students have fun speculating and arguing about the final identity of that mysterious "man of gret auctoritie." Is he an allegorical figure personified? The author himself? A pagan philosopher? A Christian saint? Or the Son of God? With these questions, however, we have arrived at my second pedagogical division—methodology.

Shocking as it will be to those with finer sensibilities, I have to confess that the Balnibarbians were not entirely off the mark for attempting "to shorten Discourse by cutting Polysyllables into one," since to a great degree the teaching of literature to architects is the discovery, often the construction, of a single vocabulary uniting these two fields of endeavor. Fortunately ambiguous words such as *loci, topos, plan, frontispiece, column, passage, stanza, section,* and *story/storey* are valuable precisely because they allow spatially oriented students to "deconstruct" the symbolic form of a literary edifice, while the term *perspective* (from the Latin *perspicere* 'to look through') similarly enables them to envision clearly and accurately the author's point of view, to organize plots, or to delineate characters. Likewise, the literary term *persona* is not as helpful or as physiognomically satisfying as the architectural equivalent *facade,* and *theme* is nowhere near to being as immediately insightful as *parterre,* a term used by nineteenth-century professors at the Ecole des Beaux-Arts (and still employed by architects) to signify the structural idea or "seed-thought" in the geometric planning of a landscape.

Lest one begin to suspect, along with Gulliver, that this approach is entirely creative rather than scholarly, I should point out that a crucial methodological precedent exists in the history of architectural criticism itself for drawing many of these same connections between buildings and books; for in the ten-part *De architectura,* the only complete extant treatise on this subject from classical antiquity, the Augustan military engineer Pollio Vitruvius derives his principles of *ordinatio, dispositio, symmetria, decor,* and *distributio* from the teachings of rhetoric (1.2), having proposed earlier in book 1 that each of the structural and decorative components of a building should embody a familiar historical and mythological narrative. Caryatids, he proffers by way of illustration, have their form and their function supporting the entablature of a temple because the city of Caryae had sided treacherously with the Persians in their invasion of the Peloponnisos. When the victorious Greeks had reduced the city and enslaved its female inhabitants, "the architects of that time designed for public buildings figures of matrons placed to carry burdens; in order that the punishment of the sin of the Cariatid women might be known to posterity and historically recorded" (1.1.5).

Rediscovered by Poggio Bracciolini in 1414, reprinted by Sulpitius in 1486, and codified, translated, interpreted, and transmogrified by every major designer from Leone Battista Alberti to Christopher Wren, Vitruvius's rhetorical matrix provided quattrocento architects and their successors with the one thing they were incapable of generating with the traditional Greco-Roman vocabulary of formalism—an equally authoritative hermeneutic system for both embodying and explicating symbolism in palaces, temples, churches, and urban plans. With his etiologic tales of divine cosmology and human metamorphoses, Vitruvius had endowed contemporary buildings with historical significance, both cultural and literary. Writing nearly two millenia before Jacques Derrida and Ferdinand Saussure, he muses prophetically in *De architectura*:

> Both in general and especially in architecture are these two things found; that which signifies and that which is signified. That which is signified is the thing proposed about which we speak; that which signifies is the demonstration unfolded in systems of precepts. (1.13)

Yet with these reflections we have been brought to my third and final pedagogical division—meanings.

Swift's philosophers were abnormally concerned, even for the early eighteenth century, about the potential for semantic abuse; thus what made their situation so remarkably comic stemmed in part from their having discriminated nicely between *res* and *verba* without any consideration to the larger discrepancy between application and explanation, common sense and abstract theory. Of course, depending on one's notions of the human condition, this viewpoint could be cause for either self-reflexive humor or scathing, self-righteous indignation. Unfortunately, though, in our century many of the descendants of these same Lagadocians have evolved to become dedicated architects; for in seeking to purify their own expressive forms of linguistic contamination by holding up to the world the intrinsic virtues of axes and grids, the Fibonacci series, Euclidean geometry, and the golden section, they isolate buildings from any social, historical, or literary context, thereby cultivating among themselves a clever preciosity and neology in place of the more demanding concern of an intelligible content. True, architects and designers should not be expected to stand in front of their works and explain them to the public, but neither should that educated public be subjected without any recourse to incestuous visions of the postmodernist arcanum or to someone's penchant for the *grotteschi* of high technology.

Herein lies a crucial difference between architecture and literature. Where the inexplicable literary work may be conveniently and deservedly ignored in the privacy of one's home or office, the inexplicable work of architecture—the home or the office itself—always stands in full public view as a disturbing monument to the failure of communication, aesthetic or otherwise. Like the all too appalling cityscape of many a recent metropolis, the Balnibarbian capital of modern Lagado, we should remember, sprawls "miserably waste, the Houses in Ruins, and the People without Food or Cloaths."

I make this polemical transition because one of the purposes of Spatial Form and Composition is to examine the production of architectural meaning itself—or, at least, to encourage my students to consider the possible *where, when, how,* and *why* of cultural history contributing in part to the final *what* in the design of a prominent building—Chartres Cathedral, Palladio's Teatro Olimpico, the Houses of Parliament, or Le Corbusier's Capitol at Chandigarh in the Punjab. In this respect, my lectures are organized chronologically for the simple reason that architects, like epic poets, are notorious for merely plagiarizing from their historical predecessors, usually modifying common structural motifs in order to satisfy the conservative expectations of a patron. Then, too, because I offer the class only in the spring semester, students will either have completed or be completing their required survey courses in the history of Western architecture. The benefits from this are twofold: practical and financial. I need not spend an inordinate amount of time in the classroom discussing significant buildings that they should already know, and my students need not spend their valuable dollars in the bookstore buying secondary studies that they should already possess.

And yet, as a glance at my syllabus might indicate, a further pedagogical consideration underlies this extensive use of secondary studies. Architects are not especially avid or voracious readers of popular literature, but they will inevitably consume and digest almost anything if only one manages to convince them that the text has something to do with a famous building or with their design studio. As a result, I devote approximately half of my course to the close analysis and discussion of major secondary studies in architectural history. My reasons for this are again pragmatic. Like interns in medicine, design students are under an extraordinary amount of pressure to master the fundamentals of their craft in a brief time. Consequently, my use of secondary studies not only helps students to maintain some semblance of morale and interest during the course of a physically grueling semester but also allows them to complete other assignments in their history and design sections. That is, the literary skills they are asked to develop for Spatial Form by carrying out research exercises, documenting sources, and writing abstracts of important articles are immediately useful to them in preparing their term papers for history and their thesis proposals for fifth-year topic studio. One standard fourth-year project is to design either a library or a public cenotaph in honor of an important figure—more often than not a poet, dramatist, novelist, or philosopher. Theory, we might say, informs the practice, but practice, in turn, helps to refine the theory.

Finally, although architects, for the most part, are remarkably sophisticated when it comes to analyzing the formal intricacies of a building, they are often shockingly ignorant if they are then asked to describe the archetypal, historical, political, or theological context within which such a structure might be erected. The average student, for example, will be able to tell the instructor more than the instructor wishes to know about the origins and the organization of the Versailles parterre—without ever mentioning that its evolution coincides with Louis xiv's program for the iconographic glorification of his personal absolutism. More frightening still is the students' failure to comprehend that Antonio Sant'Elia's futurist *Messaggio* (1914), Vladimir Tatlin's constructivist monument to the Third International (1919–20), and Albert Speer's Zeppelinfeld (1936) are just as inseparable from political ideology. It bears repeating. Design students, incredibly fluent in the vocabulary and the syntax of architectural forms, are paradoxically limited in their awareness that these same elements may be the symbolic manifestations of larger—and on occasion more ominous—religious or political orientations. Thus, a more elaborate hypothesis for teaching cultural history to architects always collapses at the precise moment that I visit the Academy of Lagado and witness the Balnibarbian Projectors trying to communicate with their scales and their blocks, their cardboard and their glue. Gulliver himself, I am reminded at such moments, could not help smiling when he noticed that "[t]here was a most ingenious Architect who had contrived a new method for building Houses, by beginning at the Roof, and working downwards to the Foundation" (153).

What Spatial Form attempts, therefore, is to introduce design students to the history of Western culture and to the practical value of contextual criticism by examining major literary works that illustrate some of the fundamental ways in which buildings and spaces have been depicted imaginatively and conceptually since our expulsion from the Edenic hut and the condemnation of our first urban high rise, the Tower of Babel. It is an edifying process, however, whose cornerstones are hardly recent; for as Caesar Augustus, Vergil's patron, was to hear from his own master builder, the architect Vitruvius:

> When, however, it is perceived that all studies are related to one another and have points of contact, they will easily believe it can happen. For a general education is put together like one body from its members. So those who from tender years are trained in various studies recognise the same characters in all the arts and see the intercommunication of all disciplines, and by that circumstance more easily acquire general information. (1.1.12)

Syllabus

Course   Spatial Form and Composition. Jesse J. Easley, English, University of Southern California.

Description   A lower-division elective satisfying general education requirements in composition and literature. Spring semester. No prerequisites, but completion of History of Western Architecture 214 or concurrent enrollment in History of
Western Architecture 215 is strongly encouraged. Meets three times a week for one
hour each session. Lectures, group discussions, written assignments, regular conferences, a final examination, and a term paper.

Objectives   To introduce design students to the general principles of literary
research while focusing in particular on major secondary studies that exemplify
cultural and historical approaches to the analysis of architecture; establish a series of
possible semiotic contexts by reading primary works in literature that develop the
themes of the Garden of Eden, the Tower of Babel, anthropomorphism, and the
earthly city as an adumbration of the heavenly Jerusalem; to propose for consideration that spatial form and composition are more closely interrelated than students
might have imagined before completing the course.

Schedule

(P) primary, (S) secondary—on reserve and required, (R) recommended
1. Spatial form and composition—an introduction.
2. Sacred and profane space. (P) Eliade.
3. Anthropomorphism and the heavenly Jerusalem. (P) Plato, *Republic* 4; Vitruvius,
   Ten Books, books 1-3; 1 Kings 6-8, 2 Chronicles 2-4, Ezekiel 40-44, Revelations
   21, 1 Corinthians 3. (R) Gutmann 1-43; Krinsky; McClung, *Architecture of
   Paradise*; Rosenau, *Visions of the Temple*.
4. The living temple and the City of God. (P) Augustine, *City of God*, books 15.1-9,
   17–19 and 18.1-26, 45–48; Chaucer, *House of Fame*; Panofsky, *Gothic Architecture*. (S) Braswell; Dougherty 23-53; Fingesten; Kendrick; Pratt. (R) Crosby 24-
   52; Freeman; Panofsky, *Abbot Suger*; Simson 3-141.
5. The castle of the body. (P) Meun, *The Romance of the Rose*; Shakespeare, *The Rape
   of Lucrece*. (S) Comito 89-147 or J. V. Fleming 54-72. (R) Stewart.
6. The Renaissance rediscovery of Vitruvius. (P) Wittkower, *Architectural Principles*.
   (S) Fraser-Jenkins; Lehmann; Taylor. (R) Gadol; Hersey.
7. Anthropomorphism and the heavenly Jerusalem 2. (P) Spenser, *Faerie Queene*,
   book 2; Campanella, *City of the Sun*. (S) Barkan 61-80, 116-74; Fletcher 11-56.
8. The living temple and the City of God 2. (P) Herbert, *Poems*; Bunyan, *The Pilgrim's
   Progress*, book 1. (S) Fish, *Living Temple*; Talon. (R) Kaufmann.
9. The English country house. (P) Carew, "To my friend G. N. from Wrest"; Jonson,
   "To Penshurst"; Marvell, "Upon Appleton House"; Waller, "On St. James's
   Park." (S) G. R. Hibbard; Wayne. (R) Girouard; McClung, *Country House*.
10. Palladio's English villa and the dispossessed. (P) Pope, "Temple of Fame,"
    "Epistle to Dr. Arbuthnot," "Ode on Solitude," "Epistle to Burlington";
    Goldsmith, "The Deserted Village." (S) Barrell 35-88. Brownell 71-325; J. Burke,
    English Art 3-89; or Mack, *Garden and City* 3-115. (R) H. F. Clark; Wittkower,
    Palladio 73-190.
11. The temple of reason. (P) Rosenblum. (R) Honour; Perez-Gomez 3-161; Rosenau,
    Boullée; Rykwert, *First Moderns*.
12. A Gothic yearning. (P) Genesis 11.1–9; Hugo, *Notre-Dame de Paris*. (S) K. Clark,
    Gothic Revival. (R) Hegel; Lessing.

13. Architecture and the crisis of meaning. (P) Dostoyevski, *Notes from the Underground*; Ibsen, *Master Builder*; Mann, *Death in Venice*. (S) Beaver; Pevsner. (R) E. Frank, *Literary Architecture*.
14. The modern search for symbols. (P) Genet, *The Balcony*; Joyce, *Portrait of the Artist*; Robbe-Grillet, *In the Labyrinth*. (S) J. Frank, "Spatial Form." (R) Foucault, *Discipline*.
15. And a return to meaning. (P) Eco, *Name of the Rose*. (S) Yates 1-172.
16. Spatial form and composition—a tentative summary. (P) Calvino, *Invisible Cities*; Rykwert, *On Adam's House*. (S) Bachelard. (R) Bloomer and Moore.

Robert Spaethling

Literature and Music

Literature and Music is an intermediate-level undergraduate course offered in the core curriculum of the University of Massachusetts, Boston. Core courses at the university are intended to introduce students to broad areas of knowledge, such as the arts or philosophic and humanistic studies and to improve their writing skills and critical thinking. Literature and Music is an interdisciplinary course that focuses on the creative interaction between two art forms and presents a documented history of their fusion, from the ancient Greek music drama to postmodern minimalism. Class presentations, assignments, and discussions follow a chronological order and derive from three thematic categories (suggested by Scher, "Literature and Music"):

1. The presence of music in literature. Includes writings ranging from parts of the Old Testament to Thomas Mann's *Doctor Faustus*; the musician in literature from the figure of Orpheus to Peter Shaffer's *Amadeus*; music as a structural device, such as counterpoint in poetry or the sonata form in the modern novella; music as a dramatic vehicle, and music as a literary metaphor.
2. The presence of literature in music. Includes the omniscient narrator in operatic music (Wagner); the soloist as protagonist in the concerto; reflections of literary styles in music, such as the musical language of the Enlightenment and Sturm und Drang; the technique of quotation in music; forms of dialogue in chamber music and symphonies.
3. The synthesis of literature and music. Includes synaesthesia and melopoeia, word music and verbal music in poetry; the German lied; Wagner's music theater.

These categories serve as a general pool of ideas, topics, discussions, and listening experiences. What students can gain from studying these materials is first of all a historical perspective on one of the oldest art forms: the blend of word, music, and dance. They will learn, too, that modes of artistic and intellectual expression—be they literary, musical, scientific, or philosophical—do not arise in isolation from one another; rather, they are concrete and relatable signs of a common cultural infrastructure. Finally, literature and music combine to add a much needed depth to human comprehension; separately and together, they have the intrinsic power to reach beyond the surface of history and individual consciousness into the wellsprings of the human mind. In so doing, they help us probe the human condition. (See Scher, "Literature and Music"; Bernstein; C. S. Brown, "Relations"; Cone; Leichtentritt; M. Brown; Winn.)

I begin the course with the proposition that music and poetic chants, combined with ritual dance, may have formed the beginning of human artistic experience; they began together even before art was known as a concept. Musicoliterary interrelations are, therefore, richly documented in early literatures, where we hear the story of creation not only as a narrative but as song, where the biblical David drives out the evil spirits from King Saul with his soothing harp music, and where Homer portrays Odysseus, his hero, moved to tears by the song of a blind minstrel. And we consider the most beautiful and symbolic myth of all: the story of Orpheus, the Thracian singer, who conquered death itself with his lyre and song.

After these readings and discussions, I introduce the first critic of the genre: Plato. Homer had already suggested the cathartic effect of music in the performance of the harper as well as its bewitching, even destructive effect in the song of the sirens. Plato sharpens this ambiguity into a specific philosophical and educational stance. In his *Republic*, he banishes artists whose art would appeal to the senses rather than the mind; poets, even the great tragedians, who feed the human passions instead of restraining them; and musicians who employ dithyrambic rhythms rather than simple, disciplined tonalities such as the Dorian mode. This last art form alone, in Plato's view, can nurture and harmonize the soul. Plato's Socratic questions touch on the essence of the musical and rhetorical experience—on the nature and function of these art forms, which are often called, for that very reason, the persuasive arts. (See Hollander.)

The questions that have drawn continuous attention from Plato (*Republic*) to Augustine (*De musica*) to Anthony Burgess (*Clockwork Orange*) are these: Do literature and music, as single or combined art forms, excite or harmonize our senses? Do they bring out the beast or the divine in us? Plato divided their effects into positive and negative forces to suit his vision of truth and education. We (in the course) must be open to the entire range of emotions that these arts elicit in us; we must accept them as guides and tools for deeper and more complete understanding.

Most of the course materials presented up to this point are based on readings. I now turn to some taped musical examples beginning with musical and poetic recitations of the ancient Greeks. This must be done judiciously, as both the performances and the instruments are reconstructed; even musical notations were generally not preserved in written form at this time, around 400 BC. (I use the *Harmonia Mundi* recording *Musique de la Grèce Antique*.) From there I take a thousand-year leap to the *Camerata Fiorentina*, a gathering of poets and musicians in Renaissance Italy who sought to re-create the ancient music theater through their own *dramma per musica*. It is here, in Florence of about 1600, that the Western opera, as we know it, was born. (See Kerman, *Opera as Drama*; Winn.)

The Greek heritage represents only one root of modern Western musicoliterary experience; the Hebrew tradition of musical declamation of prayers and scriptures is another. The Jewish custom of Torah cantillation, a "singing of speech," entered the Middle Ages by way of oral tradition and a system of manual signs passed on from generation to generation. The liturgical music heard and practiced in Western synagogues today derives from traditions established in the nineteenth century, but its roots go back to biblical times. They influenced early Christian liturgical singing and the monophonic choral offerings that became known as the Gregorian chant.

I complete the medieval section with some secular songs that were current between the eleventh and thirteenth centuries: songs of the Provence, German *Minnelieder*, the enchanting English canon "Summer is icumen in," and even a couple of bawdy drinking songs from the medieval *Carmina Burana*. If time permits I engage in a quick excursion into Irish folksong, which seems to me a legitimate heir to the medieval plainsong.

The stage is now set for the "modern" period—the poets and composers who are within easy access of the modern reader and listener. I start with the baroque, introducing the period through the visual arts: architecture, sculpture, painting. My purpose is to demonstrate the typical baroque idiom in all forms of art and science. I compare, for instance, the dramatic yet fluid style of a ceiling painting by Tiepolo to the polyphonic structure of a Bach fugue; I explain the period's proclivity for intricate structure by comparing musical counterpoint to patterns of the sonnet; most specifically, I discuss Handel's musical setting of John Dryden's poem "A Song for St. Cecilia's Day." This ode exemplifies the poetic use of music as a symbol, as a theme, and as structure. Conversely, Handel's composition exemplifies the musician's response to the challenge of setting an onomatopoeic text to music. Similarly intriguing is Haydn's *Die Schöpfung*, an oratorio based on a text from Milton's *Paradise Lost*. Haydn, of course, no longer speaks the musical language of Bach and Handel; the "learned" counterpoint has given way to simple, diatonic melodies reflecting the taste and spirit, the linearity and optimism, of the Age of Enlightenment. (See Hollander; Kerman, *Listen*.)

Then comes Mozart. He fills his music with passion and compassion; he gives music a human face. We can hear the yearning of young love in the "Adagio" of the G Major Violin Concerto (K. 216) and the voice of personal fulfillment in the B-flat Major Piano Concerto (K. 595). In Mozart's music we experience the rhythms of the dance but not orgiastic dance, the enchantment of erotic tension but not sexual destruction, melodies to witness human frailty but always, also, a voice of reconciliation. It is well known that Mozart's music is based on strict musical logic; still, the composer endowed his works with a civilizing grace and humanity, and it is these elements that make his art so affable and influential. (See M. Brown.)

Beethoven, too, prepares the ground for the Romantics: his music is both literary and philosophical, full of pathos and heroism. And he employs specific literary techniques: the "Andante con moto" in his fourth piano concerto contains one of the most distinct dialogues in all musical history; soloist and orchestra actually seem to talk to each other. But Beethoven's most significant and sublime achievement in the musicoliterary field remains the choral movement of the Ninth Symphony, where poetry and the human voice reach beyond the power of the instruments, singing the grand hymn of universal brotherhood.

The core period of German Romanticism (c. 1790–1840) is the most fertile and productive phase of artistic interrelations in the modern history of the arts. Because of the wealth of the materials, I organize this part of the course into specific issue-related aspects, so that the fundamental pattern of the course (outlined above) is highlighted here in concentrated form:

1. Literature containing musical themes or figures.
2. Analyses of concepts, such as word music, verbal music, synaesthesia, melopoeia.
3. Comparison of musical and poetic structures: for instance, comparing the ABA design in literature and music (Poe's "Ligeia" and Schumann's "Märchenerzählung," op. 132), or comparing "rondo" designs in music (e.g., ABBA, or ABACABA, or ABACAD) with rhyme schemes in poetry (abba, abab, etc.), or comparing techniques of repetition as poetic and musical devices.
4. The German lied. This emerging genre represents the climax in the Romantic fusion of poetry and music. I begin with Schubert and go on to Hugo Wolf and Mahler.
5. Richard Wagner and his *Gesamtkunstwerk*. I discuss Wagner's idea of organic style—the total fusion of word, music, and persona—especially in *Tristan und Isolde*.
6. The heritage of Wagner: positive inspirations and negative reactions—Baudelaire, Mallarmé, Joyce, Kandinsky, Nietzsche, Mann.

The reading and listening assignments listed in the syllabus for this period reflect a personal choice rather than an artistic or pedagogical rationale. It stands to reason that the entire course and in particular the Romantic period could be taught with different selections from literature as well as music. The materials selected and suggested here are meant to be typical rather than uniquely canonical. (See Aronson; Brook; Clive; Flaherty; Kerman, *Opera*; Kramer; Scher, *Verbal Music*; Stein, *Poem and Music*.)

After Romanticism, I divide the remaining class time for two tasks yet to be done: a comparative analysis of a literary text and its musical setting and the development of literature and music as an interdisciplinary subject to the present day.

For my comparative analysis I choose one great literary figure whose works have served as source and inspiration for more than a single composer. One such figure is Goethe. (See Spaethling.) Goethe's *Faust* has repeatedly attracted composers, among them Ludwig Spohr, Robert Schumann, Hector Berlioz, Charles Gounod, and Gustav Mahler. Shakespeare, too, has provided a seemingly inexhaustible source of musical ideas and settings. *Macbeth, Othello,* and *King Lear,* among others, have frequently been the subject of musical adaptations. One of the best hours in my class is spent comparing the last act of *Othello* with the same act in Verdi's *Otello.* Such comparisons and discussions stimulate ideas and insights regarding differences as well as similarities between the poetic-dramatic and musical-dramatic arts.

I present the last historical phase of the course, the period from the turn of the century to our own time, as a three-pronged development, involving intellectual, political, and mass-cultural manifestations. Despite their apparent differences, the three manifestations are all movements of liberation. Arnold Schönberg, the father of twelve-tone music, sought to free music from the worn-out harmonies of the classical-Romantic age, from Wagnerian fusions (and confusions), from the limiting aesthetics of the past. A similar development, a fragmentation of the familiar, occurs in literature and philosophy (Wittgenstein) and the visual arts (Klee). Schönberg produced a new "democratic" tonal order, but its effect proved to be so radical, cerebral, and abstract that it never became part of a common artistic language. But, if the new "serious" music was all intellect, the new dance movement was all body. The rock culture is the popular rebellion against the establishment in the arts; it is a rhythmic, dithyrambic revolt—Plato would have frowned—against society and societal aesthetics, a liberation of the dancer as well as the dance. (It should be of interest to students that rock music has its origin in the Afro-American religious song.)

The political ballad is based on the assumption that art can be an effective tool in bettering the social life of the less fortunate. The excellent materials in this category range from Brecht-Weill collaborations to the songs of Joan Baez and Bob Dylan. It is important to point out here that the relation of text and music in the political song is different from that in the Romantic lied. In the political song, the two disciplines work toward mutual alienation and critical awareness rather than toward fusion and a combined aesthetic effect.

The last two hours are devoted to an assessment of the effects of literature and music as an interart field. I base this discussion on the reading of James Baldwin's short story "Sonny's Blues" (a Harlem youngster saves himself through jazz) and on selections from Anthony Burgess's *Clockwork Orange* and Aldous Huxley's *Point Counter Point* (Spandrell's suicide to the sounds of Beethoven's A minor Quartet, op. 132). These texts provide an excellent platform for considering a final question that has gradually emerged as one of the pedagogical strands of the course: How do literature and music as a combined field of art affect us? My concluding argument emphasizes that it is important for us to know the arts, be they separate or in tandem, and that we must open ourselves to their effects. But we must not be controlled by them or by the image makers who use them. This course on literature and music is designed to increase our understanding of the arts as well as our critical awareness and reception of them.

Literature and Music is an introductory course and will, therefore, encompass a fair number of materials on a beginning (but I hope not superficial) level. It might be prudent to offer the course on a two-semester basis so that more selections, both literary and musical, can be presented in their entirety. I have also given thought to a second, more advanced sequence course that would concentrate on just one historical period, such as the baroque or Romanticism, or that would present one topic, such as The Figure of Orpheus in Literature, Music, and the Visual Arts. Such courses would not aim at broad coverage; rather, they would present materials in greater detail and completeness. My personal choice for such an offering would be the German nineteenth century. I would begin with *Die Winterreise* (or *Die schöne Müllerin*) by Schubert; next I would present and discuss Wagner's *Tristan und Isolde* (or *Die Walküre*), expanding on Wagner's influence on the arts and politics. Subsequent items might include Mahler's Eighth Symphony, with an emphasis on the choral movement based on texts from Goethe's *Faust*; samples from the Hofmannsthal-Strauss correspondence; and Mann's *Doktor Faustus*, complete with illustrations of the music described in the novel. Finally I would discuss the transformation of Georg Büchner's *Woyzeck* into Alban Berg's *Wozzeck*, emphasizing the evolution of the twelve-tone system in musical composition. This course would undoubtedly benefit from the participation of a colleague in the music department who could either be a partner or a regular guest lecturer. A collaboration of this sort would enhance the pedagogical aspects of the course and help provide a sound professional footing.

Syllabus

Course   Literature and Music. Robert Spaethling, German and Russian, University of Massachusetts, Boston.

Description   An interdisciplinary course offered every second year by the German and Russian Department. Fulfills a core requirement in the arts and may count as an elective for the German major. No prerequisites. Three class hours a week for fourteen weeks.

Objectives   To introduce students to the interrelation between literature and music, by means of a historical survey comprising three principal themes and approaches: music in literature, literature in music, and the symbiosis of the two art forms; to make students aware of literature and music as a definable interdisciplinary field, enhance reading and listening abilities, and improve writing skills.

Schedule

1. Introduction of class, aims, requirements. Examples of word-music combinations and their heightened effects: The "Marseillaise"; "Lili Marlene"; "Là ci darem la mano," from Mozart's *Don Giovanni*; "Battle Hymn of the Republic." Interart as concept and idea. C. S. Brown, "The Relations between Music and Literature"; Winn; Scher, "Literature and Music."

2. Music in ancient literatures. *Old Testament*, 1 Samuel 16.14-23; *Kalevala*, Runo 1 and 3; "The Horse Dance" in Neihardt; Homer, *Odyssey*, books 8 and 12; Plato, *Republic*, books 3 and 10; the myth of Orpheus; Ovid, *Metamorphoses*, books 10 and 11.

3. Orpheus continued. Excerpts from Monteverdi, *Orfeo*; Gluck, *Orfeo ed Euridice* (act 2, lines 18-28); Mozart, *Die Zauberflöte* ("Glockenspiel"); sonnets 1-3 from Rilke's *Sonnets to Orpheus*. The "Kol Nidre"; Gregorian chants; troubadours ("Jaufre Rudel"); Witzlaw ("Loibere risen von dem boimen").

4. Styles of the baroque. Visual materials: Tiepolo, Bernini, Balthasar Neumann; Bach: "Inventio I," "Credo" from B Minor Mass; Handel-Dryden, "St. Cecilia's Day." Enlightenment in music: Haydn, *Die Schöpfung*, numbers 1 and 30.

5. The voice of the individual. Mozart, Violin Concerto no. 3 ("Adagio"), Piano Concerto no. 27 ("Largetto"), "Contessa, perdono" from *Nozze di Figaro*; Beethoven, Piano Concerto no. 4 ("Andante con moto") compared with Gluck, *Orfeo*, act 2, numbers 18-28; choral movement of Beethoven's Ninth Symphony.

6. Romanticism. E. T. A. Hoffmann, *Don Juan*. Word and verbal music: Scher, *Verbal Music*. Poems: Goethe, "Wanderers Nachtlied"; Brentano, "Abendständchen"; Baudelaire, "L'invitation au voyage"; Poe, "The Bells"; Pound, "Langue d'Oc," "Mauberly." Poe, "Ligeia." Chopin, Etude in B Minor, op. 25, no. 10; Schumann, "Märchenerzählung," op. 132.

7. Schubert, "Gretchen am Spinnrade," "Erlkönig," *Die Winterreise* (selections); Schumann, "Mondnacht"; Wolf, "Mignon" lieder.

8. Wagner, *Tristan und Isolde* (selections, but definitely "Liebestod"). Wagner influence: Baudelaire, Mallarmé, Nietzsche, Kandinsky, Joyce.

9. Thomas Mann, *Tristan, Doktor Faustus* (selections; guest); Tolstoy, *Kreutzer Sonata* (conclusion).

10. Shakespeare and Verdi. Comparison of *Othello* and *Otello*. Goethe's *Faust* and the musicians: Berlioz, *La Damnation de Faust* (selections), Mahler, last movement of Eighth Symphony.

11. Schönberg, op. 11; *Pierrot Lunaire*; "Sprechgesang." From John Cage to American text-sound pieces.

12. The rock-music phenomenon. The Beatles; a rock mass; Afro-American spirituals.

13. Music as social criticism. Brecht-Weill, *Mahagonny*, act 2, numbers 12-15; Bob Dylan, "A Hard Rain's a Gonna Fall." Joan Baez, Pete Seeger, Wolf Biermann.

14. Baldwin, "Sonny's Blues"; Burgess, *Clockwork Orange*; Huxley, *Point Counter Point* (scene of Spandrell committing suicide while listening to Beethoven's Quartet in A Minor, op. 132). Summation.

Anthony J. Mazzella

Adaptations of Literature into Other Arts

It is art that makes *life.*
Henry James,
letter to H. G. Wells

Literature has had a significant influence on the other arts, especially as it has been adapted to other art forms—art, dance, film, music, opera, radio, television, and spoken-word recording. Indeed, it is unusual for the other art forms to be adapted to the extent that literature has been. One thinks of Tolstoy's 1891 short story inspired by Beethoven's 1803 *Kreutzer Sonata* or Martha Clarke's dance-theater piece *The Garden of Earthly Delights* (1984), based on the painting by Hieronymous Bosch; but such adaptations (if they can be called adaptations) are infrequent when compared with the range and quantity of adaptations received by, say, Shakespeare's *Romeo and Juliet*.

The term *adaptation* is here used in both a broad sense (to encompass a literary work's having influenced or inspired a work in another art form) and a narrow sense (to mean a literary work's having been translated into another art form so that the elements of literature tend to have counterparts in the adaptation). Generally, instrumental music tends to appear under the first definition and spoken-word recording, radio, film, video, opera, and vocal music under the second; dance and art (painting, sculpture, illustration, etc.) tend to appear in both, depending on the mimetic quality of the dance piece or the artwork.

Since literature has produced an avalanche of adaptations, however defined, a course exploring adaptations of literature into other arts encourages students to determine why artists seek literature as a source of inspiration and to explore what various artists have stated about the techniques and challenges of adaptation. Next to be considered might be the nature of the different adaptational media in order of increasing remoteness from the main literary forms of novel, story, poem, and play (here defined as text rather than performance, which is another matter entirely). Finally, students should receive exposure to individual adaptations in most of the eight categories listed above, adaptations that illustrate the challenges of going from literature to that particular art form. They should also become familiar with multiple adaptations of a single literary work so as to acquire some understanding of how the literary work undergoes changes in moving from medium to medium.

Artists seek literature as a source of inspiration for both aesthetic and economic reasons. Whereas Steven Spielberg may film Peter Benchley's *Jaws* because there are millions of *Jaws* readers out there, Ismail Merchant, James Ivory, and Ruth Prawer Jhabvala adapt E. M. Forster's *Room with a View* because they believe in the novel. For the audience, literature is dramatized or adapted because the adaptation offers the potential for replicating a satisfying aesthetic experience. When something in one art form gives pleasure, we tend to welcome its reappearance in another art form, hoping to re-create the pleasure derived from the original work.

The artist, of course, may have yet other motives for adapting. For example, the opera composer Thea Musgrave based her opera *The Voice of Ariadne* on Henry James's story "Last of the Valerii" for reasons that were purely musical. The Royal Opera House had commissioned a score, and she needed to find a story. That, as she said in an interview,

> is the most difficult thing in writing an opera. I began looking at short stories, reading things higgledy-piggledy, and one day I happened to be in a bookstall at Notting Hill Gate and my hand fell on a volume of Henry James. I skimmed through it and found the story . . . and I knew instantly that this was what I wanted. What attracted me was the character who isn't there—a statue. I think subconsciously I had been looking for something in which [recorded] tape could be used, and when I found the statue I thought, my God, this is it. (S. Fleming)

In this instance, necessity and serendipity were the mother of invention, the libretto being eventually written by Amalia Elguera.

Donald Wilson's experience of adaptation was different, for his challenge was to write a ten-part video dramatization of Tolstoy's *Anna Karenina*. "So here you are," he said, "at your writing table, looking at 900 pages of prose from the hand of one of the immortals. How do you start?" He speaks of having read all the English translations and not the original (feeling that the latter should be attempted only if one's "command of Russian is fairly competent"), of having "been enraptured by the characters and event," of having tried "to get closer to the author by reading all of his other work," of researching the scholarship on Tolstoy, this novel, Russian manners, customs, laws, and social conditions of the period, even train travel: "Great matters and trivial—you soak in them all."

But Wilson also cited a danger: "Research is so fascinating that it becomes difficult to cease from it and actually start writing. At some point you have to place all these books on one side for reference and go back to the masterpiece itself." When he did, he had to make the kind of decision that confronts all adapters: he had to alter the original. Sometimes the alteration is a judicial weighing of relative merits; always it results from the nature of the adapting medium. For instance, although Levin is the novel's protagonist, Anna is the pivot of the drama; so Wilson made the primary character of the novel secondary in the video adaptation. Because of the demands of the medium, he changed the novel's cliff-hanger element:

> the viewer, as opposed to the reader, must wait probably a week before the next chapter opens, so it is necessary to strengthen that element. Each *scene*, as well as each episode, ought to be constructed in such a manner as to ensure that the audience, subconsciously led from one to another, is kept in a constant state of wanting to know what will happen next. However complicated— indeed abstruse—the relationship may be between characters, utter clarity in exposition must be the goal.

Wilson concentrated ultimately on the dramatist's techniques: the novelist's narrative interruptions cannot work on video; nor can the novelist's tempo, for video can show in a moment what takes pages to describe. According to Wilson, "eliminations and cannibalism" are the answer to a novelist's building up of a minor scene and dismissal of "the vital dramatic material in one terse paragraph" and to an author's myriad characters. The action must be shown, the central roles must be reinforced, the major scenes must be written in if they are absent from the literary source. There are certain advantages to these changes: good actors will want to play the roles, and the audience is wholly involved and not a voyeur ("The narrative tells us so much of the author's feelings about his creatures and the motives that drive them . . . [that] narration exiles the viewer to a position . . . outside and at one remove from the characters"). Dialogue, too, is a challenge because, "with few exceptions, the dialogue in novels is unspeakable—in the most literal sense—apart from the rare illuminating phrase which can be reproduced verbatim and used as a guide for characterization." In short, Wilson declares the need to be "faithful always to the *spirit* of the original." (On the television adaptation of *Emma*, see Lauritzen.)

This injunction to be faithful to the spirit of the original points the way to the next phase of the course: an examination of the nature of literature and of the other arts, each as a medium of communication. What is it about literature that makes it so adaptable? And what is it about the other art forms that can encompass literature as a source for adaptation?

When we examine the media, starting with literature and moving to the other arts in order of increasing remoteness from the literary form, we find that written literature is a medium with a highly structured pattern of words on a page advancing from left to right (in English, Romance, and some but not all other languages) and top to bottom, which, through the interaction of eye and brain, can create at one time and with great latitude what all of the other art forms do singly or incompletely. Literature has had an enormous influence on the other arts because it is the most flexible, least cumbersome medium, an effect that results from its being abstract, in the sense that words constitute abstract symbols on a page.

Spoken-word recording, the adaptation medium closest to the written literary form, may be defined as an aural rendering usually through a single spoken human voice, rather than through an inner mental voice, of everything in the literary text. Radio is similar to spoken-word recording, but the text heard may be both condensed and enhanced with sound effects and uttered by more than one human voice, although a word recording can be transmitted by radio.

Film may be described as the first of the concrete media—the others being video, opera, dance, and art—since it gives a visible, spatial form to what was nonphysical in literature. Film, in this context, is the transfer of color or noncolor image and sound or dialogue from what existed in abstract form to what is concrete, from words on pages of relatively long duration (even with some short stories) to rectangular, illuminated moving images of relatively short duration. Video may be defined as an extension of film in that it is a visual and aural transfer of an abstract two-dimensional form, but video, unlike film, has a three-dimensional effect. Both literature and video may be of long duration, given the serial possibilities of television. (A film may also be telecast, but it shrinks in dimension because of screen size and loss of aspect ratio.) Opera—that is, performed opera, not recorded opera— is a variant of film and video (aesthetically, not historically) in that it is a verbal and visual rendering but one that is also highly structured aurally and occupies three-dimensional, concrete space.

Dance, art, and orchestral music are nonverbal adaptation media. Dance may be described as nonverbal concrete movement in space and time through the medium of the human body, using a form that had originally been an abstract construction of words. Art—illustration, painting, sculpture, drawing, and so on—isolates and highlights in stationary, concrete terms an aspect, scene, incident, mood, or character from a literary work. And music, primarily instrumental but also vocal, renders in significant arrangements of sound an invisible medium (the song not the singer) of an art form that was visible and abstract: those black symbols on a white page. While instrumental or orchestral music is increasingly remote from the literary form, vocal music is the closest of the adaptation media to one literary form—poetry. Radio concentrates on words as largely meaning, and music concentrates on words as largely sound.

In brief, the literary forms encompass all the other art forms by being both more, by having the ability to express thought more easily, than film, video, opera, dance, art, and instrumental music, and by being less: except for spoken-word recording, radio, and vocal music, the other art forms are visible, concrete, comprehensive, or holistic, while literature is linear and abstract. Literature encompasses all of life but cannot show it or equal its sounds. The other arts communicate life's colors, shapes, and sounds but not, at least not effectively or easily, human life's thought, analysis, reflection. Because the mental dimension of literature can encompass the showy, literature more readily lends itself to adaptation.

Studying literature and its adaptations offers students the "shuttle" benefit. By going back and forth between two art forms, the student is better able to understand the important elements of each, considering their absence from, or presence in, the one but not the other. Intriguingly, too, an element present in both may yet be different in each.

To illustrate these theoretical issues more concretely, the course investigates specific adaptations in the different categories as well as multiple adaptations of a single literary work. The objectives of the course are to become acquainted with the immense influence of literature on the other arts in the context of adaptations, to gain insight into the evolution of a literary work as it undergoes translation into other art forms, and to read the comments of some creative artists about the adaptation process.

In exploring the full range of literature's influence on the other arts in the context of adaptation, one may consider the Bible; myth, legend, and folktale; fable and fairytale; and novels, plays, short stories, poems, and nonfiction as these works have been adapted or used by painters, illustrators, choreographers, filmmakers, composers, recording artists, and radio and television producers. Three instructive groupings might be considered. The first group comprises minor literary works or those that may have been overshadowed by the adaptation (quite often operatic), such as François Ancelot's *Elizabeth d'Angleterre* and Donizetti's *Roberto Devereux*, or Beaumarchais's comedy *The Barber of Seville* and Rossini's opera. (See Hughes and also Kestner on *La Traviata* and *La Bohème*; Stern on *Norma*.) The second group includes major literary works that have remained significant and have inspired other art forms. Examples are the Bible and its influence on art (e.g., Italian Renaissance paintings) or on film (e.g., Pasolini's *Gospel According to St. Matthew*); James's *Turn of the Screw*, Jack Clayton's film, and Benjamin Britten's opera, or James's *Golden Bowl* and the James Cellon Jones–Jack Pulman six-part video adaptation; Flaubert's *Madame Bovary*, Renoir's 1934 film, Minnelli's 1949 film, and Rodney Bennett and Giles Cooper's 1975 video adaptation; Lewis Carroll's *Alice in Wonderland* and the famous Disney version.

Finally, the third group consists of extraordinary literary works, those that have inspired productions in virtually every other art form or in significant numbers: Shakespeare's *A Midsummer Night's Dream*, for instance, and its adaptation to film (1935 Max Reinhardt, 1968 Peter Hall), dance (Balanchine, Ashton), music (Mendelssohn), or *Romeo and Juliet*, the apparent champion, with at least seven films, twenty-two ballets, fifteen musical compositions, as well as paintings and video and spoken-word adaptations. In addition, one can expect to consider the reasons for the continuing appeal and interest accorded certain authors or literary works, such as *Hamlet*, which in 1976 inspired yet another artwork, John Neumeier's ballet *Hamlet Connotations*. (On Shakespearean adaptations, see Eckert; Jorgens; Kozintsev; Manvell, *Shakespeare*; Potter and Potter; and issues of the *Shakespeare on Film Newsletter*.) More recently, E. M. Forster's *Room with a View* and *Maurice* were adapted to film by Ivory and Jhabvala, *A Passage to India* by David Lean.

The principal value of a course concerned with these adaptations is probably that of an exciting diversity. The literature can range among all the major and ancillary types; the adaptation categories constitute the entire field of the arts; the specific models studied are necessarily international, interdisciplinary, and multicultural; and the effect for the student is the paradox of uniformity as multiplicity—one literary work studied as literature and then reexamined as a painting, a ballet, a film, an opera, a video dramatization, a fantasy overture, a radio serial, a word recording. To see a literary work reconceived for and embodied in another art form is to see the creative processes at work, to appreciate, in effect, literature's capacity for infinite variety. What Henry James said of art may be applied, adapted (perhaps without too much hyperbole) to literature and the arts: It is literature adapted to other arts "that *makes* life, makes interest, makes importance, for our consideration and appreciation of these things, and I know of no substitute whatsoever for the force and beauty of its process" (770).

Bibliographical Note

In addition to the scholarly works cited above, the teacher of adaptations of literature into other arts will find the following helpful: On paintings derived from literature, Rensselaer Lee's books and Richard D. Altick are especially useful. For adaptations of plays, see Harry Keyshian, William T. Leonard, and Roger Manvell (*Theater and Film*). Cinematic versions of literary works have generated much scholarly attention. Too numerous to mention here are studies devoted to films derived from individual works (e.g., *Tom Jones, The Wizard of Oz*), from a number of works by a single author (e.g., Nabokov, O'Neill, Steinbeck, Wells, Tennessee Williams), and from a literary character (e.g., Sherlock Holmes) or genre (e.g., the mystery). Scholars who have written more generally about the relations between literature and film as well as about adaptation of literature into film include George Bluestone, Joy Gould Boyum, Carol A. Emmens, A. G. S. Enser, John Harrington, Andrew S. Horton and Joan Margretta, Roy Huss and Norman Silverstein, Michael Klein and Gillian Parker, Frank N. Magill, Fred H. Marcus (*Film and Literature, Short Story/Short Film*), Gerald Mast, Stuart Y. McDougal, Gabriel Miller, Gerald Peary and Roger Shatzkin (*Modern American Novel, Classic American Novel*), Robert Richardson, Neil Sinyard, Douglas Street, Geoffrey Wagner, and Jeffrey E. Welch.

Syllabus

Course   Adaptations of Literature into Other Arts. Anthony J. Mazzella, English, William Paterson College of New Jersey.

Description   Offered periodically since 1980 as an elective in English. Uses video and audio equipment in Humanities Media Center. Meets once a week for 2 ½ hours.

Objectives   To introduce students to the range and types of adaptations of literature into other art forms; to identify problems that arise when a literary work evolves or undergoes translation into other art forms; to learn what creative artists have said about the processes of adaptation; to test the factual and theoretical knowledge gained.

Schedule

1. Introduction. Why adapt? Theoretical bases for dramatization and adaptation of literature. Quotations from artists. Nature of media—in order of increasing remoteness from the literary form. Individual adaptations. Radio and spoken-word recording. Keats's "Ode to a Nightingale"; Claire Bloom's reading (Caedmon, CDL-52011).
2. Film. "The Marquise of O": Kleist's short story; Eric Rohmer's film.
3. Film animation. *The Wind in the Willows*: Kenneth Grahame's short novel; Disney animation.
4–6. Video. *The Golden Bowl*: James's novel; Jack Pulman video adaptation. *The Taming of the Shrew*: Shakespeare's play; William Ball and Kirk Browning video production.
7. Opera. François Ancelot's play *Elizabeth d'Angleterre*; Donizetti's opera *Roberto Devereux*, with Beverly Sills. *Norma*: Alexandre Soumet's play; Bellini's opera, with Joan Sutherland, Marilyn Horne. Henri Murger's novel *Vie de bohème*; Puccini's opera *La Bohème*, with Luciano Pavarotti.
8. Opera. *The Barber of Seville*: Beaumarchais's play; Rossini opera, performed by Sills.
9. Opera. Shakespeare's *Othello*; Verdi's *Otello*, with Placido Domingo.
10. Dance. J. K. A. Musäus's story "Der geraubte Schleiter" ("The Stolen Veil"), Swan Maiden myths; *Swan Lake* ballet, choreographed by Marius Petipa, Tchaikovsky music, video performance with Natalia Makarova; *Don Quixote*: Cervantes's novel; ballet choreographed by Petipa, Ludwig Minkus music, video performance with Mikhail Baryshnikov, Gelsey Kirkland.
11. Dance. *The Nutcracker*: E. T. A. Hoffmann's story; ballet choreographed by Baryshnikov, video performance with Baryshnikov, Kirkland. Art. Bible; famous paintings of biblical scenes. Music. Goethe's *Faust*; Liszt's *Faust Symphony*, conducted by Leonard Bernstein.
12. Multiple adaptations. Hoffman stories ("A New Year's Eve Adventure," "The Sand-Man," "Rath Krespel"); Offenbach opera *Tales of Hoffman*, with Sutherland; ballet *Coppelia*, choreographed by George Balanchine, Delibes music, video performance with Patricia McBride.
13. Alexandre Dumas fils's novel and play *The Lady of the Camellias*; George Cukor film *Camille*, with Greta Garbo; Verdi opera *La Traviata*, with Teresa Stratas, Domingo.
14–16. *Romeo and Juliet*: Shakespeare's play; 1978 BBC video production directed by Alvin Rakoff; Franco Zeffirelli film; J. M. W. Turner painting; Leonid Lavrosky ballet, video performance with Bolshoi Ballet; Michael Smuin ballet, video performance with San Francisco Ballet; Tchaikovsky, Prokofiev music; Delius opera *A Village Romeo and Juliet*; Bernstein-Sondheim musical *West Side Story*.
17. Paper: (1) research of primary sources dealing with adapter's comments on adaptation challenges; (2) original study on a narrow aspect of one literary work and its adaptation to two different art forms. Exam.

Introductory Courses

James V. Mirollo

The History of Western Culture: Literature and Art

In the fall of 1972 Maurice J. Valency, as director of academic studies, introduced at the Juilliard School a year-long course entitled History of Western Culture: Literature and Art. It remained a required upper-level course until 1985, when a new president arrived with a different educational philosophy and a different curriculum. Called by an outside evaluation team "the jewel of the academic curriculum," the course could be as exhilarating elsewhere as it was at Juilliard, where it was intended to meet the needs of students of music, drama, and dance in a conservatory atmosphere. The interrelated study of literature and art supplemented and enriched these specialist majors.

Enrollment in each of the six sections of the course was limited to a maximum of twenty-five students, who met twice a week in discussion groups with their instructors. In addition, all students were required to attend my weekly slide lecture, in which we considered the literary text assigned for that week in the context of contemporary works of art or art styles and movements. While a chronological approach prevailed, the goal of mutual illumination of visual and verbal texts would sometimes entail diachronic rather than synchronic juxtapositions, as indicated below.

Since students were required to take this course in their junior year, after having passed earlier required courses in composition and introduction to literary types, the class could begin at a somewhat advanced level and take a more sophisticated approach than would have been appropriate for freshmen. The first-year composition course and the sophomore introductory literature course stressed modern works, preparing students for our classroom discussions of the literary selections and for my weekly lectures. Students were also better prepared to recognize how the culture of the present remains in dialogue with that of the past. With its focus on interart study, however, the History of Western Culture course was largely a fresh experience. A course in the history of music was also required of students, but—a possible flaw in the program—it was not dovetailed with the content or schedule of our course. Students whose interest in art was stimulated by the literature and art lectures could take elective courses in specific art periods and styles taught by distinguished adjuncts.

Classroom discussion dealt with materials of the weekly literature and art lecture and the readings required for that lecture. Since instructors attended the weekly lecture along with students, they could lead a more detailed discussion of the relations between verbal and visual texts, how one illuminated the other and how both promoted and reflected the culture.

In my first lecture I set forth the method and procedure of the course. My eclectic method initially drew on such theoretical and practical sources as René Wellek and Austin Warren's *Theory of Literature*, Ulrich Weisstein's *Comparative Literature and Literary Theory*, Jean Hagstrum's *Sister Arts*, Mario Praz's *Mnemosyne:The Parallel between Literature and the Visual Arts*, and Helmut Hatzfeld's *Literature through Art*. My "affinities" approach—emphasizing context, influence, theme, and form—became more formalist as I encountered the early work of the "anti-Lessing" theorists such as W. J. T. Mitchell, James A. W. Heffernan, and Wendy Steiner, all of whose ideas and criticism have been gathered in the volume *Space, Time, Image, Sign: Essays on Literature and the Visual Arts* (ed. Heffernan).

Thus in that first lecture I traced and explicated with slides the "recycling" of the myth of Daedelus and Icarus from its first appearance in Vergil's *Aeneid* 6 and Ovid's *Metamorphoses* 8 to its visual adaptation by Pieter Brueghel the Elder in *The Fall of Icarus* and its subsequent verbal renewal by W. H. Auden and William Carlos Williams in their poems on Brueghel's painting. I pointed out how intermedia adaptations translate from one formal language into another and how a later work may misread an earlier one in order to assert a contemporary relevance or meaning. I followed this with a complementary example of a visual image, Rembrandt's *Woman Bathing in a Stream*, as reinterpreted by Chaim Soutine in his 1931 painting *Woman Wading*. Having read in Monroe Wheeler's monograph how Soutine was obsessed by the earlier painting, James Schevill was moved to compose his poem "A Story of Soutine" on that particular obsession and the general theme of the arrogant possessiveness of art.

I also juxtaposed Williams's account of how he came to compose his poem "I Saw the Figure Five in Gold" and Charles Demuth's later painting that attempted a visual reproduction of the poem's acoustical as well as visual imagery. By showing slides of sculptures by Henry Moore and Alexander Calder and by interpreting poems written about them by Donald Hall ("Reclining Figure") and Elder Olson ("Mobile by Calder"), I emphasized not only the phenomenon of misreading but also the problem of intermedia imitation or translation, since Hall aimed at the primitive condensation and stark simplicity of Moore's figure whereas Olson opted for a philosophical meditation on Calder's gently drifting shapes rather than for a verbal reproduction of them.

To illustrate what I call the jealousy principle, I turned to X. J. Kennedy, a poet who tried to convey not only his interpretation of Marcel Duchamp's *Nude Descending a Staircase*, but also a verbal equivalent. The three quatrains of his poem, which uses the same title, follow the nude down the stairs, suggesting along the way the colors and fragmented forms of the painting by means of dissonant rhymes, repetitions, images, and puns until the final line, when, like the painting, it "Collects her motions into shape." On the other hand, my juxtaposition of Titian's *Venus and the Lute Player* and Paul Engle's poem about the painting showed that the poet did not vie with the painting's formal properties but instead gave it a reading that asserts and plays off the difference between the erotic force of "naked" and the aesthetic refinement of the classical "nude" in a way that would astonish a Renaissance neo-Platonist. My final example in the introductory lecture stressed the formal affinity of Stuart Davis's painting *Rapt at Rappaport's* and Josephine Miles's poem "Peak Activity in Boardwalk Ham Concession." The affinity here is a product of a common aesthetic rather than mutual influence or imitation. Although both works involve childhood, Davis's visual recollection of the experience of shopping in a famous toy store and Miles's evocation of a child's initiation into mortality have entirely different meanings and tones. Yet each conveys its meaning through the modernist technique of fragmentation, juxtaposition, condensation, and isolated image. (All poems in the opening lecture are collected in Drachler and Terris; see also Abse and Abse.)

In the subsequent lectures, following a more rigidly chronological sequence, I continued to emphasize cultural context, mutual influence, recycling of key myths and images, thematic and formal affinity, readings and misreadings, and intermedia translation. Where appropriate, I also introduced the phenomenon of the "double talent" (Michelangelo, Cellini, Blake, D. G. Rossetti) and the "synoptic" genres of illustrated book, emblem, pattern poems, and epitaphs or inscriptions. My discussion of another useful topic, ekphrasis or word painting, began with Homer's description of the shield of Achilles in *Iliad* 18 and continued through Pietro Aretino's verbal re-creations of Titian paintings to Keats's "Urn" and Yeats's Byzantine mosaic.

Although space limitations do not allow me to discuss the contents of all twenty-seven fall and spring lectures, I would like to take up a sampling of presentations from the two semesters that students seemed to find particularly valuable and enjoyable. Since the reading assignments divided themselves chronologically into six periods, I will choose one lecture from each of the periods.

A lecture dealing with antiquity focused on the *Iliad* and contemporary ceramic art. Following Cedric H. Whitman's explication of ring composition or concentric framing in his *Homer and the Heroic Tradition*, I showed slides of geometric-style pottery and drew analogies with the concentric structures of books 1 and 24 and the many speeches—by Nestor, Achilles, and Diomedes, among others—that are constructed on the pattern abcba. With additional slides of later pottery that featured animal and human figures, the latter drawn from the Homeric poem itself, I was able to suggest that Homer's combining of geometric structure and formulaic style with scenes of human dialogue and confrontation both reflected the ceramic art of his time and anticipated and promoted a change in the representational goals of pottery painters.

The most challenging of the medieval lectures took up the Gothic form of Chartres Cathedral and Dante's *Divine Comedy*. While in *Gothic Architecture and Scholasticism* Erwin Panofsky helpfully links architecture and culture, he does not specifically invoke the Dante parallel. And while many expert studies of Gothic and Chartres exist, few mention literary texts. I therefore focused on three key issues: geometric and numerical structure, symbolism, and light imagery. But to avoid having students think that the content and purposes of the cathedral and the poem were wholly transcendent and mystical, I emphasized the intertwining of the human and the suprahuman and, in particular, the encyclopedic character of both works. At the same time, stressing as always differences as well as similarities, I pointed out that there is no architectural equivalent to Dante's presentation of such fully realized psychological types as Farinata, Frances-ca, and Ulysses.

My favorite Renaissance and baroque lecture involved Bernini's sculp-tural ensemble in the Cornaro Chapel showing Saint Teresa of Avila in ecstasy. The literary texts included the saint's *vida* and the poetry of Richard Crashaw. Teresa's description of the transverberation she experienced insists on the paradoxical union of pleasure and pain, of the physical and the spiritual, of human and divine love. In a sculptural embodiment of this popular baroque motif, Bernini presents a Teresa undergoing simultaneously what she describes sequentially, thus collapsing before and after, suffering and joy, earthbound and levitation into a composite image of timeless ecstasy. In his "Hymn" to the saint, Crashaw offers a sequential presenta-tion of her life and works, tracing their vertical path, whereas in his "Flaming Heart," focused on a painting of the transverberation, he reveals a failure of visual paradox insofar as the painted image records her experience but does not simultaneously record her impact on us.

Early in the second semester of the course, a lecture was devoted to Pope's "Rape of the Lock" and the paintings of Watteau as exemplars of the rococo. Admitting at once the difference between Pope's satiric bite and Watteau's bemusement, I explored several areas of convergence: reduction of the heroic to the quotidian, anatomy of social attitude and gesture, and sly eroticism. Inevitably, in choosing my Watteau slides I went for depictions of musical culture, knowing that my Juilliard students would find musicians, music lessons, and concerts particularly appealing. At the same time we saw that neither Pope nor Watteau was concerned merely to record the social life of the early eighteenth century in London and Paris and that both poem and paintings contained an underlying unease and disenchantment that may be associated with the attempt to monumentalize the trivial.

A lecture on nineteenth-century materials compared Byron and Dela-croix. By this time students were learned and sophisticated enough that I could outline in a general way phenomena such as Romanticism and Byronism in order to deal specifically with two texts: *Don Juan*, canto 2, sections 72-75, and *Sardanapalus: A Tragedy*, act 5. It was possible to evoke students' previous reading, since Byron had dedicated his tragedy, written in 1821, to "the illustrious Goethe," whose *Faust* had been studied earlier. Delacroix's illustrations of *Faust* had also been discussed previously, and the contrast between the neobaroque style of the painter and the neoclassicism of Ingres and his followers was easier to explain against the background of the conflict between the followers of Poussin and Rubens illustrated earlier in the year. In any event, as we viewed slides of Delacroix's paintings of the two scenes from the Byron poems and discussed their common Romantic preoccupations with horrible suffering and death, noble and ignoble, students seemed more comfortable with interart discourse, and this impression was invariably confirmed by enthusiastic questions and comments after the lecture ended.

My final example is one of the last lectures given to the moderns, which featured excerpts from Hart Crane's "To Brooklyn Bridge" and early twentieth-century paintings of the bridge in expressionist or cubist styles by Joseph Stella, John Marin, and George Grosz. Here, naturally, I exploited the students' own experience with a familiar structure. Using the paintings and the poem, I tried to recall what must have been an awesome sight not only because of its technological accomplishment but also because of its portentous symbolism. Of course what the engineers and workers had put together the modern painters disassembled and fragmented while yet maintaining a sense of the power and majesty of the whole. Crane's poem, with its invocation of and prayer to a mythic savior of imprisoned and faithless Manhattanites, reinforces both these aspects of modernism by its epic sweep and discontinuous argument. Indeed, I found that the juxtaposition of the paintings and the poem made the latter much easier to explain than it had been previously, when I had taught the poem alone.

The need for examination on the material at midterm and endterm proved particularly vexing, since so much had been covered in the intervals. Two options were made available to section instructors to allow for simultaneous testing of both classroom and lecture discussion. The first combined short answers on the content of the lectures and an essay on class assignments. The second option, which was preferred as more challenging by most teachers and students, allowed students to apply what they had learned. The student was given reproductions of two works of art not previously studied but representative of two period styles that had been studied. After comparing and contrasting context, theme, style, and function, the student was to discuss two literary works drawn from the term assignments, using the same criteria. The student was asked to complete the essay by comparing and contrasting the conclusions drawn from the explication of the visual and literary texts.

Of the many different examination questions of this second type devised over the years, I give two representative examples. The first asked students to compare and contrast the fifth-century sculpture *Dying Niobid* and the early fourteenth-century sculpture known as the *Virgin of Paris* as instances of classical and medieval art and sculpture. The student was then to juxtapose a classical work (like the *Iliad*) and a medieval work (like the *Song of Roland*) that shared at least the same generic idiom. In the final part of the essay, the student was expected to point out not only similarities of form and content but also the limits or discontinuities in this instance of interart comparison.

The second example, from the spring semester, utilized prints of *The Street* by Ernst Ludwig Kirchner and *The City* by Fernand Léger, works in the expressionist and cubist traditions. Here the juxtaposition emphasized not only the differences between the two styles but also the contrasting representations of the city. The literary examples were to be drawn from a list of nineteenth- and twentieth-century works that focused on an urban setting or milieu, ranging from fiction by Dostoyevski to poems by Eliot. Ideally, the final part of the student's essay would draw conclusions about various ways modern artists perceive the city, whether exposing its harsh reality or translating that reality into its redemptive possibilities by the visionary alchemy of art. These "applications" of learning drew deeply from the fund of knowledge and experience acquired throughout our year-long study of the myriad and complex relations between the arts.

Syllabus

Course   The History of Western Culture: Literature and Art. James V. Mirollo, Academic Division, Juilliard School.

Description   Upper-level (normally third-year) course to fulfill academic requirement. Prerequisites: freshman composition and introduction to literature courses. Year-long course earning nine credits for both semesters. Group lecture once a week plus discussion classes of no more than twenty-five students twice weekly. Staffed by adjunct faculty members, supervised by specialist in literature and art.

Objectives   To introduce students specializing in music, drama, and dance to the other arts, their interrelations, and cultural contexts; to focus on the thematic and formal affinities of the visual and verbal arts as products and promoters of culture; to develop basic skills in discussing and writing about interdisciplinary topics; to enhance aesthetic awareness for personal enrichment and professional growth.

Texts   Required texts: Mack, *World Masterpieces*; Honour and Fleming (HF). Recommended texts: Janson; Gombrich, *Story*; Gardner; Janson and Kerman; Cleaver and Eddins; Barnet.

Schedule

Fall Semester

1. Introduction to literature and art. HF 8-26. Modern poems related to paintings: Auden, Williams, Schevill, Hall, Olson, Kennedy, Engle, Miles.
2. Bible and Near East. Book of Job. Hebrew verbal style and Egyptian visual art. HF 27-48.
3. Early Greek. Homer, *Iliad*. Homer and vase painting. HF 48-59.
4. Greek drama. Sophocles, *Oedipus*. Sophocles and the Parthenon. HF 94-121.
5. Vergil and Rome. *The Aeneid*. Roman art. HF 146-71.
6. Medieval culture. Dante, *Inferno*. Dante and the Gothic cathedral. HF 218-41.
7. Later medieval culture. Chaucer, *Canterbury Tales*. Gothic and early Renaissance realism. HF 271-300.
8. Petrarch and early Renaissance. Petrarch lyrics. Early Renaissance humanism. HF 300-15, 352-53.
9. High Renaissance 1. Castiglione, *The Courtier*; Machiavelli, *The Prince*. High Renaissance culture. HF 317-48.
10. High Renaissance 2. Rabelais, *Gargantua and Pantagruel*. Northern Renaissance. HF 349-78.
11. Mannerism. Montaigne, *Essays*. Mannerism in art and literature. HF 378-87. Excerpts from Aretino letters to Titian, Cellini's autobiography.
12. Mannerism to baroque. Shakespeare sonnets; poems by Marlowe, Raleigh, Donne, Constable. Northern mannerism.
13. Baroque. Cervantes, *Don Quixote*; poems by Shakespeare, Crashaw, Herbert, Marino, Donne, Constable, Marvell; Saint Teresa, *Life*. Baroque themes and forms. HF 426-58.

Spring Semester

1. Baroque classicism. Molière, *Tartuffe*. Versailles. HF 459-79.
2. Rococo. Pope, *Rape of the Lock*. Pope and Watteau.
3. Neoclassicism. Voltaire, *Candide*. Later eighteenth-century classicism.
4. Classicism and Romanticism. Goethe, *Faust*. Thematics and aesthetics of Romanticism. Byron and Delacroix. HF 480-507.
5. Romanticism 1. Poems by Blake, Wordsworth, Coleridge, Whitman, Thoreau, Dickinson, Hopkins. Romantic nature poetry and painting: Wordsworth and the painter John Constable.
6. Romanticism 2. Poems by Keats, Shelley. Romantic ideology and aesthetics.
7. Realism and impressionism 1. Poems by Tennyson, Browning. Late nineteenth-century trends. HF 520-46.
8. Realism and impressionism 2. Dostoyevski, *Notes from the Underground*. Realism in literature and art 1.
9. Realism and postimpressionism. Tolstoy, *Ivan Ilych*; Woolf, *The Waves*; Poe poems and Mallarmé translations; Verlaine poems; Huysmans and Moreau on Salomé. Realism in literature and art 2, symbolism.
10. Postimpressionism. Ibsen, *Hedda Gabler*. Late nineteenth- and early twentieth-century art.
11. Modern 1. Chekhov, *Cherry Orchard*; poems by Stein, Cendrars, Apollinaire, Cummings, Williams, Crane. Modernism 1. HF 564-87.
12. Modern 2. Sartre, *No Exit*; Brecht, *Mother Courage*; poems by Williams, Frost, Thomas. Modernism 2. HF 588-603.

13. Contemporary. Poems by Yeats, Eliot, Ginsberg, O'Hara, Hayden, Strand, Stone. Contemporary literature and art. HF 604-21.

Linda Dittmar

Literature as Art:
Sequencing Learning in the Core Curriculum

To the academic community of a young and rapidly developing urban university, comparative work in the arts may not be the first order of business. The Boston campus of the University of Massachusetts serves a mature, commuting, and extremely diverse student body whose pressing personal and occupational agendas tend to make an introductory core course like Literature as Art seem a luxury. It is mainly the philosophy and pedagogy of our core program that protect such work from marginalism. Like all our core electives, Literature as Art does triple duty: it introduces students to a discipline, helps them situate this discipline within its core area, and teaches them writing and critical thinking. We cap enrollment at twenty-five, emphasize student participation, assign writing frequently, and attend closely to student articulation. Our goal is to help students gain a clear understanding of their critical engagement with the material in the context of cross-disciplinary thinking. We value this teaching because it integrates knowledge and normalizes critical thinking and writing as modes of discovery and mastery that must go on at all times.

Faculty members new to core arts courses worry that they are inexpert in all but their own art, that attention to skills will conflict with teaching the arts, and that only "English" faculty members can teach skills in the first place. Still, as colleagues discovered during a semester-long faculty seminar I led soon after we established the core, such teaching is possible once one relinquishes the typically disciplinary notion of covering material in favor of a problem-centered course design. For members of my seminar, the substantive issue turned out to be not expertise but the nature of comparative interarts work. Initially, our comparative thinking was mainly thematic: we noted that Tillie Olsen's story "I Stand Here Ironing" can be taught in relation to Picasso's ironing woman and Degas's laundresses and that Brueghel's *Fall of Icarus* lines up with Auden's "Musée des Beaux Arts." But we soon discovered that the real interest of interart work lies in the study of formal and conceptual interrelations as we bring them to bear on thematic affinities and that attention to writing and critical thinking complements well this orientation. The following discussion of the course Literature as Art models a way of meeting this challenge. It concerns, first, the integration of writing and critical thinking into interart work and, next, the use and sequencing of problem-centered configurations of subject matter over a semester's duration.

Most obviously, such configurations are the thematic and formal units that constitute the backbone of this course's syllabus. Some of these units cluster their materials topically (as by gender, race, war, or coming-of-age) while others cluster around questions of genre and form. Less visibly, though not less importantly, the course's problem-centered orientation includes attention to critical method. Whatever the text, whatever the art, we note our active role in interpretation. The inscribed quality of all articulation, including our own, becomes an ongoing concern. As we foreground ways in which utterances function in the context of their production and reception, students gain access to questions of historical specificity and ideology. As we foreground a critical assessment of our own practices—including how and why we interpret texts as we do, the strategy we use to discuss them, and the assumptions that underlie the very selection and placement of each text in the syllabus—students learn to value their thinking and assume responsibility for its direction.

Over the semester, it gradually becomes easier to cross-reference examples of student writing and speaking with consciously "artistic" practices: comparative analyses of theses and their development, by several authors working in diverse media, can include student efforts; attention to syntax and paragraph structure can include student prose as well as related visual and musical arrangements; and images in student writing can link to similar or different figures in poetry or painting. One works improvisationally, whenever opportunity reveals a continuum across the arts and across levels of mastery. As students learn to think about all inscription and reception comparatively—about their own and others', about verbal and other means—they become better readers, better writers, better seers and listeners. In this way, then, Literature as Art assimilates instruction in writing and critical thinking into its literary and aesthetic preoccupations. In a course so obviously committed to the pleasures of informed comparative reception of distinct but interrelated modes of organizing and interpreting human experience, such a tool is invaluable.

Given this volume's focus on teaching literature and other arts, not writing and critical thinking, my discussion of the latter must remain brief. I mention it here only because the continuum that this course creates between skills and substance is a particularly useful model for introductory courses, where students' self-respect as thinkers is key. The important point is that, over time, through recurrent modeling within a discussion-based course, students can and do come to feel empowered. Learning to trust their minds, they become freer to master the assigned materials and develop a comparative orientation. We are always in dialogue—among ourselves, with our authors, and across works and arts. Indeed, the juxtaposing procedures of comparative work are naturally amenable to this exchange. Unfolding through a flexible process of composing, dismantling, and reintegrating knowledge, comparative work encourages active learning. Thus, my own teaching posits attention to students as self-aware participants in the generation of meanings. While this pedagogy is anything but permissively uncritical, students feel supported by the fact that the course takes seriously all utterances. We always affirm the process of responsible critical engagement.

Such empowerment occurs gradually, often imperceptibly. On the first day of class students are likely to consider fatuous any prediction of the growth, pleasure, and mastery ahead. Instead, then, that first hour goes to handing out the syllabus and clarifying expectations. We devote what little time is left to close readings of short poems, by way of signaling things to come. Thus, my two-day introductory unit focuses on poetry, painting, and photography. Starting with questions of style, tone, and organization within lines, we move on to figures and images and note how all of these generate significations. We use Carl Sandburg's "Fog" and the fog segment of T. S. Eliot's "Prufrock" to develop procedures for reading, and we then move on to a comparative discussion of the visual and epistemological suggestiveness of these two treatments in relation to paintings by J. M. W. Turner and Mark Rothko, haiku poems, Oriental landscape painting, and photography. Before returning to these issues with Robert Lowell's and Ezra Pound's imagist poems, we use Robert Herrick's "Upon Julia's Clothes" and Countee Cullen's "For a Lady I Know" to sample a more socially focused poetry that highlights questions of gender, social history, and race as these are mediated through each poem's authorial stance.

The introductory unit, then, establishes the données of the course. It begins to enact the agenda that will inform the whole course and that I will share with the class openly around midsemester, when our store of texts and critical readings is large enough to review in terms of the following issues:

1. Literary genres—poetry, fiction, drama, and exposition
2. Literary crafting—easily identified in poetry but also evident throughout the course, notably in its treatment of realism and artifice
3. Articulation across the arts—painting and sculpture, film, music, photography, theater, dance, and their various hybrids
4. The convergence of forms and of forms and themes as it guides readings—social, ideological, and personal—at moments of production and reception

Questions of genre, form, medium, and contextualized interpretation are central to Literature as Art. Taken together, they presuppose that interart work depends on the kind of generic, semiotic, and ideological analysis René Wellek envisioned in 1941 as key to the description of the common basis of the arts. Without our necessarily resorting to such labels in class, a term's duration nonetheless sees students move toward an informed application of this framework to specific works. As they learn to read critically, they become aware that the questions they raise determine what they discover.

We may discuss Ernest Hemingway's "Snows of Kilimanjaro" generically, as a short prose narrative distinct from poetry or drama. We may analyze it as a signifying system—in terms of its point of view, diction, syntax, and other aspects of its crafting. We may compare Hemingway's treatment of redemption to Edward Hopper's painting *Gas*, or the story's sparse restraint to the simplicity of a Giotto fresco. We may note, too, the historical and biographical circumstances of this story's production as they shape its ideology and interact with our own lives to shape readings.

Familiarity with a range of literary practices is necessary to such work. Questions of genre, form, medium, and context thrive on comparison. Thus, during the semester, students find themselves increasingly able to tap the comparative potentials of the course. Patterns of repetition, variation, and counterpoint gradually emerge, providing opportunities for the interconnective readings valued by all interart work. Of course, such textured learning does not come easily to anyone, let alone to students enrolled in introductory courses. Some simplification is necessary, and in Literature as Art it occurs in three ways: the literature is mostly twentieth century, the main text is a reassuringly standard anthology (Landy's *Heath Introduction to Literature*), and the syllabus's organization into thematic and generic units keeps at bay the threat of excess to which comparative work is prone.

In practice, this tidiness is more apparent than real. The works I select and place within this framework form a grid of interconnections that sets off myriad opportunities for comparison both among contiguous works and across the syllabus as a whole. When I pair J. L. Peretz's story "If Not Higher" with Shirley Jackson's "Lottery" and place them right after the first poetry unit, I do so to initiate comparison. For, seen together, this unlikely pair raises important introductory questions about prose narrative: about the plots authors choose to tell, about the information they provide or withhold, about the stances they assume toward their materials and readers, and about the narrative strategies through which those stances reveal themselves. As students learn to read fiction closely, they become aware of the ways Jackson conveys her stern condemnation of social institutions—in contrast to the faith and affection for ordinary people's capacity for redemption evident in Peretz's narrative operations. That Jackson's technique delays insight and, then, lodges it only in her readers, while Peretz's foregrounds and democratizes it, turns out to be significant, too. Either way, students learn that fiction, like poetry, must be read closely. Ferreting out the relations authors establish between readers and texts, students acquire tools and develop the critical awareness that Saki's "Story Teller" will summarize for us before we move on to Albert Camus's "Guest," Richard Wright's "Man Who Was Almost a Man," and Hemingway's "Snows of Kilimanjaro."

Thematically, these three stories gather around concepts of self—both generally, in terms of dignity and efficacy, and in the specifically patriarchal sense of masculine identity. Each is a narrative of individual maturation, and each situates personal experience at a particular point in history and, so, introduces the possibility of contextual and ideological reading. The generic unit regroups, then, to raise additional considerations. That one cannot separate the ethical dilemma of Camus's narrator from the colonial context in which it occurs, or those two elements from Camus's suppression of stylistic resonance, is key, we learn, to the story's evaluative stance. Of course, Wright and Hemingway are open to a similar analysis of interrelations among genre, form, and ideology. Furthermore, the realism evident at this point in the course lets us discuss questions of mediation and "transparency" across the arts. Representation, the material suggests, is always formed, always willed, always signifying. That Wright's protagonist ends up running away from home, bathed in moonlight, with an empty gun sagging in his pocket, alerts us to ways fiction can qualify closure. Moreover, the cultural and thematic links this story has to the blues tradition open up related issues—concerning not only Afro-American music and verbal expression but also that uniquely American mythology concerning journeys, lost Edens, and the ambiguities of coming of age in a "fallen" world.

The grid of interconnections that extends across Literature as Art depends on a recurrence of such issues. The thematic concern with the emergent self recurs throughout the course and is central to James Baldwin's "Sonny's Blues," Lorraine Hansberry's *Raisin in the Sun*, and Arthur Miller's *Death of a Salesman*. The masculine orientation of our early stories both anticipates the "war" unit and contrasts usefully with the feminine perspective of Charlotte Perkins Gilman's "Yellow Wallpaper" and the poems of Adrienne Rich, Denise Levertov, Sylvia Plath, and Emily Dickinson. *A Raisin in the Sun* summarizes usefully questions of gender, race, realism, and genre, while the shift from realism to self-reflexivity in fiction (Hemingway and Gilman) gets reiterated in the entire unit on drama. Seen comparatively, over a semester's duration, our materials challenge any uncritical acceptance of depiction as record. Instead, students increasingly learn to appreciate the ways in which our materials interpret human experience. That fiction, film, and drama, as well as poetry, music, and the visual arts, are all mediated utterances defines the critical orientation of our work throughout the semester.

The Afro-American unit of Literature as Art illustrates most fully the comparative work this course undertakes. The unit is particularly well integrated thematically: the subthemes that come into play within its sustained focus on Afro-American expression interconnect well among themselves and tie in with preceding and following writings. This unit is also rich formally, covering all genres and arts. That it is placed at midsemester and that students respond to its materials with special warmth are obviously helpful, too. Of course, any well-designed unit is likely to be a success at this point, resting as it does on several weeks' worth of preparation. For introductory courses in particular, this is an excellent opportunity to review past work, rearticulate goals, and clarify students' growth as readers of literature and other arts. Still, I value this unit also because its focus on Afro-

American art at once foregrounds that important achievement and puts in question canonic notions of "fine" and "popular" arts.

"Sonny's Blues" is the entry point and the heart of this unit. As a sustained and well-crafted narrative, it helps us review questions of genre and representation; but its special contribution concerns the recurrent allusions to Afro-American music that Baldwin embeds in it—ranging from gospel to bebop and diverse kinds of jazz. These prove important thematically, as a context for this story's account of redemption and a coming of age, and formally, as interrelated modes of musical and verbal articulation. Listening to recordings of pieces akin to those Baldwin describes, we analyze the operations of each medium as a distinct yet related modality. Next, we test our insights against a cluster of poems: Gwendolyn Brooks's "We Real Cool," Langston Hughes's "Dream Deferred" (the source of Hansberry's title *A Raisin in the Sun*), and Hughes's "Boogie-Woogie" poem cycle. As we listen to boogie-woogie music, discuss dance and Mondrian's painting "Broadway Boogie-Woogie," and screen Dudley Murphy's jazz dance film "Black and Tan," we focus increasingly on questions of form. Narrative representation is negligible in Murphy's film. Its interest lies in the ways diachronically unfolding images refract, duplicate, and reorganize the visual track in response to Duke Ellington's music. By the time we turn to Carl Sandburg's "Jazz Fantasia," to paintings by William Johnson and Jacob Lawrence, and to sculpture by William Edmondson, students have a strong appreciation of formal arrangements as these articulate personal and social meanings.

There is much in Baldwin's story that touches students very personally: the narrator's struggle with the imperative to be his brother's keeper; the relation between actual and surrogate fathers and sons; the interaction of drugs, music, and spiritual regeneration within a community; and the basic, nonnegotiable human need for expression, mastery, and self-respect. Students are often deeply attached to the music we discuss, too, for many have experienced it as formative in their lives. Most important for the purposes of this course, though, is the fact that through all this students learn to appreciate diverse aesthetic practices as separate yet interrelated ways of reformulating experience. Noting the respect with which our authors treat their materials (Baldwin's virtuosity with prose, for instance, or Brooks's poetic reclaiming of slang) and seeing this respect carried over into our own work in class (e.g., our reclaiming of the funky music played on Baldwin's jukebox and our giving it equal time with canonic art), students develop a new, flexible, and more confident sense of art as their birthright.

Seen over the course of a semester, the thrust of the organization and pedagogy of Literature as Art is to encourage students to become critical readers of texts and to discover the creative potentials of comparative thinking. Beyond doubt, this work helps them understand each art more clearly in terms of its medium's capabilities and to understand the creative impulse generally in terms of the myriad aesthetic forms it assumes. But, beyond that, the organization and pedagogy of Literature as Art work to empower students. The Afro-American unit empowers them in special ways, for it summarizes and builds on past work most explicitly, and it does so by tapping students' own artistic literacy as a way of opening doors to uncharted territory. In the following weeks there is less pressure to justify our work, greater ease about simply doing it. But, in fact, what goes on in this unit is typical of the course as a whole. For as students learn to trust their own tastes and respect their own thinking, they become ready to take on cultural artifacts responsibly. Some move on to specialized courses in literature and other arts. Some become English majors. For some Literature as Art remains the only course they will have had in the arts. But all experience this comparative work as an exciting introduction to the ways the human imagination generates meanings and to the ways art intertwines with daily living.

Bibliographical Note

For works that inform the theoretical foundations of the course, see, among others, John Berger, *Ways of Seeing*; Roy Pascal; Tzvetan Todorov; and René Wellek, "Parallelism"; those that help shape its pedagogical approaches include Ann E. Berthoff; Claus Clüver, "Teaching"; Paulo Freire; Thomas P. Kasulis; Jerry K. Stonewater; and Robert J. Yinger.

Syllabus

Course   Literature as Art. Linda Dittmar, English, University of Massachusetts, Boston.

Description   An introductory elective counting towards the core arts requirement. Taught regularly by English department faculty members. No prerequisites or set syllabus, but the same objectives and similar procedures for all sections. Classes meet twice a week for seventy-five minutes.

Objectives   To introduce beginning students to the pleasures and methods of reading literature in relation to other arts; to explore ways the imaginative shaping of articulation in literary and other media shapes meanings; to pursue comparatively questions of theme, genre, form, expressivity, and context across works and across arts; to improve writing and critical-thinking skills.

Text   Landy.

Schedule

1-2. Introduction. Poetry: "Fog" (Sandburg), lines 115-22 of "Prufrock" (Eliot), "Upon Julia's Clothes" (Herrick), "For a Lady I Know" (Cullen), "The Sick Rose" (Blake), "Wind and Silver" (A. Lowell), "In a Station of the Metro" (Pound).

Paintings by Turner and Rothko. Oriental landscapes, flowers, and haiku. Photography.

3-5. Fiction: "If Not Higher" (Peretz), "The Lottery" (Jackson), "The Story Teller" (Saki), "The Guest" (Camus), "The Man Who Was Almost a Man" (Wright), "The Snows of Kilimanjaro" (Hemingway). Paintings by Hopper and Giotto. Photography by Steiglitz and Sheeler. Blues music and lyrics.

6-7. Women writers: "The Yellow Wallpaper" (Gilman), "Aunt Jennifer's Tigers" (Rich), "Losing Track" (Levertov), "Morning Song" (Plath), "Tell all the Truth" (Dickinson). Fantasy and surrealism in visual arts. Women's domestic and fine arts, music.

8-9. Afro-American writing: "Sonny's Blues" (Baldwin), "We Real Cool" (Brooks), "Harlem" and other selections from *Montage of a Dream Deferred* (Hughes), "Jazz Fantasia" (Sandburg). *Black and Tan Fantasy* (film by Dudley Murphy, music by Duke Ellington). Jazz and boogie-woogie. Mondrian's *Broadway Boogie-Woogie* and art by William H. Johnson, Jacob Lawrence, and other Afro-Americans.

10-11. Review and midterm exam.

12-15. Drama: *A Raisin in the Sun* (Hansberry), *Death of a Salesman* (Miller), and *The Good Woman of Setzuan* (Brecht). Visit to a live performance when workable.

16. Film and fiction. *An Occurrence at Owl Creek Bridge* (Ambrose Bierce and Robert Enrico).

17. War poetry: "The Man He Killed" (Hardy), "An Irish Airman Foresees His Death" (Yeats), "The Naming of Parts" (Reed). Painting and music. Photography, reportage, and expository prose.

18. Poetry. "The Unknown Citizen" (Auden), "Papa's Waltz" (Roethke), "In the Back of the Real" (Ginsberg), "I Wandered Lonely as a Cloud" (Wordsworth), "The Pennycandy Store beyond the El" (Ferlinghetti), "in Just-" (E. E. Cummings).

19. Summation.

Jean–Pierre Barricelli

The Quest for Values

All too frequently, incoming freshmen walk through the hallowed portals of their chosen college campus, their intellectual baggage fairly empty, their minds unburdened and light from innumerable cultural deficiencies. By *cultural* I mean what concerns the arts—their nature, history, and significance. Civilization builds roads, runs governments, grows food, cures diseases, and administers justice. Culture makes all that laudable enterprise worthwhile. But more and more, when one speaks of education—and the pronouncements coming nationally from Washington and locally from school boards abet the slant—one assumes science and mathematics without the seminal counterparts of literature, the visual arts, music, and their related expressions. Yet it is the arts that last *aere perennius* and keep interpreting and defining generations, that enrich and invigorate life, revaluate its standards of human sensibility and sustain traditional wisdom, and, most important, that provide the most trustworthy lens through which to measure, assess, and understand social movements and historical periods of civilization—in short, ourselves and the world in which we live. Civilization without culture is tantamount to a body without a soul. Societies stifle without cultural air. The arts are central to their very act of breathing. If the center cannot hold, in Yeats's phrase, all the freeways and vaccines will not stave off a troglodytic future, rumblings of whose imminence we hear around us increasingly today. The spiritual must share at least equal esteem, and perhaps more, with the material in a world where individuals define themselves too much by what they have and not by how they think or feel.

The above is a résumé of my opening lecture; yet, platitudinous as it may sound, it does not necessarily fall on understanding ears. The spectacle of those freshmen, who after four years enter the outside world trained but not educated, must be the saddest vision a caring humanist can witness.

It has been such a vision for me, campus after campus, and, like a desperado who defiantly exaggerates, I devised a course, which I now give every year, called The Quest for Values. It is nothing less than a cultural intellectual history of the world based on the arts and supported by history, philosophy, religion, and law. The challenge is to demonstrate the validity of my opening remarks. Offered under the aegis not of a department, but of a committee on interdisciplinary studies, the course does not propose to study poetry, painting, and sculpture as artistic disciplines in themselves. (Such study I present in an optional one-quarter introductory course entitled The Arts: Their Meaning and Interrelations.) Rather, it uses the arts to get at something beyond, something the student can relate to more immediately: the constant shift in values, in self-cognizance, aggregate social attitudes, and overall worldviews—like the swinging of the pendulum from generation to generation, period to period, dynasty to dynasty—which the arts, despite the universality and timelessness of true genius, unmistakably reflect. When we grasp the essence of these attitudes and views, the social sciences seem to pale by comparison. In broadest terms, the shifting modes involve the search for order and the search for freedom in our persons and in our institutions; these twin ideals appear to be as valid a duality, governing changing human impulses and needs, as there is.

Except where appropriate, I avoid the terms *classicism* and *Romanticism,* since they pertain mainly to the West and since my course ventures—as now toward the end of the twentieth century it should—into China, Japan, India, Islam, and Africa. More appropriately, I have adopted Nietzsche's designations *Apollonian* and *Dionysian.* I have focused on society and the individual, the rational and the imaginative, the prescriptive and the permissive, the absolute and the relative, the logical and the emotional—modes that perpetually occupy human thinking and feeling—as disclosed by the arts. The perfect existence of any sentient, organic entity shows an interpenetration of the Apollonian and the Dionysian (that is, of order and freedom), but perfection is an ideal, by definition never a lasting achievement. Only Periclean Greece basked in the harmony of order and freedom—and then only for a few decades—and perhaps the Sung dynasty during its apogee did so as well. The modes may blend, as in central African cultures; or they may coexist, as in areas of Islam or in the mixture of Hindu and Moslem/Moghul expressions in India; or they may exist in juxtaposition, as during the European Renaissance and Enlightenment. Functioning societies may lean to the right or to the left on the order-freedom axis; they are always the healthier as they approach a balance at the center. On the left and on the right—say, European Romanticism or the T'ang dynasty on the one hand and ancient Rome or the Tokugawa period on the other—one mode usually dominates; but to remain viable, the prevailing one ought never to suppress its opposite. If it moves in the suppressing direction, it heads for a deadly extreme, for too much order leads to totalitarianism and suffocation, while too much freedom leads to irresponsibility and anarchy. Reflecting the times, the dominant aesthetic manner in the arts during any generation suggests, not always consciously, the values espoused by that particular historical mentality.

Though the Dionysian counterforce is always present when the Apollonian force prevails (Euripides did emerge from the rational Greek culture of Aristophanes, Sophocles, and Praxiteles), it is the prevalence of one or the other that persuaded me to arrange the course not chronologically but by mode, emphasizing during the first half the Search for Order and during the second the Search for Freedom (the course's subtitles). In each instance, the counterforce is not dismissed; it is simply not identified as the directing force. The Apollonian quarter begins conveniently with Western antiquity: unruly, democratic Greece was guided from Aeschylus to Plato and the Parthenon by ideals of stability and the good life, while private temperament and state came face to face in *Antigone.* Rome's system of laws and roads and its emphasis on the family villa advanced a prescriptive mentality to which Vergil, Cicero, and Horace lent their quills, the innuendoes of Catullus and the later barbs of Juvenal and mockeries of Petronius notwithstanding.

Using the same pattern, I swing to the Han dynasty in China with its strong Confucian moralism and, skipping over the Dionysian T'ang and the liberalization of Buddhist thought, engage the mixed Taoist, Buddhist, and Confucian ("Elizabethan") Sung dynasty. In Japan, I consider the "classical" Muromachi period, including the Noh theater ideals as set forth by Zeami, and the isolationist Tokugawa period, not forgetting the populist puppet and Kabuki theaters as practiced by Chikamatsu and the Genroku era but hurdling the slightly less conservative Momoyama. In India, I present the early, fundamental Vedic philosophies through literature and sculpture and the sophisticated Sanskrit age of Kālidāsa and its culmination during the Gupta empire. Throughout, music, dance, painting, sculpture, and architecture occupy a selective but integral part of the discussions, underscoring the beliefs, likes, dislikes, and pursuits—the values—of the times. The Indian segment allows me to move into Islam briefly, after which I return to the European Renaissance. There order was the ideal despite (or perhaps because of) the violent disorders in the streets, on the seas, and in the taverns and despite the indomitably explorational spirit of self-rediscovered humanity. I proceed to the neoclassical age and the Enlightenment, with only passing reference to the baroque, which for me harbors more Dionysian than Apollonian qualities. I finally arrive at the landing point of both halves of the course, the confused twentieth century, whose values, in the arts as in politics, in social credos as in business behavior, betray as many despicable inconsistencies as laudable goals.

The second quarter, the Search for Freedom, I see as the reverse of the first, a filmic negative of the previous quarter's picture. I begin with the Faustian impulse, Western Romanticism, and the nineteenth century. *Faust,* as it bridges the Apollonian and Dionysian, opens the floodgates. In its wake appear effusions of the imaginative over the rational, sentiment over logic, the infinite over the finite, the relative over the absolute. In so flowing, the Dionysian permits glimpses of past periods that also evidenced irrational, lonely, mystical, titillating drives (as represented even in the Middle Ages, with its shadowed Gothic cathedrals erected amid scholastic absolutisms, and in the demonstrativeness and distortions of the baroque and mannerism), as well as rebellious, existential, and libertarian impulses (like the revolutionary upheavals recorded so strikingly in all the arts). Géricault replaces David as Liszt replaces Cherubini.

The second half of the course also moves beyond the West to cover the more emotionally liberated T'ang dynasty, with its imaginative releases of Buddhism and nature-bonded Taoist creeds (the inappropriately named "classical" period of Chinese poetry and its lavish pictorial expression), and the later Ming expansiveness after the age of the Great Khan. In Japan, I consider the more democratized Meiji period, not to mention the agitated modern one. Apart from the written word, artistic works on silk, screen, and stone always tell much of the story. Comparative questions arise all the time. In China, the pendulum swings more dramatically than in Japan. Why? What do the *ch'i* (inner vitality) of portraiture and the poetic *tz'u* (poetry with rigid tonal [musical] requirements, verse patterns, and rhyming scheme) say about the ancient Chinese view of humankind, and what happens to this view when Chinese and Korean artists are imported into Japan? What do Shinto and *giri* (moral duty) say about the Japanese view? How does Buddhism relate to both? Where do art, literature, and jurisprudence cross? If there is a ready-made stimulus for discussion in the course, it sometimes lies less in the materials themselves than in the use to which they are put.

Again, the landing point remains the twentieth century, where so many aspects of the modes considered confront one another or attempt coagulation—a new Hegelian synthesis. After reasoning about the pendulum and the axis, students are startled to confront the stately and intellectual mysticisms of the Arabic manner. Even more bewildering is the black African precolonial homogeneous stability that bespeaks a fusing of Apollonian and Dionysian modes from tribes and nations whose cultural movements are so dissimilar from those of the Western world and the Orient. Particularly in Africa, there is no swing like that from neoclassicism to Romanticism, Han to T'ang, Tokugawa to Meiji that we can follow. What do the arts reflect in these cases, from Firdausī to Hāfiz to today, from the griot and mvet epics to writings of colonial times and later? What happens when Portuguese bronze is introduced to the African sculptor or when the guitar intrudes in animistic musical expression? And what do Chinua Achebe, Alex La Guma, Ngugi wa Thiong'o, and Wole Soyinka bring to the search for values? Only the language of culture offers viable answers to these queries.

Obviously, mine is not a course to draw the enthusiasm of purists or blindered specialists, who tend to rigidify in their minutiae and may entertain an entirely contradictory sense of, say, the baroque. The purpose of the course has got to be fairly blunt; it is not to engage in shades of meaning and intellectual ultrarefinements, and it is not served by becoming a battleground for ideologies, particularly the Marxist or the modern literary-theoretical. All those matters can come later, when the student decides to take a more specialized course. But for now, we must consider the freshman who has not even faced the artists, let alone the nomenclature and the intricacies of periodization. And while we are at it, we must consider the discipline-oriented, historical, unintegrated, separatist—and up to now often unproductive—ways we have been trying in a materialistic society to make the future engineer and sociologist and salesperson aware of the arts as concepts and spiritual forces. The fact remains that we have failed to convince the public at large of the centrality of the arts for the good life, and we have failed to make exposure to them—except in isolated fashion and even then only for the foresighted few—an integral presence in the curriculum.

Also debatable may be my arbitrary separation of Apollonian and Dionysian stresses into two halves of the course. A straight chronological methodology might produce better results. This I am not prepared to argue; I offer the possibility simply as an option. I can only say that many of the students I have now had the pleasure of introducing to this course have found it refreshing and rewarding not to be restricted to the same chronological timetables they face in almost every other course in the humanities. They have appreciated the freedom of pursuing an idea topically—the use of nature images in Giacomo Leopardi and Li Po—as a comparatist might do, or thematically—the conflict between love and duty in Western and Japanese drama—as a philosopher might, and with a little effort they have been able to cope with the civilizational leaps and acknowledge the principle of the pendulum. With even greater interest, in applying value systems to themselves and to their society, they have put to significant use the axis diagram in order to measure—and argue about— where they stand as persons or as generations in relation to its center.

It is the arts whose criteria are utilized in these debates. This aspect of The Quest for Values has proved most fruitful. For the arts speak both overtly and covertly, manifestly and subliminally. They offer clues the historical detective seeks; they reveal secrets to the well educated and insights to the discerning. I wish my students to realize that over the centuries the artistic impulse has created works that have much more to say about human nature and values than do all the nonhumanistic disciplines put together. When I suggest to them at the outset that the music we like tells us who we are and by what philosophies we live, even such an unoriginal statement falls flat. But after students have heard about the African bull roarer, the aeolian harp, the Gregorian chant, the madrigal, the biwa and shamisen, the Ninth Symphony, bel canto, the Viennese waltz, the Dorian scale and the *Tonreihe*, the satara and zamr, tabla and rock and roll, my suggestion does start to make sense. More important, the students come to realize that true artistic creation represents an act of respect for humanity. Civilizations pass, but cultures endure. And in the flux of values, our concepts of ourselves and history change, and cultures acquire—thanks to the arts—their most salient and lasting hues.

Syllabus

Course   The Quest for Values. Jean-Pierre Barricelli, Comparative Literature, University of California, Riverside.

Description   Lower-division elective course capable of fulfilling humanities requirement. Winter and spring quarters. No prerequisite but prior (fall-quarter) course recommended: The Arts: Their Meaning and Interrelations. Meets three hours a week. Three films shown evenings and discussed each quarter. (Films have included *Antigone*, *La dolce vita*, *Lord of the Flies*, *Satyricon*, *The Andalusian Dog*, and *Lonely Are the Brave*.)

Objectives   To understand how the arts speak for the individual and mirror society's values, swinging like a pendulum between a search for order and a search for freedom; to appreciate the significance of the rational and emotional in Western and non-Western literature, visual arts, and music as they reflect changing modes of thinking and feeling—altering worldviews—in the movement of civilizations and cultures.

Comments   Complex course, with fourteen-page syllabus and daily hand-outs, including lists of titles, names, terms. Assignments in literature only; visual arts and music covered in class. Often I make drawings and play the piano in class to illustrate various points, but while "performance" of this sort enhances, it is not necessary. Readings amount to an average of eight hundred pages a quarter. Optional readings suggested. Required each quarter: eight reports, six quizzes, midterm, final. Textbooks are a problem; most anthologies deal only with the West. Reading materials put on reserve in the library. Since there is not enough space to itemize all works studied, I limit myself to a breakdown by segment and section with suggestions for readings throughout and sample units for the first segments of each quarter, the spirit of which is repeated in subsequent segments.

Schedule

The Search for Order

1. Western antiquity
   a. Ancient Greece (see sample units below)
   b. Ancient Rome (see sample units below)
2. China and Japan
   a. China: Han and Sung dynasties (e.g., Ssu-ma Ch'ien, Chang Heng, Li Ch'ing-chao, Su Shih)
   b. Japan: Muromachi and Tokugawa periods (e.g., Noh theater; Zeami, *Atsumori*; Kabuki theater; Chikamatsu, *Courier from Hell*)
3. India and Islam
   a. India: Hindu texts and Gupta era (e.g., *Mahabharata*, including *Bhagavad Gita*; Valmiki, *Ramayana*; Kālīdasa, *Shakuntala*)
   b. Islam: overview (e.g., Sa'di, *Gulistan*; Hāfiz, *Ghazals*)
4. European Renaissance, Enlightenment, neoclassicism
   a. European Renaissance (e.g., Dante, *Paradiso*; Machiavelli; More; Pico; Petrarch;

Sidney; Spenser; Rabelais; Montaigne; Erasmus; Shakespeare; Cervantes; Descartes)
  b. European Enlightenment and neoclassicism (e.g., Racine, Molière, Pope, Jefferson, Beccaria, Lessing, Hölderlin, Foscolo, Vico, Bacon, Goethe, Voltaire, Alfieri, Manzoni)
5. Africa: Black continent, traditional (e.g., griot and mvet epics)
6. Twentieth century in the West (e.g., Tolstoy, Shaw, Valéry, Chekhov, Faulkner, Fitzgerald, Mann, Pavese, Yeats, Eliot, Rilke, Joyce, O'Neill, D'Annunzio, Sartre, Zamyatin, Lawrence, Rulfo, García Márquez, Sábato, Carpentier, A. Miller, Hemingway, Camus, Buzzati)

The Search for Freedom
1. European Romanticism and Middle Ages
  a. European Romanticism (see sample units below)
  b. European Middle Ages (e.g., Dante, *Purgatorio*; Boccaccio; Petrarch; Villon; Chaucer; Walther von der Vogelweide, *Tristan and Isolde*; *Aucassin and Nicolette*; Rojas, *La Celestina*)
2. China and Japan
a. China: T'ang, Ming, Ch'ing dynasties and modern period (e.g., Wang Wei; Li Po; Tu Fu; Ts'ao Hsüeh-ch'ing, *Dream of the Red Chamber*; Han Yü; Lu Hsün)
  b. Japan: Momoyama, Meiji, modern periods (e.g., Murasaki Shikibu, *Tale of Genji*; Chikamatsu, *Love Suicides at Sonezaki*; Basho; Akutagawa; Kawabata)
3. India and Islam
  a. India: Moslem, colonial, modern (e.g., Tagore, *Stray Birds*, *Gitangali*; Narayan, "The Financial Expert")
  b. Islam: Modern (e.g., Firdausī, *The Story of Bahram Gur* 5; *Thousand and One Nights*: "The Lady and Her Five Suitors")
4. Africa: Black continent, modern (e.g., Achebe, *Things Fall Apart*; Ngugi, *Petals of Blood*; Soyinka, *Death and the King's Horseman*; La Guma; Senghor; Neto)
5. Twentieth century in the West (e.g., Unamuno, Montale, Neruda, Darío, Borges, Solzhenitsyn, Robbe-Grillet, Bellow, Brecht, Svevo, Calvino, Hamsun, Heller, Levi, T. Williams, W. C. Williams, Stevens, Eliot, Gide, Kafka, Burgess, Pirandello, Wells, Dick)

Sample Units

The Search for Order: Western Antiquity (including contrastive works)

Literature: Homer, *Iliad* 18; Pindar, "Olympian Ode 1"; Aeschylus, *Eumenides*; Sophocles, *Antigone*; Aristophanes, *Frogs*; Thucydides, *Peloponnesian War* 2.34-46; Vergil, *Aeneid* 6; Cicero, *First Oration against Catiline*; Horace, *Odes* 1; Lucretius, *On the Nature of Things* 4:1037-287 and 5.91-508; Seneca, *The Trojan Women*. Other: Sappho, *Odes* 4, 5, 88, 94, 96, 98, 114; Plato, *Republic* ("Allegory of the Cave"); Aristotle, *Ethics* 5-9; Euripides, *Bacchae*; Ovid, *Metamorphoses* 1; Catullus, *Lesbia* cycle; Juvenal, *Satires* 10; Petronius, *Satyricon* 5.

Visual arts: Cycladic musician; Crete: Knossos house and interior; Mycenae: Agamemnon's palace and gate; Agamemnon's mask; protogeometric amphora; geometric pitcher; dipylon amphora; geometric funerary krater; lyre; kouros from Melos; kouroi: Kroisos, Aristodikos; woman wearing peplos; naked wrestler; sports in relief sculpture; Acropolis; Propylaea; Nike; Erectheum; Parthenon; kore mirror handle; funerary stela of Hegeso; Demeter and

Persephone with Triptolemus; Poseidon of Artemision; youth of Antikythera; Poseidon of Melos; youth from Antikythera; Aphrodite and Pan (Delos); monument with horse; horse jockey of Artemision; white official lekythos; fisherman fresco.

Music: First Delphic Hymn; Dorian, Phrygian, Lydian, and Polylydian modes; Seikolos Song; lyre, kithara, aulos, tuba.

The Search for Freedom: Western Romanticism (including contrastive works)

Literature: Rousseau, *Confessions* 1. 1712-19 and *Reveries* 5th promenade; Goethe, *Faust*: "Prologue in Heaven," "Faust's Study 2," "Walpurgis Night"; Wergeland, "Napoleon," or Manzoni, "The Fifth of May"; Keats, "Ode to Melancholy," "Ode on a Grecian Urn," "Ode to a Nightingale," and "To Autumn," or Wordsworth, "Tintern Abbey" and *Prelude* 119-310; Leopardi, "The Infinite" and "Night Song of a Wandering Asian Shepherd"; Hugo, "To Albert Dürer" and "The Sadness of Olympio," or Baudelaire, "Spleen" 2, "Spleen" 4, "Her Hair," and "Litany to Satan"; Nietzsche, *Beyond Good and Evil* 2.24-44, or Schopenhauer, *The World as Will and Idea* 3 ("On Genius" and "On Madness"); Byron, *Manfred* or *Cain*; Radcliffe, *The Mysteries of Udolpho* (selections from 1); Balzac, *Gambara*, or Lermontov, "The Demon"; Pushkin, "The Bronze Horseman," or Poe, "The Cask of Amontillado"; Mazzini, *The Duties of Man* 8 or Emerson, *Society and Solitude*, "Art." Other: Echegaray, *The Great Galeoto*; Burke, *Reflections on the French Revolution* 4; Jefferson, *First Inaugural Address*; Dostoyevski, "Dream of a Ridiculous Man"; Goethe, *The Sorrows of Young Werther* 2; Wergeland, "Myself"; Hugo, *Notre Dame de Paris* 10.4; Keats, "Fancy," "Welcome Joy Welcome Sorrow," "The Sea"; Lermontov, *A Hero of Our Time*, "Introduction to Pechorin's Journal"; Lamartine, "The Crucifix"; Foscolo, *Last Letters of Jacopo Ortis* (letter of 23 May); Vigny, "The Mount of Olives" and "The Bottle in the Sea"; Shelley, "Ode to the West Wind"; Whitman, "When Lilacs Last in the Dooryard Bloom'd"; Thoreau, "Haze" and *Walden* (selections); Coleridge, "Kubla Khan"; Heine, "The Silesian Weavers"; Chateaubriand, *René* or *Atala*; Tolstoy, *The Kreutzer Sonata*; Hoffmann, "Murr the Tom-Cat" or "The Sandman"; Schiller, *The Robbers*; Novalis, "Hymns to the Night" 4; Pellico, *My Prisons* 7, 53, 76, 86-89; Manzoni, *The Betrothed* 9-11.

Visual arts: David, *Oath of the Horatii, Death of Marat, Battle of the Romans and the Sabines, Mme Récamier, The Coronation of Josephine, Mars Disarmed by Venus and the Graces*; the Madeleine (Paris); Arc de Triomphe (Paris); Guérin, *The Return of Marcus Sextus*; Guérard, *Psyche Receiving a First Kiss from Cupid, Napoleon at the Battle of Eylau*; Gros, *Christine Boyer*; Friedrich, *Abbey in the Oakwood, Hun's Grave in the Snow, Morning in the Riesegebirge*; Runge, *Lily of Light, Rest on the Flight to Egypt*; Girodet, *Entombment of Atala*; Géricault, *The Raft of the Medusa*; Ingres, *Jupiter and Thetis, Mme Blanc, Portrait of Granet*; Delacroix, *Abduction of Rebecca, Arab Rider Attacked by Lion, Lion Hunt, Liberty Leading the People*; Constable, *Stoke-by-Nayland, The Hay Wain*; Palmer, *Coming from Evening Church*; Turner, *Dido Building Carthage; Rain, Steam, and Speed; The Burning of the Houses of Parliament, Interior at Pentworth, Interior of a Theater in Venice*; Millais, *Ophelia*; Burne-Jones, *Chant d'amour*; Durand, *Catskill Clove, Kindred Spirits*; Cole, *Oxbow of the Connecticut River*; Bierstadt, *The Rocky Mountains*.

Music: Beethoven, Symphony no. 6.1 and 4, Symphony no. 5.1, Symphony no. 3.1 and 2; Schubert, "Gretchen at the Spinning Wheel"; Schumann, *Manfred*

Overture; Chopin, Nocturne in E-flat, Revolutionary Etude, Polonaise in A-flat; Wagner, Prelude to *Tristan and Isolde*; Berlioz, *Symphonie fantastique* 5 ("Witches's Sabbath"); Liszt, "La Campanella"; Brahms, Symphony no. 2.1; Verdi, *Nabucco* (chorus, end of act 3); Boïto, *Mefistofele* (epilogue); Tchaikovsky, Symphony no. 4.4; Mahler, Symphony no. 1.1; R. Strauss, *Till Eulenspiegel*; Sibelius, *Tapiola*; Puccini, *Turandot* ("Nessun dorma").

Period Courses

Joseph Gibaldi

The Baroque in Europe

Although the study of literature by period has provoked numerous questions and objections in twentieth-century scholarship (see, e.g., Weisstein, *Comparative Literature* 66-98), the approach remains, and justifiably so, among the most common methods of analyzing and evaluating, not to mention teaching, literary works. In their *Theory of Literature*, René Wellek and Austin Warren define a "period" as "a time section dominated by a system of literary norms, standards, and conventions, whose introduction, spread, diversification, integration, and disappearance can be traced" (265); as such, they contend, "the concept of period is certainly one of the main instruments of historical knowledge" (268). More recently, Wendy Steiner has added a strong contextual argument supporting periodization. "We need period concepts," she writes, "not only to write history but to know what a work is—for it is nothing in isolation from all norms, values, and other relational concepts" (*Colors* 194).

Interestingly, for both Wellek ("Concept") and Steiner (*Colors* 184-85), the baroque, once the subject of intense terminological controversy, is among the more useful of period concepts, especially for interart study. After rigorously reviewing the major scholarship devoted to the baroque, Wellek writes of the term, "It raises the problem of periodisation, of the analogies between the arts; it is the one term for the style between the Renaissance and classicism which is sufficiently general to override the local terms of schools; and it suggests the unity of a Western literary and artistic period" (127).

For the teacher of literature and other arts, a course on the baroque seems inevitable, for no other period perceived a more intimate association among the arts. The celebrated baroque poet Giambattista Marino (1569-1625), for example, declares, "Music and Poetry are two sisters. . . . The world has no arts more beautiful or more soothing to exhausted minds than these" (477-78). Of another "sisterhood," he states, "so alike are these two dear twins, born of one parturition, that is Painting and Poetry, that no one knows how to differentiate between them. . . . Poetry is called a speaking Picture, Painting a mute poem" (qtd. in Mirollo, *Poet* 201). Many other contemporary writers echo such sentiments. "Music," concurs Henry

Peacham in *The Compleat Gentleman* (1622), is "a sister to Poetry" (Strunk 331), while Charles Alphonse Du Fresnoy in his *De arte graphica* (1668) adds, "Painting and Poesy are two Sisters, which are so like in all things, that they mutually lend to each other both their Name and Office. One is called a dumb Poesy, and the other a speaking Picture" (Holt 164). In addition, no other period more consistently and, for its time, more daringly mingled these "sisters," producing such amalgams as the ceiling painting, the emblem book, and the opera.

Significantly, one of the first modern scholarly works to treat the mutual illumination of the arts, Heinrich Wölfflin's *Renaissance und Barock* (1888), focused primarily on the baroque and its relation to the Renaissance. Indeed, Wölfflin's comparative approach continues to provide the teacher with a helpful way to introduce the baroque. As Frank J. Warnke concisely and cogently puts it, the baroque is essentially a "hyperextension" (3) or "hyperdevelopment" (58) of Renaissance style rather than a revolt against it. To understand the baroque, therefore, one must know thoroughly the Renaissance and its arts.

The ideal way to teach the baroque is, of course, to establish a European Renaissance course as prerequisite. If this is not feasible, a helpful alternative is to set each baroque work studied, whatever the art, against its Renaissance "model." For instance, begin by placing a slide of Michelangelo's *David* side by side with a slide of Bernini's *David* and ask students to describe the differences they see between these two sculptural depictions of the same biblical subject. Invariably, even if they have never even heard of the scholar, they will begin using many of the very same terms Wölfflin employed to distinguish between Renaissance and baroque styles—the perfect and completed versus the restless and becoming, closed versus open form, static versus dynamic, and so forth. Additional comparisons that reinforce these or introduce other aspects of the baroque include Raphael's and Caravaggio's *Deposition*s; church facades of Alberti (e.g., S. Maria Novella) and Bernini (e.g., S. Andrea al Quirinale); Sigismundo d'India's monodic and Claudio Monteverdi's complexly madrigalesque settings of the Petrarchan lyric "Hor che'l ciel" or the opening pages of the Gloria from Palestrina's *Pope Marcellus Mass* and the first section of Vivaldi's Gloria in D; and Petrarch's sonnet 199 and Marino's poem "Il guanto," poetic treatments of the *bella mano* theme (on Renaissance, mannerist, and baroque poems about the beloved's "hand" and "glove," see Mirollo, *Mannerism* 125-59).

In theoretically oriented courses, this approach to "reading" or "decoding" the baroque would naturally relate to reception aesthetics, with its interest in the original readers' "horizon of expectations" (Jauss 25-28); reader-response theory and its investigations into how we experience a text and discern innovation (Iser, *Implied* 29; *Act* 131-34); semiotics, with its "intertextual frames" and "inferential walks" (Eco 31-32); genre theory, with its concern for "generic signals" (Fowler 88-105); E. H. Gombrich's theory of "schema and correction" in the making and viewing of art (*Art and*

Illusion); and Harold Bloom's quasi-oedipal conception of literary history (*Anxiety of Influence*).

Among the various approaches for teaching the baroque, ranging from the stylistic (e.g., Wölfflin) to the political (e.g., Maravall), one pedagogical device I have found especially helpful—and one that touches the heart of many of the theoretical approaches noted above—is to focus attention on the "beginnings" of the works studied. As James Lees-Milne has rightly observed in discussing seventeenth-century architecture, "the Baroque aims at making a tremendous impact upon first sight" (107), a notion James V. Mirollo has transferred to baroque lyric poetry, finding "an analogy between the desire of an architect to grasp his viewer's interest immediately and the similar intention of a Marino to 'stupefy' and raise the eyebrows of his reader with an opening conceit or an impressive verbal display" (*Poet* 276).

In their concern for effective beginnings, baroque artists reflect their intense interest in classical rhetoric. Virtually all rhetoricians from Aristotle, Cicero, and Quintillian through such Renaissance and baroque writers of rhetorical treatises as Pierre Fabri, Leonard Cox, Francesco Sansovino, Thomas Wilson, Giason De Nores, and Guillaume Du Vair discuss at length the importance of the first part of the oration, the *prooemium* or exordium. According to these writers, the successful exordium establishes the appropriate relationship between speaker and audience; the repertory of exordia is vast, selection from it depending on the rhetorical situation; the exordium may be direct or indirect (*insinuatio*); it should be brief and should contain the essence of the presentation; the exordium must cohere with the body of the work.

Study of the baroque arts uncovers a pattern of beginnings marked by brilliance, ingenuity, audacity, and virtuosity. Among literary works appropriate for classroom study, the most obvious examples of baroque exordial exuberance include Shakespeare's *Macbeth* (compare its first scene with the more "classical" prologue of the earlier, more "Renaissance" *Romeo and Juliet*) and, set against the Petrarchan tradition, lyric poems by Marino ("La donna che cuce"), Luis de Góngora ("Oh claro honor del líquido elemento"), Richard Crashaw ("The Weeper"), John Donne ("To his Mistris Going to Bed," Holy Sonnets 7 and 10), and Andreas Gryphius ("Uber die Geburt Jesu")—the openings of which are characterized by extraordinary dramatic, metaphoric, and linguistic effects that immediately arrest the attention and provide an effective "entranceway" coherent with the work as a whole. More indirect, or insinuative, though equally engaging, are the openings of many of Jean de La Ceppède's meditative lyrics (e.g., "Cette rouge sueur" and "Voicy-L'Homme," both conveniently in Warnke 98-101), which seem to assume at the outset the physical presence of the speaker as well as the reader at the biblical scenes described.

In each of the above beginnings, the poet simultaneously invokes a Renaissance norm and ingeniously transforms it. This quintessential quality of the baroque helps us understand why baroque art was and remains a "popular" style, for it calls forth the familiar yet treats it in a thoroughly fresh and surprising way. It also helps to explain why both church and state so aggressively adopted the baroque as the official style of the status quo, as a medium for preserving "inherited structures" (Maravall 263).

In each of the above works, too, the beginning, while serving to seize the reader's attention, coheres stylistically and thematically to what follows, as class analysis of the relation between the opening and the body of the work consistently demonstrates. The first scene of *Macbeth*, for instance, drawing on macabre interests of audience and patron (James I), startles with the sudden appearance of the witches, accompanied by "Thunder and lightning." Beyond its shock value, the scene also establishes the supernatural mood that dominates the play; it presents, with its fair-is-foul, foul-is-fair pronouncements, major themes of the work (e.g., the reversal of values, the conflict between appearance and reality); and, as Stephen Booth notes (117-18), it sets forth "a surprisingly complex alliterative pattern that runs across the whole play," continuing with the "fair-foul" echo in Macbeth's very first line (1.3) and concluding with the famous "full of sound and fury" soliloquy in act 5.

This focus on exordiums is particularly helpful in interart study because the idea of "beginnings" is relevant to arts that exist in both time (literature, music) and space (architecture, visual arts). The overture to Monteverdi's opera *Orfeo* provides a good example of an exuberant baroque musical beginning. Compared with the more static opening of earlier monodic music dramas, such as Giulio Caccini's *Euridice*, Monteverdi's overture makes use of a dynamic military fanfare played three times by the full ensemble, unusually large for its time even though the work was originally performed privately in a small room. Again, the overture not only grasps the attention but provides unity and coherence to the whole. The downward scale of the overture supplies thematic material for the ensuing ritornello, a theme subsequently repeated several times throughout the opera (see Donington).

Other exuberant musical openings include those of Monteverdi's madrigals "Altri canti di Marte" and "Ardo, avvampo," Bach's Toccata and Fugue in D Minor, and almost anything by Vivaldi, whether secular (*The Four Seasons*) or sacred (Gloria in D). A good example of an insinuative beginning is the striking opening of Monteverdi's setting of Petrarch's sonnet "Hor che'l ciel," in which the six voices of the madrigal, slowly in *parlando* fashion and in their lowest register, create an almost supernatural mood expressive of the stillness of nature as described in the text.

In speaking of beginnings, we are, of course, speaking of the relationship the artist wishes to establish with the audience. Baroque artists, as we are seeing, sought fully to involve their audiences intellectually, emotionally, even physically with the work. Nowhere is this tendency more evident than in baroque architecture. With its multiple facades and dramatic volutes, Baldassare Longhena's S. Maria della Salute in Venice is, as typically viewed from the other side of the Grand Canal, a dazzling attraction. In such

Roman baroque churches as Francesco Borromini's S. Carlo alle Quattro Fontane, Pietro da Cortona's S. Maria della Pace, and Bernini's S. Andrea al Quirinale, the entranceways thrust forward to meet the spectator. In Bernini's piazza of Saint Peter's, composed of huge oval-shaped colonnades symbolic of the embracing arms of the Church, the transition between architectural space and the approaching viewer's space is imperceptible.

This kind of spatial continuity between work and spectator is common, as well, in Bernini's sculpture, such as the *David*, poised to send his shot toward an unseen Goliath, and the bust of Cardinal Scipione Borghese, caught in the act of speaking. Both these figures "seem to demand an actively participating audience to complete the action" (H. Hibbard 90). In the statues of Longinus, Daniel, Jerome, and Gabriele Fonseca, among others, Bernini depicts figures in such extreme emotional states that the niches intended to enframe them can no longer do so, since the statues penetrate beyond their traditional space into that of the spectator.

In *Baroque*, an excellent introduction to the period and a required text for the course, John Rupert Martin discusses extensively the use of space in baroque art. He notes the aim of the baroque artist "to break down the barrier between the work of art and the real world" by representing the subject as "existing in a space coextensive with that of the viewer" (155). In painting, Martin finds the integration of real and fictive space in, for example, Caravaggio's *Supper at Emmaus* and Rembrandt's *Night Watch*. Like Bernini's statues, the figures in both paintings seem to protrude beyond the surface of the canvas into the viewer's space.

Martin also treats the baroque tendency to create a sense of infinite space "by means of emphatic recessional movements" (161). This tendency is best exemplified by baroque ceiling paintings, such as Baciccio's in the Gesù and Andrea Pozzo's in S. Ignazio, both in Rome. Such works blend real architecture with feigned architecture, and sculpted figures with painted figures, so that the viewer cannot tell where "real" space ends and the painting begins. In other words, the spatial continuum begins in the spectator's space and continues, illusionistically, through a series of recessional movements upward into infinite space.

We find similar exordial complexity and narrative (rather than visual) complexity in the baroque tradition of the play within a play (see Nelson 1–61), which includes Beaumont and Fletcher's *Knight of the Burning Pestle*, Lope de Vega's *Lo fingido verdadero* (*Acting Is Believing*), Calderón's *La vida es sueño* (*Life is a Dream*), and Pierre Corneille's *L'illusion comique* (*The Theatrical Illusion*), all of which are currently available in paperbound editions. In the Beaumont and Fletcher drama, we find another example of spatial continuity between work and viewer as the play's would-be formal prologue is rudely interrupted by disgruntled members of the audience, one of whom joins the cast of the play. At one or more points in all these plays, actors unite with audience to watch a drama unfold.

Similarly, Giambattista Basile, breaking with the Boccaccian tradition, uses as cornice for the novellas of his *Pentamerone* not the traditional "narrative situation" (e.g., a plague, a flood, a pilgrimage) that prompts storytelling but an actual tale as engaging as any of the tales it enframes. In fact, as the storytelling reaches its end, the novellas and their frame merge, the tales themselves becoming an intrinsic plot element of the cornice tale.

Along with such plays within plays and tales within tales, George Herbert in "The Collar" and Henry Vaughan in "The World" offer poems within poems, for each has a "correcting voice" that interrupts a misguided speaker to set his words into a more appropriate context. Such multiple beginnings take on new meaning with John Milton. "Lycidas" contains three separate invocations (lines 15, 85, 132) and *Paradise Lost* four distinct prologues (books 1, 3, 7, 9). Significantly, both works conclude with "beginnings"—the mourning shepherd off to a new pasture; Adam and Eve, hand in hand, to a new world. With Milton, we find that the idea of beginning becomes not just artistic strategy but theological truth.

Whatever approach one uses, a successful course in the baroque will enable students not only to understand and appreciate the period's artistic achievement and learn something about the age that generated it but also to gain insights into the evolution of "tradition" by seeing how artists respond to and transform the norms and forms of their artistic predecessors. Students will note the process by which the "receiver" of the aesthetic experience (the reader, the viewer, the listener), in attempting to decode works of art, encounters a type of surprise that, in turn, produces pleasure. They will discover the nature of "popular art"—an art that draws on the familiar yet finds fresh ways to present it—and the manner in which such art may be exploited for political and ideological ends. A course on the baroque also illuminates the relations among different national literatures and, more to the point of this volume, among the major arts of an important historical period.

Syllabus

Course   The Baroque in Europe. Joseph Gibaldi, Humanities, New School for Social Research.

Description   Upper-level elective course to fulfill humanities requirement. Spring term. No prerequisite but prior (fall-term) course recommended: The Renaissance in Europe. Meets once a week for two hours. Occasional guest lecturer. Includes visit to a museum; attendance at a concert and/or play.

Objectives   To introduce students to the major intellectual, cultural, and artistic trends of the baroque; to study major literary genres of the period—lyric poetry, epic, novella, drama—and explore literary interrelations with painting, sculpture, architecture, and music; to probe baroque arts through a number of critical approaches: historical, political, thematic, generic, rhetorical, reader-response, semiotic; to understand and appreciate the baroque artistic achievement as well as the artistic process in general.

Schedule

1. Reading and decoding the baroque. Renaissance norms and baroque transformations. Michelangelo and Bernini (statues of David). Raphael and Caravaggio (paintings of Christ's deposition). Alberti and Bernini (church facades). Palestrina and Vivaldi (settings of Gloria). Sigismundo d'India and Monteverdi (settings of Petrarch's "Hor che'l ciel"). Petrarch and Marino (poems on the *bella mano* theme).
2. Introduction to baroque. Wellek, "The Concept of Baroque in Literary Scholarship." Etymology, early uses, Wölfflin, twentieth-century scholarship. Relations among Renaissance, mannerism, baroque. Baroque and Counter-Reformation. Meditative tradition. Baroque and rhetoric. Baroque fusions of the arts.
3. Secular lyric poetry. Marino, Góngora, Donne, et al.
4. Sacred lyric poetry. Saint Ignatius of Loyola, *Spiritual Exercises* (excerpts). Marino, Crashaw, Gryphius, La Ceppède, Donne, Herbert, Vaughan, et al.
5. Drama. Shakespeare, *Macbeth.*
6. Music. Monteverdi, madrigals. Vivaldi, *Four Seasons.* Bach, Toccata and Fugue in D Minor. Handel, *Royal Fireworks Music.*
7. Opera. Monteverdi, *Orfeo.* Purcell, *Dido and Aeneas.*
8. Architecture. Bernini, Borromini, Longhena, et al. Varriano.
9. Sculpture. Bernini. Saint Teresa of Avila, *Vida* (excerpts). Crashaw, "Hymn to St. Teresa." Petersson.
10. Painting. Titian, Annibale Carracci, Rubens, Caravaggio, Rembrandt, et al. Mary Magdalene theme. J. R. Martin.
11. Drama. Calderón, *Life Is a Dream.*
12. Epic. Tasso, *Jerusalem Delivered* in baroque painting and music. Lee, *Ut Pictura Poesis*, especially chapter 7. Poussin, Tiepolo, et al. Monteverdi, *Battle of Tancredi and Clorinda.* Gemignani, *Enchanted Forest.* Handel, *Rinaldo.*
13. Epic. Milton, *Paradise Lost* (excerpts).
14. Short fiction. Basile, *Pentamerone* (excerpts in Smarr).
15. Drama. Corneille, *Theatrical Illusion.*

Robert K. Wallace

Nineteenth-Century Fiction, Music, and Painting

Housed in the English department, the course Nineteenth-Century Fiction, Music, and Painting attempts to bring the arts together at a university that has traditionally kept them apart. It was originally conceived as an enrichment course for English majors, enabling them to explore the degree to which the stylistic transition to Romanticism in literature had parallels in other arts. Today, the course also serves as an enrichment elective for majors in fine arts and in the humanities generally.

Nineteenth-Century Fiction, Music, and Painting began as a "period" course but has become increasingly "interart" in method; it is now, I hope in the best sense, both at the same time. In early versions of the course, I would begin by teaching *Pride and Prejudice* and *Wuthering Heights* as examples of the transition from neoclassical to Romantic in English prose fiction. Then we would study instrumental works by Mozart and Beethoven as examples of the transition from classical to Romantic in Viennese music, after which we would move on to Goya and Turner as examples of the transition from neoclassical to Romantic in oil painting. The current course retains this emphasis on one period of stylistic transition, but its method has now become interart in an integrated rather than a parallel sense. Here I discuss some of the assumptions, methods, and goals underlying the course syllabus.

Earlier versions of the course tended to begin with a rather formal overview of Romanticism in the separate arts, along with a theoretical overview of difficulties inherent in comparing the arts. Now I prefer to begin the course with three works of art. Edgar Allan Poe's "Ligeia" and Frédéric Chopin's "Octave" Etude are easily assimilated by students of any academic background. Students who hear the étude after reading the story immediately see a parallel in the three-part structure (a:b:a) of each work. They also perceive the unity of effect each artist achieves by juxtaposing highly contrasting materials (Ligeia and Rowena, the outer and inner sections), and note the ambiguous meaning of each work, despite its structural clarity. Because Théodore Géricault's *After Death* is a painting, it does not share the three-part temporal dynamics of the story or the étude. In subject matter, it does resemble "Ligeia" in its presentation of the main subject "after death." But students tend to see a more interesting potential for comparison in

Géricault's unity of effect and structural ambiguity. This opening exercise shows students that they can handle material in all three arts. Discussion of the three works brings out naturally—by drawing on students' own perceptions—the kind of theoretical observations that I had lectured on in earlier versions of the course.

From the short three-part form of "Ligeia" and the "Octave" Etude, we plunge into the long three-part structures of *Pride and Prejudice* and Mozart's Piano Concerto no. 9, K. 271. After studying volume 1 of the novel, we turn to the first movement of the concerto (the starting point for Rosen's brilliant and accessible analysis *The Classical Style*). As with the Poe and Chopin pieces, certain structural comparisons are obvious on the surface of these works, often becoming more intricate and interesting the deeper one goes. But students are seldom content to compare the structures. They feel that the spirit, the tone, the balance, the wit—in short, the style—of these works is in some important way comparable. Discussion always leads to a comparison of the functions of Elizabeth Bennet in the novel and the solo voice in the concerto. During the next week, we pursue these issues as we compare the concluding parts of the novel and the concerto.

Teaching music to the uninitiated is tricky, especially for a teacher of literature. But I have found that students can go far on their own if they are encouraged to use their own ears and minds. I once required Joseph Machlis's *Enjoyment of Music* for my interart courses, but it was expensive, ponderous, and only peripherally relevant. I now have that book on reserve, along with Cuthbert Girdlestone on the Mozart concertos, Rosen on the classical style, Romain Rolland on Beethoven, and my own comparisons of Jane Austen with Mozart and of Emily Brontë with Beethoven. Such reference works are often useful to students writing about music, but they are generally not needed at the earlier stage in which the primary works are themselves being compared in the classroom.

To ensure that students engage with the music before we discuss it in class, I ask them to prepare brief written responses to each piece, outlining their perceptions of structure and emotional or spiritual content. (All the musical works are put on reserve on cassette tapes, which students can easily copy for study at home.) This assignment helps them follow the skeletal outlines of structure that I present in class and that they later find more fully described in reference works, which I encourage them to consult when they need help in clarifying what they have intuited on their own.

Once they understand Mozart's classical use of the sonata-allegro form in the first movement of K. 271, students easily sense the vehemence with which Beethoven disrupts that form while also preserving it in the first movement of the *Appassionata* Sonata, op. 57. Similarly, they see how Brontë, in the first volume of *Wuthering Heights,* both disrupts and preserves the novelistic form perfected by Austen. Our discussion of this Brontë volume and Beethoven movement, as well as that of the subsequent volume and movements, is almost by definition a four-way comparison: Brontë and

Beethoven in the context of Austen and Mozart. For their first paper, students are required to write an interart comparison involving those four artists. Most choose an Austen-Mozart or Brontë-Beethoven parallel, but some will plunge right into a four-way comparison. Occasionally someone will compare Austen with Beethoven or Brontë with Mozart.

The next section of the course builds quickly from Brontë and Beethoven to Goya. We begin by considering the mystical visions experienced by Catherine and Heathcliff shortly before their deaths (supplemented by appropriate Brontë poems), along with the mystical transcendence of strife expressed in Beethoven's last piano sonata, op. 111. This comparison, interesting in its own right, leads directly to the world of Francisco Goya. Students always respond to the deafness that afflicted both Goya and Beethoven, but our primary focus is on Goya's parallel stylistic evolution, from the decorative world of his early cartoons through the court paintings, the war paintings, the black paintings, and the late luminous work in Bordeaux. As the students quickly see, Goya's painterly career recapitulates the stylistic transitions we have traced from Austen to Brontë and from Mozart to Beethoven.

In a paper on Goya students are asked to compare one or more of his paintings with one or more works already studied in the course. Because of Goya's extraordinary human and technical range and his stylistic breadth, possible topics are almost limitless. In the comparative papers for this course, students must refine their language to write accurately about the individual arts and at the same time broaden their conceptual range to articulate that which the arts have in common.

Now at the midpoint of the semester, one could profitably return to Poe, Chopin, and Géricault, juxtaposing representative short works by these artists with Hector Berlioz's *Symphony Fantastique*, Honoré de Balzac's *Père Goriot*, and major canvases by Eugène Delacroix. All six of these artists build on themes prominent in the Goya, Beethoven, and Brontë part of the course and dramatize the distance the culture had come, by the 1830s, from the world of Austen, Mozart, and early Goya. Currently, however, I follow the Goya paper with the paintings of J. M. W. Turner, both to provide an extended comparison and contrast with Goya's evolution into Romanticism and to prepare for a close reading of Herman Melville's *Moby-Dick*.

Turner's career in landscape, no less than Goya's in societal subjects, reflects the stylistic transitions in prose fiction and instrumental music traced earlier in the course. Study of his career enriches our general sense of the transition to Romanticism while offering another highly individualistic embodiment of that development. In Melville's *Moby-Dick* we find a prose aesthetic that parallels Turner's painterly aesthetic. We read the text slowly for its richness of texture in the context of the issues discussed throughout the course. As their assignment for this portion of the course, students keep a running journal. *Moby-Dick* lends itself to such an exercise even in isolation, as I argue elsewhere ("Teaching"), but its richness as the subject for a journal is strongly enhanced in the context of Austen and Brontë, Mozart and Beethoven, and Goya and Turner.

Completion of the *Moby-Dick* discussion and journal brings us to the most interesting and perhaps even the most valuable part of the course, the presentation by students of their own interart comparisons. Students may discuss works by artists already studied, but only if the topic departs from subjects taken up in class. They are encouraged to range, within the boundaries of nineteenth-century fiction, music, and painting, as widely as their instincts and capabilities allow. As the syllabus seldom extends beyond 1851, many turn to the second half of the century in order to follow up trends of particular interest from the first half. Students tend to be apprehensive about this requirement early in the semester, but by the time we get to the actual presentations, they invariably have conceived of a comparison they are eager to explore in some depth. After making an oral presentation to the class, each has until final-exam day to write up the comparison as the last formal requirement of the course. The student presentations always add considerable diversity to the materials of the course as presented in the syllabus.

Nineteenth-Century Fiction, Music, and Painting deals primarily with analogies and parallels among the arts. It is not self-consciously theoretical. It does not work the student through the hybrid art forms (the art song, verbal music, concrete poetry, the *Bildgedicht*) that are often emphasized in interart courses. Nor is it much concerned with influence studies—though a bit of this perspective does come out in the Brontë-Beethoven and Melville-Turner sections. Yet these limitations, too, are balanced by certain advantages. Students are surprisingly able to discover methodological pitfalls on their own, without being told in advance what is legitimate or not. If works are carefully chosen, students will see what is comparable and what is not; if works are humanly and artistically rich, they will find more comparability in them than any teacher can predict. Hybrid works are valuable for a certain kind of interart study, but they are not necessarily the most representative of their period or the most worthy of classroom scrutiny. If comparisons can be made among autonomous works in the separate arts, then that which is being compared is perhaps what is most human and, hence, most humanistic about them.

Syllabus

Course Nineteenth-Century Fiction, Music, and Painting. Robert K. Wallace, Literature and Language, Northern Kentucky University.

Description Offered in alternating years as upper-division elective for humanities and honors students. No prerequisites but strong background in one of the three arts recommended. Meets twice a week for seventy-five minutes each meeting.

Objectives   To introduce students to three separate arts in the nineteenth century through detailed comparisons of selected masterworks; to trace the transition from classical (or neoclassical) to Romantic in prose fiction, instrumental music, and oil painting; to understand the similarities and differences in artistic media by making detailed comparisons between and among them. Students present their own interart comparisons in the closing weeks of the class.

Schedule

1–2. Introduction to Romanticism and the arts. Poe's "Ligeia," Chopin's "Octave" Etude, Géricault's *After Death*.

3–4. Austen, *Pride and Prejudice*, volume 1; Mozart, Piano Concerto no. 9, movement 1. Sonata-allegro form.

5–6. Austen, volumes 2 and 3; Mozart, movements 2 and 3.

7–8. Brontë, *Wuthering Heights*, volume 1; Beethoven, *Appassionata* Sonata, movement 1. Organic form.

9–10. Brontë, volume 2; Beethoven, movements 2 and 3.

11. Austen/Mozart/Beethoven/Brontë paper due.

11–12. *Wuthering Heights*, chapters 15, 16, 31–34, and Beethoven's Sonata op. 111, especially *Arietta*. Mystical vision.

13-14. Goya: early, middle, and late (Abbruzzese).

15. Goya paper due.

15–16. Turner before 1819 (Reynolds, chs. 1–2) and after 1819 (Reynolds, chs. 3–4).

17–18. Turner (Reynolds, ch. 5) and Melville, *Moby-Dick*, chapters 1–3.

19–20. Melville, chapters 4–41.

21–22. Melville, chapters 42–85.

23–24. Melville, chapter 86 to end.

25. *Moby-Dick* journal due.

26–29. Students present interart comparisons orally to the class (15 to 20 min. each).

30. Final examination. Paper derived from student presentation due.

J. Theodore Johnson, Jr.

The Year 1913: An Interdisciplinary Course

The inspiration for this course came from Zdenka Volavkova, who was a member of the research team responsible for the impressive three-volume *L'année 1913* (ed. Brion-Guerry). While serving as a visiting professor in our art history department, Volavkova persuaded Jeanne Stump and me to create a team-taught course on 1913—an extraordinary year. We two, specialists respectively in French art and literature of the late nineteenth and early twentieth centuries and both strongly inclined toward interdisciplinary courses and approaches, had given guest lectures a number of times in each other's classes before deciding to collaborate on this course.

The course focuses on 365 dazzling days in the history of Western civilization—a period of blazing creativity just before the long night of the Great War, with its barbed wire, trenches, mustard gas, aerial attacks, and death. A *course*, as the etymology of this term reminds us, is linear. Yet linear logic implies cause-and-effect relationships, and to see 1913 in such a framework would falsify its organic, dynamic nature. Therefore, we view the course as a giant kaleidoscope, turning like the Grande Roue, a gigantic ferris wheel by the Eiffel Tower, which figures so often in the painting and poetry of 1913. Each class brings new configurations as additional materials pass over the backgrounds of previous materials, which, in turn, are seen with different depths of field and focus. This kaleidoscopic structure allows us to spend a considerable amount of time "looking at beautiful forms" (*kalos* 'beautiful' plus *eidos* 'form' plus *skopos* 'look at') in painting, sculpture, architecture, cinema, costume and scenic design for the ballet, and fashion. We also stress the kaleidoscopic aspects—in terms of images and structures—of the poetry of Guillaume Apollinaire and Blaise Cendrars and the prose of Marcel Proust and André Gide.

What of the ideas and theories of 1913? The word *idea* derives from the Greek *idein* 'to see,' while the word *theory* comes from the Greek *theōrein* 'to look at,' and ultimately from *thea* 'the act of seeing.' Thus we examine the various ways of seeing in 1913, which are implied in sixteen futurist manifestos that appeared that year, and we compare them with Gino Severini's *Dynamic Hieroglyphic of the Ball Tabarin* (1912) and Umberto Boccioni's *Dynamism of a Cyclist* (1913) and *Unique Forms of Continuity in*

Space (1913). (On the futurist movement, see Perloff.) During the semester we read volume 2 of *L'année 1913*, which includes articles about the periodicals of the era, and volume 3, which comprises many manifestos and theoretical texts in philosophy, aesthetics, architecture, sculpture, painting, music, literature, theater, dance, and cinema. We also hear guest lecturers who discuss psychology and the sciences as well as historical, political, and social developments. By the end of the semester we all feel that we are beginning to see the world of 1913 the way contemporaries must have seen it. Terms such as *Geistesgeschichte, Weltanschauung,* and *Zeitgeist,* unfashionable though they are, make sense in relation to that year's phenomena.

The year 1913 has, of course, attracted the attention of numerous scholars with diverse approaches. Virginia Cowles, for example, devoted a chapter to each of the great centers of 1913—London, Berlin, Saint Petersburg, Vienna, Rome, Paris, and New York. Elisabeth Hausser selected the significant or picturesque events of the year in Paris day by day. Because of our research specialties, Jeanne Stump and I focus on Paris, for to this international center had flocked painters, writers, musicians, and dancers from around the world: Gertrude Stein and Isadora Duncan from America; Marc Chagall, Igor Stravinsky, Sergei Diaghilev, Vaslav Nijinsky, and the Ballets Russes from Russia; Arthur Honegger and Blaise Cendrars from Switzerland; Juan Gris and Pablo Picasso from Spain; Gabriele D'Annunzio and numerous futurists from Italy; and Louis Marcoussis from Poland.

Any one of the numerous artists at work in Paris could give us access to the exuberant spirit of the year. Among those we choose to discuss is Guillaume Apollinaire (born in Rome to a Polish mother and unknown father), who became the self-styled impressario of cubism (and other movements), spoke about orphic cubism at the Robert Delaunay exhibition in the Der Sturm gallery in Berlin in January 1913, and published in that year the manifesto *L'antitradition futuriste,* essays such as *Méditations esthétiques, les peintres cubistes,* and a major volume of poetry entitled *Alcools* containing a cubist portrait by Picasso. He also wrote the poems that were soon to be collected in *Calligrammes, poèmes de la paix et de la guerre (1913-1916),* another important volume. The opening poem of that collection, "Liens," first published in the new review *Montjoie!* in 1913, has the lines "Nous ne sommes que deux ou trois hommes / Libres de tous liens / Donnons-nous la main." Liberation from shackles of any sort to form human bonds is a theme that courses through much of the artistic production in the Paris of 1913.

We ask students to read a wide variety of texts. Besides placing many books on reserve in the library (e.g., Bertrand; M. W. Brown; M. W. Martin; Shattuck, *Banquet Years*; Sypher, *Rococo to Cubism*; Tuchman), we use as art history text Werner Haftmann's two-volume *Painting in the Twentieth Century* for its emphasis on this period and for its numerous reproductions. With the understanding that those who can will read the literary works in French, we also assign Roger Shattuck's *Selected Writings of Guillaume Apollinaire*; Marcel Proust's *Du côté de chez Swann* (1913), the first volume of

A la recherche du temps perdu; and André Gide's *Les caves du Vatican* (*Lafcadio's Adventures*), written in 1913 and published early in 1914. Gide's concerns with society, intellectual responsibility, mores, ideas, elegance in expression, and a young person's *formation* or development—and his views, so often contradicting those of the church and his milieu—make his playful yet serious *sotie* an important book for the course. After gratuitously pushing Amédée Fleurissoire out of the train, Lafcadio remarks that "ce vieillard est un carrefour" 'This old man is a crossroads.' In so many ways, the writings of Apollinaire, Proust, and Gide were *carrefours* for the artistic activity and thought of Paris in 1913.

We also look closely at Blaise Cendrars's *Prose du Transsibérien et de la petite Jehanne de France, dédiée aux musiciens,* a poem published in 1913 in an edition about two meters tall, printed with numerous type fonts and in four colors. Adjectives denoting one color are printed in another, so we see "*Place Rouge*" printed in orange, "*lunettes bleues*" in green, and so forth. This typographical technique sets up a buzzing, synesthetic cognitive dissonance in the mind and the senses of the viewer-reader. The whole was to have been promoted by Sonia Delaunay-Terk's *affiche* in words of various colors as "PREMIER LIVRE SIMULTANE / PRESENTATION synchrome / TEXTE peinture *simultané.*"

Simultaneity was central to 1913 (see Bergman); thus our nonlinear, kaleidoscopic, simultaneous course 1913 becomes a *carrefour* for the interchange of disciplines. The diverse materials keep intersecting like the materials in the papiers collés of Braque and Picasso, which create those *passages* that give cubism (as Sypher puts it) its high irridescence, joyfully allowing words and images to overlap and fuse. These new materials, new insights, different methods of inquiry, histories, traditions, anecdotes, trivia, and various forms of discourse seem to barrel, like the metropolitan subway trains connecting Montmartre to Montparnasse in 1913, through our fixed classroom space in the basement of the Kansas University Art Museum. We find this aspect of the course intellectually stimulating and thoroughly in keeping with futurism and with the new montage and flashback techniques in the increasingly dynamic medium of the cinema.

In the opening lectures of the course, I deal with the transition from the nineteenth century and naturalism to the new perspectives of [the "reel" world of] the cinema (subsequently we screen two representative films by D. W. Griffith, *The Battle of Elderbush Gulch* and *Judith of Bethulia,* as well as several shorts and documentaries, all of 1913) and with the experiments in color by the fauves and the German expressionists. We then hear a guest lecture analyzing Stravinsky's *Rite of Spring.* Later lectures deal with the new organizations of time, space, and visual rhythms devised by the futurists and the cubists; the Ballets Russes of Diaghilev; and the riotous performance of Stravinsky's *Rite of Spring,* choreographed by Nijinsky, with decor and costumes by Léon Bakst, in Auguste Perret's newly opened Théâtre des

Champs-Elysées, with its handsome decorations by Maurice Denis, Edouard Vuillard, and others. Just two weeks earlier, the premiere of Claude Debussy's *Jeux*, with choreography by Nijinsky and sets and costumes by Bakst, had taken place in the same theater.

Through sobering period films and the erudition of a guest lecturer, we behold the outbreak of the Great War. Returning to Apollinaire, we see that before the war, in January 1913, and in conjunction with the exhibition of his friend Robert Delaunay's *Fenêtres simultanées* (for which he had written the catalog preface in the form of a poem, "Les fenêtres," an *ars poetica* of orphic cubism), Apollinaire lectured about orphic cubism at the galleries of the new magazine *Der Sturm* in Berlin. Apollinaire enlisted in December 1914. During his time at the front, he wrote *Calligrammes*, a brilliant and heart-rending poetic testimony about war and peace. Orphism is central to Apollinaire's poetics (see Johnson). He had seen himself as Orpheus and Christ in his collaborative effort with Raoul Dufy in their *Bestiaire, ou le cortège d'Orphée* of 1911. Chagall's *Hommage à Apollinaire* of 1911–12, where each couple becomes a new Adam and Eve as they create their unique time and space, shows how important the blurrings of myth, metempsychosis, relativity, and simultaneity were for these artists and writers (as they were for Einstein in physics and for Freud and Jung in psychology). In the opening paragraphs of *A la recherche du temps perdu*, Proust's narrator becomes what he reads about—a church, a quartet, the rivalry of François I and Charles V. In 1913, James Joyce was just beginning *Ulysses*, where Bloom will take a day-long Homeric odyssey through the streets of Dublin.

After the joyous excitement of the first part of the course, which brings the students to the Great War and their first examination, the second part begins by emphasizing the written word as opposed to the visual. Yet the visual and the rhythmic are always present, especially in futurism, concrete poetry, the brilliant synthetic collaboration of the Russian Sonia Delaunay-Terk and the Swiss Blaise Cendrars in *La prose du Transsibérien et de la petite Jehanne de France* with its triumphant resolution in the colors of the French flag, the Great Wheel, and the Eiffel Tower.

We now read Proust, who was very much aware of the enormous transitions he was witnessing—the advent of electricity, the bicycle, the motor car, the telephone, the airplane—as well as of the gradual and constant upheavals in social orders. A "painter of the heroism of modern life" in the tradition of Baudelaire, Proust presents society in a brilliant display of styles that range from Balzacian realism through impressionism to a painstakingly rigorous overlay of images that resembles analytic or synthetic cubism. We stress not the art nouveau, turn-of-the-century, belle époque qualities of the man and the work, which certainly are there, but rather the vigorous artist who admired Claude Monet (now in that final phase where he was producing the enormous *Nymphéas*) and who saw himself as quite different from Henri Bergson. It was Proust who, in the same sense that plane geometry is different from solid geometry, strove to develop the difference between plane psychology and what he called psychology in time. We also hear a guest lecture on Edwardian literature and the stratified British society of the period we have come to know from the television series *Upstairs, Downstairs.*

In the third part of the course, we look at the United States. A guest lecturer introduces popular songs and voices of the period: Irving Berlin, Victor Herbert's *Sweethearts,* and Charles Ives's symphony *Holidays*—as well as a kaleidoscope of references to, among others, the comic-strip characters Happy Hooligan, Buster Brown, Krazy Kat, and Jiggs and Maggie in *Bringing Up Father* by George McManus. The Armory Show (1913) brought to the American public—in New York and then in Chicago and Boston—some thirteen hundred art works by European and American artists such as Alexander Archipenko, Constantin Brancusi, Arthur B. Davies, Marcel Duchamp (whose *Nude Descending the Staircase* of 1912 was as scandalous as *September Morn* by Paul Chabas, which had to be removed from the window of a Fifth Avenue art gallery), Henri Matisse, Claude Monet, Edvard Munch, Jules Pascin, Francis Picabia, Pablo Picasso, and Odilon Redon. For our purposes this exhibition effectively synthesizes the wide diversity of 1913.

Another guest lecturer describes Germany in 1913 as returning to the irrational—to metaphysics, myth, and mysticism—in such countermovements to naturalism as impressionism, the new romanticism, and expressionism. Carl Sternheim's play *1913,* a satirical critique of society, focuses on the parvenu industrialist Christian Maske. In 1913 Thomas Mann published *Death in Venice,* and in January of that year the opera *Der Rosenkavalier* by Richard Strauss with libretto by Hugo von Hoffmannsthal, judged indecent in 1911, was first performed at Covent Garden. From the elegant final trio in *Der Rosenkavalier,* we turn to a guest lecture reviewing Lenin's works on Karl Marx, Friedrich Engels, Georg Hegel, and the American, French, and Russian revolutions.

As the second part of the course opened with a guest lecture on the various developments in physics (Nils Borg, Einstein, Marie Curie, and the Nobel prize), the course closes with another lecture on aeronautics. In 1903 Orville Wright flew 120 feet, in 1909 Louis Blériot crossed the English Channel, and in 1913 Roland Garros flew 453 miles across the Mediterranean. Night flying began in 1913, and the first loop-the-loops were executed in August and September of 1913. Robert Delaunay's huge *Hommage à Blériot* of 1914, begun in 1913 and now in Basel, relates to the generalized theme of *machinisme* in the arts of the period (part of *modernolatria*) as well as to his academic, theoretical *Formes circulaires* of 1913, which help lay the groundwork for abstract art.

During the final part of the course we deal with such brief topics as popular music, Scott Joplin and the rag, jazz, various dance forms—the turkey trot, the grizzly bear, the fox trot, the bunny hug, and the scandalous tango, defended and given full dignity in a speech by Jean Richepin of the

Académie Française at the end of 1913. Yvette Guilbert's career as diseuse took a new direction from that of the gay-nineties cabarets in the Montmartre of Henri Toulouse-Lautrec. The Montmartre piano player and composer Erik Satie was particularly prolific in the years 1912–14, and his *Le piège de Méduse*, described as a *comédie lyrique en un acte*, looks forward to surrealism and some of the theater work of Eugène Ionesco, Boris Vian, and Fernando Arrabal. Satie's *Trois valses distinguées du précieux dégoûté* of 1914 (a total of 2 ½ minutes long) pokes fun at Maurice Ravel's *Valses nobles et sentimentales* of 1911. These miniature but abstract waltz compositions can be compared with Picasso's *Guitar and Music Sheet "Waltz"* (1912–13), where we find not quite two measures of music pasted on the composition. In this papier collé, Picasso collapses, abstracts, and edits nineteenth-century linearity and the time-space continuum of the ballroom, flattening it out over printed wallpaper, with its floral motifs and borders turned in various directions to syncopate even further this new conceptual space. How far we have come from the flow of Johann Strauss's *Blue Danube Waltz* (used in Stanley Kubrick's *2001: A Space Odyssey* precisely to establish a coherent time-space continuum in the opening sequences in space), in which couples in elegant belle époque clothes waltz counterclockwise to strings fluid and surging but always in three-quarter time. In 1913 the strings became percussive in Stravinsky's *Rite of Spring*, and the orchestra appears as fragments of a guitar in Picasso's papier collé.

From the course are omitted hundreds of important names and titles of works for a number of countries in volume 2 of *L'année 1913* (see the chronology on 1174–1235); and *1913*, an exhibition catalog, brings to light much valuable information and many fresh sources. A semester course devoted solely to the French literature of 1913 would be full and would include *Le Grand Meaulnes* by Alain Fournier; *La colline inspirée* by Maurice Barrès; *Jean Barois* by Roger Martin du Gard; *Les copains* by Jules Romains; *L'envers du music-hall, L'entrave*, and *Prrou, Poucette et quelques autres*, all by Colette; *La révolte des anges* by Anatole France; and Valery Larbaud's *A. O. Barnabooth: Ses oeuvres complètes, c'est-à-dire un conte, ses poésies et son journal intime*. Theatrical performances of 1913 included *L'annonce faite à Marie* and *Protée* by Paul Claudel; D'Annunzio's *La Pisanelle ou la mort parfumée*, with Ida Rubenstein in a decor by Bakst; and on the boulevard one could see *L'habit vert* by Proust's friends Robert de Flers and G. Arman de Caillavet. A simple baker's dozen of poets would include Francis Carco, Paul Claudel, Jean Cocteau, Arthur Cravan, Léon-Paul Fargue, Paul Fort, René Ghil, Max Jacob, Francis Jammes, Pierre-Jean Jouve, Anna de Noailles, Charles Péguy, and Victor Segalen. The first poems by André Breton, Paul Eluard, and Pierre Reverdy also appeared in 1913. The first complete edition of *Poésies* by Stéphane Mallarmé was published in 1913, as were the songs "Trois poèmes de Mallarmé" by Claude Debussy. Henri-Martin Barzun, leader of *Simultanéisme*, one of the many "isms" that flourished at the time, published *La révolution polyrythmique moderne: Trois poèmes simultanés* and other works in 1913.

One always feels at the end of such a course that students and teachers alike could begin the course all over again, this time with different materials and different guest lecturers. We often think of other years that could be explored in much the same way: 1889, with the centennial celebration of the French Revolution and the Eiffel Tower; 1900; the twenties, with emphasis on 1925; the thirties, with emphasis on 1937; or 1968. The infectious enthusiasm generated by the students and teachers participating in an interdisciplinary course turning kaleidoscopically around the single year 1913 grows naturally within the classical, academic tradition of a university as a community of scholars.

Syllabus

Course   The Year 1913. J. Theodore Johnson, Jr., French and Italian, and Jeanne Stump, History of Art, University of Kansas, Lawrence.

Description   First offered in spring term, 1975. Cross listed as Humanities 500, French 600, and History of Art 605. Three credits. Prerequisites: junior standing or above; research paper for graduate students. Class meets three times a week for fifty minutes, with an additional evening for screening period films.

Objectives   To focus on the burst of artistic creativity in Europe (with an emphasis on France) and America early in the twentieth century, a creativity that reaches its height in the year 1913 and then is tragically interrupted by World War I; to acquire an overview of the visual arts, including film and photography, painting, sculpture, architecture, theater design, ballet costumes and sets, and literature; to read relevant French texts in English translation (though students are encouraged to read them in the original); to hear guest lectures in such diverse areas as music, history, physics, English literature and society, American studies, German literature and society, philosophy, and aeronautics.

Schedule
1. Introduction.
2. From naturalism to the "reel" world.
3. The "reel" world: the cinema to 1913.
4. Experiments in color: fauves and the German expressionists.
5. Guest lecture: Stravinsky and *The Rite of Spring*.
6. Developments in cubism.
7. Orphism and orphist painting. Screening of Griffith's *Battle of Elderbush Gulch* and *Judith of Bethulia* and several shorts and documentaries of 1913; samples of early cinema.
8. Russian artists in Paris.
9. Architectural program of the Théâtre des Champs-Elysées.
10. Performance at the Théâtre des Champs-Elysées.

11. Guest lecture: European turmoil in 1913.
12. Films: *Sinking of the Titanic* and *Great War*, part 1.
13. Examination 1.
14. Guest lecture: the world of physics in 1913.
15. Futurist painting.
16. Crosscurrents in French literature in 1913.
17. Concrete poetry from Mallarmé to Cendrars, with particular reference to *Prose du Transsibérien et de la petite Jehanne de France* (Cendrars and Delaunay-Terk).
18. Architecture and sculpture in 1913: a brief survey.
19–20. Introduction to Apollinaire, *Alcools*, essays, and *Calligrammes*.
21. Film: *Recovery of the Mona Lisa*.
22. Art circles: Picasso and Stein in Paris in 1913.
23. *Pittura metafisica*; England and the "New Spirit."
24. Guest lecturer: Edwardian literature—the long Indian summer.
25–27. Introduction to Proust's *A la recherche du temps perdu* and specifically *Du côté de chez Swann*; relations with visual arts and music.
28. Review and discussion.
29. Examination 2.
30. Guest lecture: the American scene in 1913.
31. The Armory Show.
32. Guest lecture: Carl Sternheim's *1913*.
33. The Blue Rider.
34. Guest lecture: philosophy, revolution, and Lenin.
35. Developments leading toward abstract art.
36–37. Introduction to Gide and *Les caves du Vatican* (*Lafcadio's Adventures*).
38. Guest lecture: aeronautics in 1913.
39–42. Brief presentations on a variety of subjects: Satie, especially his *Le piège de Méduse*; Scott Joplin and the rag; Yvette Guilbert; the Paterson, New Jersey, Strike Pageant of 1913.
43. Final examination.

Betty Jean Craige

Twentieth-Century Ideas in Literature and Painting

Marco Polo describes a bridge, stone by stone.
"But which is the stone that supports the bridge?" Kublai Khan
asks.
"The bridge is not supported by one stone or another," Marco
answers, "but by the line of the arch that they form."
Kublai Khan remains silent, reflecting. Then he adds: "Why do you
speak to me of the stones? It is only the arch that matters to me."
Polo answers: "Without stones there is no arch."
> Italo Calvino, *Invisible Cities*

To interpret well the particular texts we call literary in a given period, we must understand the paradigm in which they were written. And, circularly, to understand the paradigm, we must read the texts, where we may glean knowledge of the interests, values, and model of reality of the period's thinkers: "Without stones there is no arch."

But how can we know the arch if we look at the stones in isolation from one another? In traditional undergraduate courses in Western literature, we generally examine only one kind of text—the literary work—which we study as a "masterpiece," acclaimed by readers over time as a work of aesthetic value to the culture. Since the scientific revolution, we have separated literature from science, and under the influence of Kant we have separated aesthetics from politics. Such standard textbooks as *The Norton Anthology of World Masterpieces* and Macmillan's *Literature of the Western World* reflect our discipline's assumptions that "literature" constitutes its primary subject matter and that coverage of the field, achieved by a representative sampling of a wide variety of works, is the primary function of an undergraduate course. These textbooks, because they are anthologies of literary works, tend to keep in place the traditional canon and reinforce the notion that our purpose is to interpret the individual text as an aesthetic entity.

An interdisciplinary course for a period of history—whether it be Literature and the Visual Arts, Literature and Music, or Literature and Science—has a different purpose; to explore the model of reality in texts of that period through an examination of various kinds of texts in relation to one another. And it has a different philosophical presupposition: that meaning is contextual. Since both the concept of masterpiece and the possibility of coverage have been challenged in recent decades—in the acknowledgement that masterpieces are not repositories of universal values, that the traditional canon itself has an ideology, and that objectivity is a lost illusion—we may serve students well by reintegrating imaginative texts into their historical context and by exploring them for their social significance as well as their aesthetic qualities. In designing the course's syllabus, therefore, we must employ some principle of selection other than presentation of masterpieces or coverage of a field. One way of organizing material for such a course is to trace a few prominent ideas through their diverse expressions in literary and other texts.

Literature and the Visual Arts, as I have taught it, has as its subtitle Twentieth-Century Ideas in Literature and Painting. Underlying the course is the assumption, common to recent critical theory, that the end of Cartesian dualism means a relativity of values, a world in which meaning in any text depends on the text's context, which includes the reader. In the past several decades—with the recognition that no discourse is value-free and that every text implies a set of values—scholars have begun to question the category of the aesthetic and the practice of isolating the literary work for study; in so doing, they have begun to ask why some texts and artworks have been canonized and others not. According to these scholars, if there is no objectivity, there is no intrinsic meaning to texts or art objects and no disinterested reading of them: meaning is contextual, and context includes the reader.

In the critique of objectivity, history discloses its relativism: it is narrative written from particular interested points of view. And the canon of Western literature discloses its values as well, values that do not appear universal to the women and minority groups not represented in it. In other words, literature is not free of ideology. So what do we do with our discipline, founded as it is on the belief that the appreciation of literary masterpieces benefits individuals morally and intellectually? Do we keep adding new works to the "canon" (that is, to the anthologies used in the classroom), in the hope that eventually we shall represent everybody? Do we abandon the notion that some texts are greater than others? Do we still believe in the category of literature? What about the visual arts? Are not its monuments—those objects that appear in museums and textbooks, that command high prices in auctions and therefore our attention as apprecia-tors—determined to some extent by the economics of the art world and the political interests of the critics?

Because we no longer accept René Descartes's division of the world into *res cogitans* 'thinking thing' and *res extensa* 'extended thing' (121), we cannot continue to teach literary history as if it were unproblematical or literary texts as if they transcended politics. Nor can we confidently continue to analyze literature independently of other kinds of writing without regard to context. It is more logical, in the holistic paradigm, to seek to understand the variety of systems in which we find texts. Since we shall be involved in quarrels regarding the composition of the canon for as long as we assume that our purpose is to teach literature alone, we should perhaps devote ourselves to teaching ways of interpreting texts of all kinds, literary texts alongside paintings, articles written by philosophers, and accounts of contemporaneous scientific discoveries. Paradoxically, in combining a wide variety of texts in a single course, we may increase students' interest in what we have called the literary work, for we shall be showing its relevance to texts of the "real" world. We may thereby avoid promulgating values—under attack by critics of the traditional canon—that many believe function to oppress certain classes. In teaching students to look to a text's source and to a text's context when interpreting a text—that is, by alerting students to ideological implications of texts—we may instill in them a habit of critical thinking and an awareness that our knowledge of the world depends on the questions we ask.

I have taught Literature and the Visual Arts four times in recent years, initially as a survey course of the period from the 1880s through the 1980s and finally as a concept-oriented course that did not pretend to offer coverage. In the survey course, I found myself frustrated in trying to find representatives in literature and painting of impressionism, expressionism, surrealism, and so on that lent themselves to comparison. This made me realize that I was developing a very inadequate history course, one that excluded many interesting works because they did not fit into the traditional categories. I saw that I was operating with the outmoded philosophical assumption that "history" was somehow "out there" and that my responsibility as a teacher was to present this entity to the class. Moreover, I saw that as long as I focused on the various works' aesthetic form and sought to compare works of different media to one another on that basis alone, I was overlooking, almost intentionally, the philosophical and political forces behind the production of those works. What was I trying to accomplish? This question led me to think more about the pedagogical implications of the shift in paradigm from Cartesian dualism to holism—a shift expressed by the very literature and art that I was teaching. As a result, I abandoned the practice, implicit in the interdisciplinary survey approach, of comparing works directly with one another and adopted the practice of studying them as expressions of philosophical and political ideas.

For the concept-oriented course, I focused on a few profound, culture-shaping ideas, a familiarity with which I believe is necessary to an understanding of twentieth-century discourse: the "death of God," relativism and the principle of indeterminacy, the concept of an unconscious, and the critique of patriarchy. (Another time, I shall include Marxism.) To introduce the ideas, I chose the following documents for the syllabus: Friedrich Nietzsche's parable of the madman in *The Gay Science*, Jean-Paul Sartre's lecture titled (in English) "Existentialism," John Dewey's essay "The Influence of Darwinism on Philosophy," the first chapter of Werner Heisenberg's *Physicist's Conception of Nature*, Sigmund Freud's "Creative

Writers and Daydreaming," and Virginia Woolf's *Room of One's Own*. To relate the theories to literature and painting, I added Carl Jung's "Psychology and Literature," André Breton's *Manifestoes of Surrealism*, Harold Rosenberg's "Action Painting," Jonathan Culler's "Linguistic Basis of Structuralism," Tom Wolfe's *Painted Word*, and Stanley Fish's "Is There a Text in This Class?"

After selecting those texts, I looked for expressions of the ideas in the two arts, and I found a multitude of works from which to choose. Having relinquished the goals of surveying the masterpieces and providing a chronological history of the century, I turned to literary texts and paintings that manifested the ideas in particularly exciting ways; then I used them as examples rather than as monuments in and of themselves. For instance, instead of giving coverage of French impressionism, I focused on Claude Monet as a representative of the movement in whom an attention to point of view, to light, to the indistinguishability of object and environment, and to the medium of paint on canvas revealed intuitions of decenteredness. We studied Monet after reading Dewey's "Influence of Darwinism on Philosophy," which describes the effect Charles Darwin had on our conception of reality in the late nineteenth century: how the world suddenly appeared to be in flux and how that perception affected the confidence of philosophers, painters, and novelists in what they had thought was an objectively definable external reality. We discussed Monet in relation not only to Darwin but also to Woolf, whose novel *The Waves* expresses in its structure the notion that reality is subjective. And then we moved into Heisenberg's chapter, in which Heisenberg writes: "Science no longer confronts nature as an objective observer, but sees itself as an actor in this interplay between man and nature" (29). My purpose was to offer the students a conceptual framework whereby they could make sense of texts and artworks they might encounter elsewhere.

Instead of testing their knowledge of particular works, I required term papers that would demonstrate the students' ability to relate one of the basic concepts that we had discussed with at least one work each from literature and the visual arts that we had *not* discussed. One of the students wrote on the breakdown of Cartesian dualism in relation to Edgar Degas and James Joyce, without comparing them with each other; another wrote on cultural self-reflection in relation to Kurt Vonnegut and Roy Lichtenstein, again without comparing them with each other. At the end of the course I gave the students a series of questions to prepare for their final exam on the various major ideas we had studied; at the time of the final, I asked them to analyze specific artworks in connection with one or two of those questions.

Interdisciplinary courses facilitate the transition from a discipline defined by its subject matter (literature) and still influenced by the New Critics' methodology (which has dominated our teaching through textbooks that anthologize literary works alone) to a less easily defined discipline characterized by a holistic methodology in which we reorient ourselves from literature to processes of contextual interpretation. Twentieth-Century Ideas in Painting and Literature is such a course, because it enables students to see the relevance of aesthetic expression to major intellectual forces of the period. It seems to give students confidence in their powers of interpretation—with respect not only to Monet and Woolf but also to Freud and Heisenberg—and an enthusiasm for seeing the big picture. By the end of the quarter, they appear eager to discuss the stones in relation to the arch and the arch in relation to the stones.

Syllabus

Course   Literature and the Visual Arts: Twentieth-Century Ideas in Painting and Literature. Betty Jean Craige, Comparative Literature, University of Georgia.

Description   Combination upper-level and graduate course of interest to comparative literature majors and graduate students as well as art majors and graduate students. Prerequisites: two sophomore literature survey courses. Two-hour meetings twice a week on the quarter system.

Objective   To introduce students to the ways in which major ideas of the twentieth century manifest themselves in the arts and the ways in which various artworks may be discussed in relation to one another.

Schedule
1. Introduction. From Cartesian dualism to holism. Dewey, "The Influence of Darwinism on Philosophy."
2. The breakdown of dualism. Monet and French impressionism.
3. The breakdown of dualism. Woolf, *The Waves*.
4. The end of representation. Heisenberg, "The Idea of Nature in Contemporary Physics." Picasso and cubism.
5. The end of representation. Stein, "Picasso," "Susie Asado." Queneau, *Exercises in Style*.
6. The unconscious. Freud, "Creative Writers and Daydreaming." Jung, "Psychology and Literature."
7. The unconscious. Surrealism. Breton, *Manifestoes of Surrealism* (1924). García Lorca, "Scream toward Rome" (Craige).
8. The unconscious. Dali and surrealism in painting.
9. The death of God. Nietzsche, *The Gay Science* 3. 125. Sartre, "Existentialism."
10. Radical subjectivism. Sartre, *Nausea*.
11. Radical subjectivism. Rosenberg, "Action Painting." De Kooning and abstract expressionism.
12. Structuralism. The prisonhouse of language. Culler, "The Linguistic Basis of Structuralism."
13. Decenteredness. Calvino, *The Castle of Crossed Destinies*.
14. Cultural self-reflection. Warhol and pop art.

15. Narrative self-reflection. Robert Coover, "The Magic Poker."
16. Feminism. Woolf, *A Room of One's Own*.
17. Feminism. Judy Chicago, *The Dinner Party*.
18. The end of art. Wolfe, *The Painted Word*.
19. The end of literature. Fish, "Is There a Text in This Class?"
20. Holism. Earth art, conceptual art.

Term paper. An essay (12 to 15 pages typed, double-spaced) on a major twentieth-century idea (preferably one discussed in class) as expressed in a literary text and an artwork.

Final examination. Essay questions on the interrelations of the various texts and artworks discussed during the course.

Texts. Students will purchase the following books, as well as a volume of material copied and bound: *The Waves, Exercises in Style, Nausea, The Castle of Crossed Destinies, A Room of One's Own,* and *The Painted Word*.

Courses on Themes and Topics

Marcia Green

The Demonic Pact:
The Faust Myth in Music and Literature

The Demonic Pact: The Faust Myth in Music and Literature is a course taught for San Francisco State University under the auspices of the NEXA program. Over a decade ago, NEXA was conceived as a science and humanities convergence program whose goal (according to its catalog) was "to break across the artificial barriers between areas of scholarship and to provide a model of education of the whole person." When NEXA began to incorporate convergence within the creative arts as well, the steering committee invited me to design a course that would combine music and literature. Like all NEXA offerings, this course is team-taught by two instructors—one from the music department and one from the English department. Both participate in all class sessions so that their team effort will be coherent and cooperative, allowing for interart discussions.

I decided to use the Faust myth as the theme for developing the course on music and literature. (For other interart courses on this myth, see McMillan.) The Faust legend comprises a multitude of metaphoric possibilities—the quest for ultimate knowledge, the desire to live outside one's life in immortality, and the oppositional impulses to good and evil, to name only a few. But for the purposes of this course, the Faust story presented itself as a vision of organic unity—the meeting of irreconcilable realms and the interrelations of dissimilar art forms. The Faust myth offers a stimulating starting point from which the general education student can embark on an investigation of music and literature. No specialized knowledge of either music or literature is required, but most students do have some idea about a man who made a pact and sold his soul to the devil.

The idea of naming the course The Demonic Pact came from the multiple use of pacts within the context of the class. There is the pact between music and literature and the pact between composer and librettist—two relations of primary importance in the course. There is the pact between the two teaching partners and NEXA (that is, to serve as a team for at least three years with renewal options). There is the pact between the two instructors concerning the division of class time, teaching methods, and assignments and grading procedures. There is the pact entered into by all

NEXA students who, according to the catalog, are asked to be ready to "take the risks of a completely new approach to learning. . .[to] expect to be challenged and to have [their] way of looking at the world [and themselves] changed."

The course is structured on still another pact, the one students must sign during the first class. It looks particularly demonic, with its illustration of the palm of a hand across which run ancient musical notations (the "Guidonian hand" was a pedagogical aid to sight-singing developed by Guido d'Arezzo, c. 995–c. 1050). The pact is written in angular calligraphic script detailing the conditions of the contract: that the students "enter freely into this covenant in order to increase their knowledge of music and literature"; that they "begin the course with an assigned grade of A (4.0)"; and that "each successive assignment as well as attendance and participation will be measured against that grade either to bolster its continuance or to diminish it accordingly." The pact is signed and dated above the inverted words *Consummatum est*, the words Faust utters on signing his pact with Mephistopheles in Christopher Marlowe's version of the tragedy. The pact provides a frame for the class and enables the students to conceive of their work as being of a piece with the material they are studying.

In designing this course, I wanted to encourage students to think synthetically about artistic disciplines instead of privileging one art form over another. To accomplish this goal, I needed to do two paradoxical things: first, to separate through interpretive analysis what is intuitively perceived as a unity—both literary and musical works of art—and, second, to synthesize or bring together these disciplines, which are perceived as distinctive. Another goal is to help students understand musical and literary language well enough to be able to explore further the cultural and aesthetic values exemplified by the various settings of the Faust myth.

The class is held once a week for three hours. The approach to teaching the class varies depending on the material. Overall, there is an interrelation of musicological analysis (e.g., tracing a particular musical theme or set of themes) and textual interpretation in a lecture-discussion format. Some class sessions discuss the literary texts first and then the music, and others begin with the musical selections. However, when we discuss a musical work and the literary work from which it was derived (e.g., Goethe's *Faust* and the compositions by Gounod, Boïto, Berlioz, and Schumann), there is a purposeful Faustian interplay between the instructors. Not only are the scenes from the play discussed and then compared with the corresponding scenes in the musical version, but the instructors themselves try to "break across the barriers of scholarship" by crossing over into the opposite discipline—offering insights, criticisms, comments, and questions. Discussions of this type often encourage students to think more innovatively about literature and music and their interrelations.

Most students taking the course are not music or literature majors, and many may never have taken a course in music or literature before. It is important, then, to gear the discussion toward a general understanding of the material so that all students may participate and may gain insights into ways of responding to and integrating the musical and literary works. But it is also important to incorporate sufficient specialized material so that students who do have some knowledge of music and literature may be encouraged to experiment with the new approaches presented in the class.

The range of the course takes the student from early opera to contemporary popular culture. One connecting theme is the way musicians use musical motifs to suggest characters or situations. In Gounod's *Faust*, for example, a musical theme is introduced by the orchestra during the scene in which Mephistopheles produces a vision of Margaret that he hopes will entice Faust to sign the pact. This same theme appears later on in a vocal duet when Faust and Margaret are pledging eternal love to each other ("O nuit d'amour!"). The class discussion centers on how the composer uses music subliminally to connect characters and situations—in this case, Mephistopheles's enticement of Faust to sign the pact is coupled with Faust's seduction of Margaret. Later in the course the theme of subliminal musical suggestion will recur as we consider the modern use of subliminal techniques in advertising.

Another important integrative concept is the effect of time on creativity. Faust, in his bargain with the devil, is given twenty-four years in which he may have any desire fulfilled. This concept of time is projected into the class in various ways. The more obvious effects of time would be the number of weeks the class meets, the three hours of each individual class, the division of time between instructors, and the amount of time allotted between the receiving and completion of assignments. The issue of the effect of time on creativity becomes most relevant during discussions of musical texts derived from literary ones. For example, the class compares Goethe's version of the poetic song "King of Thule" to the musical versions in Gounod's *Faust* and Berlioz's *La damnation de Faust*. Having read Goethe's version in class, we listen to each composer's rendition of the song. Berlioz's text is in French and begins with the word *Autrefois*, which has three syllables. The students begin to see that the rhythm of the music also has a corresponding movement in three. When copies of a page of the music are distributed among the students, it is noted that within each measure are two beats subdivided into units of three.

Gounod's version is also in French; however, his song begins with the words, *Il était un Roi*. Each syllable is given a musical beat within a measure containing four beats—producing a feeling of movement in two. The discussion centers on how each composer, in writing music for the same scene, may have been influenced by the rhythmic time of the libretto. The students also discuss the correspondingly different dynamic levels of the pieces: Berlioz's introduction is soft, almost timid, while Gounod's is loud and flamboyant.

After these discussions, we conduct a three-part experiment on the effects of time on composition. In the first part, the students are given twenty-four minutes to write their own Faustian stories. The stories must be complete, so the students need to pace themselves accordingly. For the second part, the students are given the same assignment, but this time they have twenty-four hours to finish their stories. In the third part, each student is asked for a written discussion on the effects of time on creativity.

A further objective is to help students realize that literary and musical texts embody multiple concepts of time. The literary text is read within one historical time while evoking a different narrative time. Music is governed by musical time, which functions within chronological time. In opera—where music and text are combined—at least three concepts of time are in effect: the musical, functioning within the chronological, serving to display the narratological.

Gounod's version contains all these aspects of time. It begins with Margaret singing about the faithful King of Thule. In the middle of the song she breaks off her singing and begins to interject her thoughts about Faust. These thoughts are musically represented by a recitative style—that is, a freer style not governed by strict musical time. When she finishes expressing her thoughts, she continues to sing her song only to break off once again within the musical time of the song so as to interject her thoughts within the recitative's more chronological time. This alternation dramatizes Goethe's story within narrative time.

The phenomenon of musical versus chronological time culminates with the discussion of George Crumb's *Black Angels* (*Thirteen Images from the Dark Land*), a piece written for electric string quartet. The players are governed initially by chronological time; that is, the notes on the page are to be played within the specific number of seconds indicated on the musical score. The pauses between sections are also governed by chronological time, the musicians being instructed to wait thirteen seconds before beginning the next section. The score for the second section, "Absence," contains a version of Schubert's melody "Der Tod und das Mädchen," written in regular notation with the appropriate time signature. Here the musicians are governed by musical time instead of chronological time. The composer may even be consciously referring to the difference between these two senses of time, because above this section he has written the instruction to play the notes as if they were the voice of an ancient music.

Course assignments reflect the material being discussed in class. The first assignment generally deals with how art relates to life or morality. The students' arguments must be supported by references to at least one musical work and one literary work. The second assignment calls for a more specific discussion of the relation between music and literature. The assignment is twofold. One section concerns the mediums of literature and opera and asks students to discuss the demonic balance between music and text and the shared responsibility of the two for the success of the drama. The second section questions whether the instrumental works of Liszt and Wagner demonstrate this responsibility to drama.

The final projects of the students must integrate music and literature. They may be critical discussions of the interrelations between music and literature. One paper presented a critical study of Faustian elements in the works of the great blues guitarist Robert Johnson. Most projects, however, have been creative works using Faustian literary elements and music. Presentations have included films and videos; puppet plays with original music; storybooks with original drawings and accompanying musical tapes; live performances of original songs; a play containing musical clues to the solution of a mystery; short stories read to the accompaniment of music; a board game incorporating a pact with the devil, assorted good- and bad-deed cards, and the achievement of eternal salvation through the answers to musical and literary questions; multimedia works consisting of dance, narrative, and ambient sound images; a photographic creation of the Faust myth using members of the class (instructors included) as characters in a story, with narration and musical selections taken from the required listening list; and original paintings derived from the musical and literary Faust settings.

These wonderfully creative and integrative projects indicate the high degree of relevance that students find in the literary and musical versions of the Faust legend. This type of interart educational environment, where two disciplines can be examined independently and collectively, fosters a new appreciation of these art forms. In sensing the positive interplay between two academicians, one from music and one from literature, students become motivated to take risks and "break across barriers." Their innately innovative ideas begin to take shape with the convergence of music and literature in this class.

Syllabus

Course The Demonic Pact: The Faust Myth in Music and Literature. Marcia Green, Music, San Francisco State University.

Description Open to all students through the NEXA program. Team-taught by a professor of music and a professor of English. Spring term. No prerequisites. Class meets once a week for three hours; attends a play and an opera.

Objectives To familiarize students with the disciplines of music and literature; to explore similarities and differences in the artistic statements of the disciplines and investigate the comparative techniques by which each discipline seeks to achieve artistic meaning; to define the essence and significance of the Faust legend through history; to trace the progression of the Faust legend and its ability to evoke and express the cultural and aesthetic values of each era.

Texts   Ellmann and Feidelson (EF); Strunk.

Schedule

1. Introduction to elements of music. Schubert's setting of Goethe's "Erlkönig." Fact versus fiction. Historical Faust—who was this man whose name has come to mean so much? Mythical Faust—the longing for infinity as a basic trait of Western civilization. The concept of Faustian culture.
2. Meet the devil. Outline of the devil through history. Jeffrey Burton Russell's four books on the devil. Musical modes and their effect on human personality. Plato's *Republic* (Strunk 3–12). Boethius's *De institutione musica* (Strunk 79–86). Tritone as "diabolus in musica." Chanting versus invocation. "Dies Irae." Tartini's Sonata in G Minor, *Devil's Trill*.
3. Renaissance Faust. Marlowe, *Tragical History of Doctor Faustus*. What is drama, dramatic form, blank verse? Renaissance music. Development of chromaticism. Madrigals by Gesualdo: "Moro lasso al mio duolo." Beginning of the demonic pact between music and text leading to opera.
4. What is opera? The beginnings of opera: Camerata. Monteverdi's *Orfeo*. Purcell's *Dido and Aeneas* (chorus of the witches). The demonic pact between music and text, composer and librettist, aria and recitative.
5. Marlowe's *Doctor Faustus* and Busoni's *Doktor Faust*. An examination of the philosophical similarities between the sixteenth-century text and the twentieth-century opera.
6. Marlowe and Busoni, continued. Cordier's "Belle bonne" (Grout 135), music written in the shape of a heart (c. 1400), and Crumb's *Makrokosmos: Twelve Fantasy Pieces after the Zodiac*, music notated in symbolic shapes (1972).
7. What is Romanticism? Schopenhauer (EF 391–397), Kant (EF 34–39), Coleridge (EF 39–47). Byron, *Don Juan*. Mozart, *Don Giovanni*.
8. Goethe, *Faust*, part 1. Berlioz, *La damnation de Faust*.
9. Goethe, continued. Gounod, *Faust*.
10. Goethe, *Faust*, parts 1 and 2. Boito, *Mefistofele*.
11. Goethe, *Faust*, parts 1 and 2. Schumann, *Szenen aus Goethes Faust*.
12. Absolute versus program music. Essays: E. T. A. Hoffmann, "Beethoven's Instrumental Music" and "The Poet and the Composer" (Strunk 35–57). Liszt, "Berlioz and His 'Harold' Symphony" (Strunk 107–33). Music: Liszt, *A Faust Symphony*. Wagner, *A Faust Overture*.
13. Mann, *Doktor Faustus*. Faust as musician. Is the devil dead? Beethoven, *Ninth Symphony*. Stravinsky, *L'histoire du soldat*.
14. Film of Murnau's *Faust*.
15. Blues as the devil's music. Robert Johnson, "Crossroads Blues," "Me and the Devil Blues," "Hellhound on My Trail" (*King of the Delta Blues Singers*, Columbia, CL 1654). Faust on Broadway. Sondheim, *Sweeney Todd: The Demon Barber of Fleet Street*.
16. Contemporary Fausts. Space exploration as outcome of basic spiritual drive of a "Faustian culture." Crumb, *Black Angels*.
17. Final exam session, reserved for students who wish to present live original performances of their final projects.

Estella Lauter

Images of Women in Contemporary Arts: Interart Discourse with a Social Dimension

First developed in 1974, the interart course I teach grew out of my commitment to interdisciplinarity and my fascination with the emerging field of women's studies. The problem-centered focus of my university encouraged me to consider the social role of the arts, so I decided to inquire what role artists had played in relation to the limited cultural images available to women. For my exploration, I chose the postwar period, in part because our students needed exposure to recent work, but also because feminist art history had not yet shown how much women had accomplished in earlier periods. The course has evolved in response to the wealth of new information concerning women's contributions to art and culture, so that now, instead of comparing men's and women's representations of women, it examines the ways women have intervened in the image-making process to extend and change culturally accepted images. My account here focuses on the issues that women's studies has raised in my thinking about interrelations among the arts.

At the outset I believed—with Gotthold Lessing and Susanne Langer (*Feeling and Form*)—that each art offers something different, something not easily translated into or subsumed under language, however attractive the idea of language might be as a model to understand the structure of an art. Since my students, for all their knowledge of specific art disciplines, were in no way prepared to deal directly with theoretical questions concerning the interrelations of the arts, I hoped to lure them into theoretical discussions by using images as a lightning rod to attract attention to differences among the media. I wondered myself if in the development of images we would find one medium ahead of another—one more open to experimentation, less bound by cultural taboos, or less responsive to market considerations. Despite the formalist bias of aesthetics at the time, I saw the arts as vehicles for cultural change and wanted to compare their relative strengths for such a task.

Since most of the students were familiar with neither the study of women in the arts nor a contextual approach to interpretation, I needed a format that would generate information quickly and provide room for individual experimentation with interpretation. Thus I chose to begin with slides of visual works that present recognizable images of women. Most of us understand the term *image* best in this way, and I wanted to build on a solid base of iconographical knowledge before I asked students to identify patterns of images in other arts and, eventually, to apply the term to phenomena that are not so clearly representational. (See Mitchell, *Iconology* 10, for a useful diagram of the term's range of meanings.) I worked, typically, with no more than thirty slides at a time. After prefacing them in some way to focus attention, I said just enough about each image to elicit responses and questions from the group, often simulating one or more approaches of reader-response criticism.

The central problem at first was how to organize the presentation of images without unduly prejudicing the discussion. I decided to begin with overlapping schemas of art history and archetypal psychology but to introduce both as provisional frameworks built on limited cultural bases. Art history has privileged images of the nude and the Madonna (we do not know what other images the methods of social history may yet uncover). Likewise, archetypal psychology has focused on the anima or transformative feminine figure (who may be either a bewitching seductress or an inspiring muse) and the mother (who may also be either negatively controlling or positively nurturing). I pointed out (using Berger's argument in *Ways of Seeing*) that in both systems, the presumed audience is predominantly male. As the students became more capable of recognizing images, seeing patterns, and clarifying differences, I added Toni Wolff's descriptions of the amazon and the medium to expand the number of patterns under consideration.

The quandary was, of course, how to examine patterns without conveying the idea that they represent unchanging universals. My own redefinition of Carl Jung's concept of the archetype arose from these discussions. I have come to see the archetype as the tendency to form an image in relation to recurrent experiences rather than as a preexistent form that determines our lives.

Together, the students and I discovered that women artists have indeed altered archetypal images, often by presenting them from the vantage point of experience lived by a woman. Just before World War II, for example, Käthe Kollwitz, in her sculpture *Tower of Mothers*, extended the scope of the mother's imagined strength; in her prints, she also clarified the degree of the mother's vulnerability. By ranging outside art history into the relatively uncharted territory of works by women, we discovered other patterns of female imagery besides the Madonna/nude opposition or the seductress/mother/muse triangle. The "independent woman" documented in *Feminist Archetypal Theory* (Lauter and Rupprecht) is a case in point, one whose manifestations in earlier centuries deserve to be studied. The related figure of the female artist is another. We also found ourselves wishing for the development of images we experience in life more fully than we do in art: the sister, for example, or the woman who defines herself in relation to a female collective. These discussions have led naturally to the consideration of relations between art and life.

The collaborative role of an audience in bringing about cultural change was never more apparent than in our study of theatrical works, which illuminated the differences between what we can accept on the page or in the gallery and what we can absorb when we are confronted with a four-dimensional simulation. What an artist can do in any medium depends on what an audience can receive, and images develop as audiences become capable of receiving them. The process of cultural change is one of constant adjustment between these creative and receptive forces.

As we moved from one medium to another (typically from the visual arts to short fiction to poetry to theater), we found no stable answer to the question of which art serves best to extend or change culturally accepted images. Images of lesbian women in literature, perhaps because they detail the psychological benefits of the relationship, seemed to enable us to receive the more visceral visual images of the seventies. Other visual images, however, seemed to facilitate the release and recognition of strong emotions. I think of the transformative anger presented in Betye Saar's mixed media box *The Liberation of Aunt Jemima* (1972), for example, where the "nanny" who normally presides over the kitchen and the children carries a gun along with her broom. The justice of the image was apparent to most female viewers and made possible a more sympathetic reading of poems expressing the depth of women's anger and desire for empowerment that were written at the same time. No medium is privileged, we decided, by virtue of its inherent properties.

Cross-cultural material, particularly from U.S. minority populations, has proved indispensable in constructing meaning from comparisons. What is perfectly "natural" in a "muted" culture (see Ardener and Ardener) often requires a major shift from the dominant vision. The image of the "woman warrior" that occurs in Maxine Hong Kingston's as well as in Audre Lorde's work would bear study in this context. In the absence of a positive visual image of the woman warrior in the dominant culture, how do readers "see" these images from Chinese American and black American sources? Are they precisely the same?

As more works by women have become available for classroom use, I have found it increasingly difficult to maintain the comparison between male and female visions as a high priority. The new works have brought with them all the excitement of an archaeological find. Their freshness came in part from their position outside the established art world, no doubt, but also from their revaluation of women. Their differences from cultural expectations were apparent without reference to specific visions recorded by men. Their refreshing quality was spoiled by constant comparisons to the received canon.

Besides, since the images by men often came closer to expressing conventional expectations, the comparison implied that men alone had determined the cultural code and were alone concerned with upholding it. Since many of the images were negative, they, in turn, implied that the entire culture held a negative attitude toward women. This implication may turn out to be true, but I came to see that the attitudes of, say, Willem de Kooning, Richard Lindner or Tom Wesselmann might be better understood as the product of a misogynist strain in modernist aesthetics. I am awaiting a spate of studies concerning this issue in modernism before pursuing the comparison further.

Whereas in earlier versions of the course I spent hours attempting to rationalize the views of de Kooning and others, I now simply acknowledge their existence in a background lecture on images of women that have received some measure of cultural acceptance; then I go on, spending the time on, say, a reader's theater production of Megan Terry's *Calm Down Mother*. A choice such as this begins to shift the grounds of aesthetic evaluation from the formal concerns of the mid twentieth century to a more affective and socially responsive base. In relation to images of women created by women, de Kooning's famous *Women* series, for example, now seems too limited, too much a matter of formal manipulation of bugbears. The approach to images that I am attempting to teach is deeply contextual, reaching back into prehistory and forward through the works of many individuals to the shifting boundaries of our future. In this river, I prefer works that carry us forward.

I do case studies of women now, primarily to show how a woman artist embodies an image in her life. For many, Georgia O'Keeffe has become a cultural symbol of female independence. Since the culture has had no viable image of the woman artist (even in literature, she has been one of many insignificant "scribbling women"), the simple fact of a woman producing a body of work begins to make a new image. In addition, it turns out that many women in the arts have drawn their creative inspiration or courage from female figures imagined or real (see De Shazar concerning the role these figures have played for twentieth-century poets). Explorations of this kind bring the power of the image into focus in a way that transcends what can be done in traditional iconographical analysis.

Indeed, the course takes seriously the theoretical issues of interart discourse by showing how they matter in the process of cultural change. Distinctions among arts of space and time, or the relative power of an artistic medium to represent, abstract, or combine with other media, become tools that an artist can use to move an audience into a new perspective. The differences among the arts become complementary channels in which new ideas can find expression, often by being introduced in one medium and developed in another, sometimes in conscious dialogue. The fact that patterns exist across different artistic media becomes an indication that an image is sufficiently important to require exploration to the full depths of human capacity for understanding.

Once involved in the discussion, students respond remarkably well to the full range of issues (theoretical, interpretive, and political) raised by the course. They are usually predominantly female, and so the subject matter, though strange in its high valuation of women, is also familiar. Male students often find their cultural training as connoisseurs of women good preparation. The course does require the psychological strength to cope with change, and it helps to have some returning adult students in the classroom—individuals for whom change is simply a fact of life. I also often have the special joy of working with students who are themselves artists and who may carry the process of revision we study further in their own work.

The key to success lies in the word *discussion*—the more open the better. In order to ensure that it remains open, I require students to keep a journal for responses to the images we work with in class and for interpretations, questions, theories, and notes on reading or on research. The journals help me to identify issues for further discussion in subsequent classes and to counsel the students more wisely in their independent research.

The most important assignment of the term, however, requires the student to choose a particular image and investigate its development in the work of artists not covered in class. I encourage students to cross aesthetic boundaries in this research, but they may also choose a single artist as long as they compare that artist's work to work in another medium they have seen in class. In this assignment, students usually find the center of their interests in the subject matter and method of the course. One student may grapple with the image of the androgyne, while another may test the limits of the term *image* in abstract painting, and still another may think independently for the first time about the artist's cultural role as image maker.

Images of Women in Contemporary Arts stimulates critical thinking and demonstrates the impact of the arts on our lives. It challenges traditional iconographic and comparative methods of interpretation by expanding the range of contextual elements (gender, race, class, effect on an audience) to be considered in the construction of meaning. It could, of course, be transposed into other periods (the modernist one is ripe for study) and other media. Colleagues in far more traditional settings than mine may find it a useful way to vitalize a basic curriculum.

Syllabus

Course   Images of Women in Contemporary Arts. Estella Lauter, Humanistic Studies, Communication and the Arts, University of Wisconsin-Green Bay.

Description   An upper-level elective that counts toward an interdisciplinary minor in women's studies or aesthetic awareness. Designed for a fourteen-week semester. Typical enrollment: fifteen students. Junior standing or consent of instructor required for registration. Meets three hours a week.

Objectives   To examine images of women created after 1945 by painters, sculptors, poets, writers of fiction, and playwrights, starting from descriptions of patterns offered by art historians and archetypal psychologists; to focus on the conventional images of the mother, the seductress, and the muse, seeking to understand the degree to which artists can alter cultural images; to ask whether works by women significantly alter our images of women; to examine the kind and degree of change that is possible in each medium of art; to see, by working systematically through the various media, what happens to an image or pattern when it appears in other than visual form.

Schedule

1–2. Introduction to course objectives and requirements. Exchange of information among students and discussion of media images of women. Introduction to analytical framework.

3–4. Introduction to iconographic analysis using images of women with a high degree of cultural acceptance. Reading: excerpts from K. Clark, *The Nude*; Neumann; Berger, *Ways of Seeing*; Guitton; Lawrence.

5–6. Slides from Petersen and Wilson, *Women Artists: Images, Themes and Dreams*. Discussion of patterns discovered in art by women. Browse in art histories devoted to women: Fine; E. Munro; Nemser; Rubenstein; Slatkin. Lauter, chapter 7.

7–8. Slides from Peterson and Wilson, *Twentieth Century* and *Third World*; Petersen and Stofflet, *Twentieth Century, Photography, Sculpture*. Reading: excerpts from Downing; N. Hall; Harding; Lauter; Lauter and Rupprecht; Wolff for additional interpretive frames. Journal due.

9–12. Case studies of two artists who embody different images and illustrate different approaches to image making (e.g., Judy Chicago and Georgia O'Keeffe). Reading: books by the artists.

13–14. Stories by Morrison, Walker, Bambara, and Brooks in Washington. Differences that arise from minority views.

15–18. Poems by Atwood, Grahn, Levertov, Lorde, Piercy, Rich, Rose, Sexton, and Wakoski in Howe and Bass or on reserve. Lauter, chapter 8; Bennett. Differences that arise from medium. Take-home exam.

19–22. Plays by Childress, Churchill, Hansberry, Lessing, McCullers, Moore, Shange, and Terry in Moore, or in Sullivan and Hatch, or on reserve. Differences that arise from medium. Journal due.

23–28. Brief presentations of research for paper to enlarge discussion of contributions by women artists and to assess strengths of various media. Review. Evaluation of our discoveries. Paper due.

Sidney H. Bremer

The City in American Literature and Art: Images, Situations, and Pluralism

A college course has a life of its own. The particular impulses that conceive it often give way to other, deeper purposes informing its growth and maturity. When The City in American Literature and Art was just a gleam in my scholarly eye, I wanted simply to trace the historical sequence of urban images in American literature. The course could not quicken as an immaculate scholarly conception, however. I would have to unite my idea with the needs of our Department of Urban and Public Affairs if the course was to have any chance of coming into existence. Adding visual arts would engage the visual skills of our preprofessional students in urban and environmental design. Broadened to include visual as well as literary arts and to explore issues in our cultural environment, the course could also fulfill a general education requirement. Thus I secured a departmental home and legitimacy for my brainchild, along with the blessings of our general education program. That meant adequate student enrollments to sustain the life of the course.

Despite this mixed parentage and sponsorship, my original conception has left its mark on the syllabus. It is organized around the four patterns that I had discovered in literary images of the city. Briefly summarized, an *aristocratic city-town* cultivates natural and cultural resources to express its society; an *economic city* fragments society and destroys nature with its industrial machinery; a *megalopolis* then invades the psyches of individuals and extends beyond city limits with its electronic media; and an *ethnic neighborhood city* creates an organic, countercultural community within that alienating world. The addition of visual images to literary ones has even clarified these patterns. For example, the outsize people who make the street their playground in *Sunday Afternoon*, a painting by the Italian American Ralph Fasanella, provide a visual analogue for the block-party participants who tear down the brick wall of their dead-end street in *The Women of Brewster Place*, by the African American Gloria Naylor. This parallel points toward the artist's and writer's shared participation in the ethnic neighborhood pattern of urban imagery.

But in the process of course development I have discovered other, more basic purposes, extending well beyond my original conception. As I reflect on The City in American Literature and Art in its maturity, then, I affirm its essential threefold commitment: to the power of image in human awareness, to the importance of contextual situation in human creativity, and to the pluralistic richness of the human condition. Emerging at the heart of the course, these concepts of the image, situation, and pluralism shape both its academic subject and its pedagogical process.

When I conceived the course, I already knew a lot about the power of image to inform art, culture, society, and personhood. I had even learned to theorize about that power: literary and artistic images offer "presentational discourse" (Langer, *Philosophy* 79-102) and "metaphorical ways" (Gordon) of knowing about realities that logical discourse misconstructs, while such images also shape the basic operational myths (Janeway 195-96) of our "symbolic universe" (Cassirer 24-25). In the throes of bringing this particular course to life, however, I forgot all that. No matter. When the development of the course mixed literature and the visual arts together around the theme of the city, it released the power of image. For image commands attention. It epitomizes what we know, exposes what we do not yet know, and embodies possibility. It concentrates human awareness.

The primary subject matter of the course, then, is the *image* of the city. It takes even the city itself and its physical components not as places but as icons. Thus Chicago and the Brooklyn Bridge become analogous to works of art in their capacity to symbolize hopes and fears about the economic city (Bremer 32-33; Trachtenberg vii-viii). They become analogous to works of art in their value as symbols. In turn, they lend their incontrovertible, consequential reality to other works of art in the course. *The Day of the Locust* by Nathanael West articulates the underlying idea about the reality of images in ways that today's students easily understand. It dramatizes how mass-media images promote false expectations, destructive behavior, frustration, even cataclysm. At the end of West's megalopolitan novel, the "dream dump" of Hollywood explodes in a "savage and bitter" riot; a "civil war" over images erupts out of the frustration of "the people who come to California to die" in the motion picture "lynchings, murder, sex crimes, explosions, wrecks, love nests, fires, miracles, revolutions, wars" that have "cheated" them of normal lives (97, 78, 157).

As the focusing instrument for analyzing works of art, the image highlights structure as well as iconography, particularly when verbal and visual images are juxtaposed. Paintings that interrelate built and green environments—for instance, along the balanced diagonal in *The Architect's Dream* by Thomas Cole—help students see how Kate Chopin frames, balances, and interlocks her urban and seaside settings in *The Awakening*. Similarly, the explication of conflict between private and public space in F. Scott Fitzgerald's essay "My Lost City" (Pickering 167-74) directs attention to the windows that simultaneously divide exteriors and interiors and expose them to each other in so many of Edward Hopper's paintings, such as *Nighthawks* and *Morning in a City*. Structurally, those windows delineate space, mediate light, and establish perspective in Hopper's work. They also communicate a strong sense of exposed isolation. Thus content and form merge in the image.

The success of a particular kind of imagery—like urban imagery—as a focus for analyzing art depends, of course, on its resonance and pertinence. The particular theme must have symbolic resonance or cultural significance. Images of the city will surely bear more interpretive weight than will images of the shoelace. Joyce Carol Oates has even argued that the city is "an archetype of the human imagination" (11). But even broadly construed, images of the city are more pertinent to Henry James than to Mark Twain, to Georgia O'Keeffe's *New York with Moon* than to her *Black Iris*. Focusing on a particular imagistic frame means either skipping or skewing important works of art that do not fit. But then, any conceptual framework or critical theory implicitly does the same. Thematic or imagistic criticism merely makes the filter explicit. It announces the principle of selection.

Images are powerful tools, too, as part of classroom process. They model intellectual skills we usually ignore in favor of logical discourse. The making of metaphors, for example, has proved especially helpful in raising students' awareness of the urban images they themselves assume. I begin the course by having students imagine what kind of music, plant, vehicle, or clothing a city might be. The predominance of mechanical, alienating images among their metaphors prepares the class to spot similar patterns in American films and novels, paintings and poems. Then, too, because my students are more visual than literary—raised on TV, not books—I have formed the habit of sketching blackboard maps for the city-town, economic city, and megalopolis. The maps have clarified the structure and content of these patterns for the students. They have also helped to free me from common academic assumptions, so that I could see, for instance, city-town elements in women's literature from turn-of-the-century Chicago, a setting conventionally understood to epitomize the economic city.

By grounding the course in the students' images of the city, I also direct attention to our situation in a particular national culture. Students discover, while struggling to decide whether or not the term *city* applies to our own medium-sized, relatively homogeneous locale of Green Bay, Wisconsin, that our culture biases the very terms we use to define our subject matter. They then explore how the physical and social situation of living here affects their attitudes toward cities. At best, they realize that culture, location, class, gender, ethnic-group membership, and one's status as native or newcomer all affect one's urban expectations, experiences, and visions—the urban images one carries, enacts, and creates.

If the image is the subject of the course, then, the city is the context. Besides examining the imaginative cities *in* American literature and art, I ask the class to consider the changing urban environment *around* American literature and art—the importance of situation for artistic creation. The City in American Literature and Art demonstrates the proposition that we can understand how both cities and art work—informing each other through human experience and creation—only if we recognize their situational connection. More generally, the course implies that we can understand the nature of human knowledge and creation only if we recognize the role of situation. Any author or artist, like any student or teacher, will discover some realities and miss others by virtue of his or her place. In that double sense, all our human truths and images are qualified. To use Ralph Ellison's terms, the "universal" in any creative work is embodied in its "specific circumstance" (322), the situation of its creation. Thus the particular thematic vehicle for this course on literature and other arts, the city, drives home an epistemological point. The city is the setting and context, as well as the pedagogical vehicle, for the art.

As such the city has particular power. First, the physical and social phenomena to which urban images refer are just what students view as "real life." Second, because the city has been studied and conceptualized primarily within the social sciences, The City in American Literature and Art straddles a major interdisciplinary fault line and must confront the overlaps between the social sciences and the humanities and arts. Particularly because most of my classes are first-generation college students concentrating in the social sciences, they continually challenge me to explain the relevance of the literary and visual images to life and to other disciplinary paradigms. I cannot use some formalistic appeal to dismiss the content of the images' urban references—nor their personal and public implications (Bremer 33-35). In Hans-Georg Gadamer's terms, I have no established disciplinary "method" that can ward off the potentially revolutionary "truth" of nonacademic perspectives. My students and I must, for example, face the brick wall in *The Women of Brewster Place* as a physical and economic barrier dividing ghetto from downtown and as an internalized symbol of Afro-Americans' oppression—in our own real-life world as well. Urban context keeps the dialogue with art real.

This realization implies a pluralism that can teach teachers as much as it can teach students. The course's urban context and its interdisciplinary situation undermine my disciplinary privilege and empower students to challenge me from other perspectives. Conversely, its subject matter—literary and other artistic images—brings the limits of real-world and social scientific assumptions into clear view. For instance, when several students objected that I was turning our urban studies class into women's studies by including *The Awakening*, I realized how radically many women artists' images of the city challenge our established understandings about what cities are. Chopin's image of New Orleans as expressive of human vice and virtue, as centered in familial connections, and as open to natural settings and forces does not fit the paradigm of the city as, at best, a social scientific problem or, at worst, an antihuman, antinatural machine. Conversely, we accept Upton Sinclair's Chicago novel *The Jungle* into the literary canon—despite the supposed flaw of its final collective vision—partly because it presents the city in just these terms, "like it is," in our students' idiom. So the interdisciplinary pluralism of the City in American Literature and Art challenges the aesthetic canon, too.

If its subject matter is the image and its context the city as situation, then, its thrust is toward pluralism. The course values diverse academic and nonacademic perspectives; it undermines the canonical boundaries that often tend to exclude scholarly and creative work by women, men of color, and working-class men. Social scientific understandings of institutions, minority status, oppression, cultural hegemony, and our consequently biased "social constructions of reality" (Berger and Luckmann) make clear that the exclusion of minority works from our culture has been no isolated fluke or inconsequential oversight. The capacity of literary and visual arts to probe the affective structures and subjectivity of human experience suggests just how deep our loss might be. We need to value and respect the heterogeneity that characterizes human life—particularly in this nation of natives and immigrants, particularly in its cities. The course highlights specific dimensions of that heterogeneity, such as the organic imagery in the work of women artists and the artistic and urban politics of the Harlem renaissance. The purpose is pluralism, not a melting-pot mush.

That pluralistic purpose informs the way I teach and ask students to learn, too. Discussion is the primary mode of classroom discourse. I ask students to contribute questions as well as information, good listening as well as insight, and I hold them responsible for their daily contributions in grading their course work. I urge them to follow their special interests and even to stretch the course's implied definitions of literary and other artists in choosing the subjects for their class presentations. So they have chosen groups as well as individuals, Hallmark poets as well as documentary photographers, architects as well as rock lyricists. I ask them to learn by imitating the aesthetic process, too: at the start of the course, by making metaphors for their own urban images; later, by combining slides of paintings into a visual essay on *The Jungle*; and, finally, by composing a dramatic dialogue for their final examination, in which they discuss the urban images of Nathanael West and Gloria Naylor.

Putting together literature and art about the city has had many unanticipated benefits. My students have learned to appreciate what these literary and artistic images can teach about urban experience. Together they and I have developed a dynamic understanding of the creative process—of art as part of human living, not some transcendent realm of privilege. They have received support for the diversity of their own insights and styles of learning; they have been challenged to respect those of others; and I have expanded the range of materials I consider worthy of attention. All this has been possible because The City in American Literature and Art has developed the power of image in human awareness, the importance of situation in human creativity, and the pluralistic richness of our human condition.

Syllabus

Course   The City in American Literature and Art: Images, Situations, and Pluralism. Sidney Bremer, Urban and Public Affairs, University of Wisconsin-Green Bay.

Description   Lower-level elective to fulfill general education requirement and to attract interdisciplinary majors for urban and public affairs. Offered occasionally. No prerequisites. Ninety minute classes meet twice a week.

Objectives   To introduce students to historically important images of the city in the United States; to focus on major, diverse American writers and painters; to analyze aesthetic structure and urban iconography in works of literary and visual art; to analyze what they imply about historical patterns, individual experience, and value conflicts in American cities; to explore how cultural and artistic images relate to our urban experience, visions, and possibilities; to develop skills of literary and visual interpretation, oral and written communication.

Texts   Davidson; Pickering (P).

Schedule
1–2. Personal and popular images: advertisements.
3. Contemporary values and experiences in literature. Jackson, "Pillar of Salt"; Malamud, "The Cost of Living" (P).
4. Historical values and metaphors. John Winthrop, Henry Thoreau, Eldridge Cleaver.
5. City, country, and nation in art. Davidson, Chapter 4. Thomas Cole.
6. Historical sampler. Davidson, Chapter 2. Francis Guy, John Lewis Krimmel, Mary Cassatt, John Sloan, Joseph Stella, Charles Sheeler, Elizabeth Bishop, Edward Hopper, Reginald Marsh, Ben Shahn, Georgia O'Keeffe, George Tooker, et al. Short paper (1-2 pp.) compares and contrasts images of city and country in "Pillar of Salt" and discusses their cultural significance.
7. The aristocratic city-town: expectations. Hawthorne, "My Kinsman, Major Molineux" (P).
8–9. The aristocratic city-town: experience. Chopin, *The Awakening*.
10. The aristocratic city-town: remembrance. Fitzgerald, "My Lost City" (P).
11-12. Review. Midterm examination requires students to explicate urban images and to place them in their cultural contexts.
13. The economic city: crossings. Whitman, "Crossing Brooklyn Ferry"; Davidson, Chapter 7. John Sloan, John Marin, Joseph Stella. *Brooklyn Bridge* (film).
14. The economic city: epitome cities. The Eight, Theodore Dreiser, Carl Sandburg.
15-16. The economic city: the machine. Sinclair, *The Jungle*. Jacob Riis.
17. Women's organic images. Florine Stettheimer, Elizabeth Bishop, Georgia O'Keeffe, Louise Nevelson.

18. The megalopolis: the exposed isolato. Edward Hopper, Walker Evans.
19-20. The megalopolis: nightmares. West, *The Day of the Locust.*
21. Suburban extensions. Oates, "The Children," "Normal Love," "Extraordinary Popular Delusions" in *Marriages and Infidelities.*
22. The ethnic city: Harlem and black literature. Fisher, "The City of Refuge," and Johnson, "My City" (P). Langston Hughes, Gwendolyn Brooks.
23-24. The ethnic city: family and neighborhood. Naylor, *The Women of Brewster Place.* Ralph Fasanella.
25. Re-vision. Lorenz, Mumford, and Copland, *The City* (film).
26-27. Student presentations on development of urban imagery in the lives and works of other artists (musicians, architects, dramatists, etc.).
28. Personal responses. Kazin, *The Writer and the City* (film).
29. Final. Take-home dialogue (8-10 pp.) discusses which visual artists' images of the city are most or least like West's and Naylor's.

Appendix:
Additional Syllabi

Literature and the Other Arts
Stephen C. Behrendt
English, University of Nebraska

Description Undergraduate elective course applicable to college humanities requirements and to humanities minor. Normally offered in alternate years. No prerequisites. Meets three hours a week for fifteen weeks. Discussion format, occasional guest artists or lecturers. Two examinations; one brief formal analysis of a painting or sculpture; one research or critical paper examining an example of the intersection of literature and another art; voluntary student presentations. Class sessions heavily supplemented with slides, music, some film.

Objectives To introduce students to the investigation and discussion of interdisciplinary relations among the arts; to focus on literary texts that attempt to adapt and incorporate materials, techniques, and formal features from other arts; to sharpen students' skills in both formal and thematic analysis of related works in different media.

Schedule
1. Introduction to field of inquiry. Perception, cognition, interpretation. Define the aspects of the work of art in various media.
2. Some theories of relations among the arts. Langer, "Deceptive Analogies"; Hermeren; Aldrich; McFarland; Horace, *Ars Poetica.*
3. Form and content in the work of art: visual examples. R. Fry.
4. Verbal and visual aspects of the literary work. Concrete poetry, concrete music. Selected poems of Cummings; W. C. Williams, "Pictures from Brueghel"; Solt; Gomringer (in Solt); Thomas.
5. The "pregnant moment" and the contextualizing fiction. Paintings by Giuseppe Arcimboldo, John Singleton Copley, Benjamin West, Grant Wood, et al. Poems by Keats, Yeats, et al. Lessing; Addison.
6. Perception and the contextualizing fiction in longer literary works. Robbe-Grillet, *Snapshots*; Hawthorne, "Young Goodman Brown"; Barth, *Lost in the Funhouse.*
7. Structure and movement in visual works. Literary reflections of visual art. Paintings by David, Fuseli, Goya, Curry, Picasso. Stevens, "Relations"; Weisstein, "Literature."
8. Poems on pictures, pictures on poems. Originality and influence 1: visual-visual, visual-verbal, verbal-visual relations. Selected poems. Paintings by Brueghel,

Delacroix, van Gogh, Picasso, Manet, et al. Vickery; Behrendt, "Community Relations."

9. Longer prose work thematically and structurally related to the visual arts: Woolf, *To the Lighthouse*.

10. Audience entrapment in the arts. Originality and influence 2: "borrowings" in music. Behrendt, "Art"; Schwartz and Willbern; Copland, "How We Listen."

11. Musical form and the literary work. The fugue as musical form and basis for poetry. Celan, "Todesfuge"; Plath, "Little Fugue," "Daddy," from *Ariel*; Scher, "Literature and Music".

12. Longer literary work exhibiting musical form: Cather, *The Professor's House*; Burgess, *Napoleon Symphony*.

13. Other varieties of response. Verbal responses: imitation, parody, critical essay. Selected examples of imitations and parodies. Eliot, "Tradition"; Calinescu.

14. Visual responses to literary texts: the illustration, the "derivative decoration."

15. Multimedia responses and art forms: theater, opera, dance, film; stage and musical comedy adaptations.

Literature and Music
Mildred Meyer Boaz
English, Millikin University

Description   Offered to undergraduates for general education credit. Designed for the non-English major. No prerequisites. Meets twice a week for seventy-five minutes. Directed listening in class; tapes or cassettes on reserve for out-of-class listening. Some piano demonstrations. Quizzes, two papers, two tests, one final exam, an optional oral report.

Objectives   To introduce students to an interdisciplinary study of music and literature; to read and discuss short fiction, poetry, a novel, and a play; to listen and respond to music, from traditional ballads to contemporary works; to examine the literal relations between words and music, the use of musical allusions and motifs in literature, the use of literary sources in music, and structural parallels.

Texts   Kennedy; Copland, *What to Listen For*; Cassill.

Schedule

1–2. Introduction: definitions, methodologies. Kennedy, "Entrances"; Copland, "How We Listen," *What to Listen For*. Music: Bach, Beethoven, Chopin.

3. Creative process, audience. Kennedy, chapter 2; Copland, chapter 3; Kafka, "The Hunger Artist" in Cassill.

4. Unit 1: words and music. Kennedy, chapters 7 and 9; Copland, chapter 4. Music: ballads; madrigals; Lennon and McCartney, "Eleanor Rigby."

5–6. Songs. Kennedy, chapter 7. Poetry: "Sir Patrick Spence," Shakespeare sonnets 8 and 128, "Full Fathom Five," "When Daisies Pied." Copland, chapter 5. Music: madrigals, Schubert lieder, Stravinsky.

7–8. Tone, tone color, voice (differences and similarities). Kennedy, chapter 2; Copland, chapter 7. Poetry: Browning, Dickinson, Eliot. Music: Ravel, Britten, Debussy. Test on vocabulary, analysis of poem, essay on interrelations.

9. Unit 2: musical allusions and motifs. Kennedy, chapter 8. Welty, "Powerhouse"; Baldwin, "Sonny's Blues" (Cassill). Music: jazz, blues.

10. Allusions. Kennedy, chapters 3 and 4. Poetry: Marianne Moore, "Mind Is an Enchanting Thing"; Stevens, "Peter Quince." Novel: Chopin, *The Awakening*. Music: Chopin, Wagner. Assigned paper on musicality of imagery and sound patterns.

11–12. Image as motif. Kennedy, chapters 5 and 6. Chopin, *The Awakening*.

13–14. Unit 3: dramatic and narrative values. Opera, myth. Kennedy, chapter 13; Copland, chapter 15. Music: Gluck, Mozart, Verdi, Tchaikovsky, Wagner.

15–16. Film music. Copland, chapter 17. Music from films (e.g., *Platoon*, *Alexander Nevsky*). Paper. evaluation of effect of music in film or play.

17–18. Unit 4: structural parallels. Kennedy, chapter 10; Copland chapters 8 and 9. Poetry: Thomas. Fiction: Oates, "How I Contemplated the World" (Cassill). Music: Haydn, Mozart, Chopin, Stravinsky.

19–20. Forms. Copland, chapter 10–13. Fiction: Woolf, "Kew Gardens"; Coover, "The Baby Sitter"; Poe, "The Fall of the House of Usher" (Cassill). Music: Bach, Mozart, Beethoven, Copland.

21–23. Free forms. Copland, chapter 14 and 16. Kennedy, chapter 10. Poetry: Levertov, Cummings, W. C. Williams, Stevens. Fiction: Barthelme (Cassill). Music: Berio, Bartok. Test: comparable to first (see sessions 7-8).

24–25. Music as means to understanding. Williams, *The Glass Menagerie*; Eliot, "Preludes" and "The Love Song of J. Alfred Prufrock"; Joyce, "Araby." Music: Sinatra, Chopin, Satie, Bartok.

26. Interpretation. Kennedy, chapters 15–17; Copland, chapter 18. Criticism: Plato; Sontag.

27. Final exam: students compare and contrast structural patterns, examine responses of listeners and readers, discuss interrelations among literary and musical elements.

Pen and Pencil: The Illustrated Work
Gail Lynn Goldberg
Maryland State Department of Education

Description   One of a series of comparative arts courses developed by instructor at Webster College. No prerequisites. Cross-listed by English and art departments as elective meeting humanities credit requirement. Two weekly meetings, 1½ hours each. Several visits to rare book collections. Whenever possible, assigned readings drawn from easily available paperback texts or from photocopies of material not under copyright. Students expected to consult books placed on reserve. Duplicate set of instructor's slides also placed on reserve. (Course currently under consideration by Maryland Institute College of Art.)

Objectives   To establish the position that the graphic accompaniment to literary texts has often been considered by writers and artists, and by their audiences, to be a means toward enlightenment, elucidation, and exemplification; to examine selected works of poetry, fiction, and nonfiction prose, along with their illustrative counterparts, and explore the wide variety of ways in which design and text have been conjoined from medieval to modern times.

Schedule
1–2. (Middle Ages) The image and the Word: the Bible and illuminated or illustrated manuscripts. *Utrecht Psalter* and Caedmon's *Genesis* (Junius xi), with illustrations.
3–4. (16th c.) Early printed works: popular literature. Elizabethan "rogue" pamphlets including Robert Copland's *Hye Way to the Spyttel Hous* and Robert Greene's *A Notable Discovery of Coosnage*.
5–6. (17th c.) Emblem books and the emblem tradition. Francis Quarles's *Emblems*; George Wither's *A Collection of Emblemes*; poems by Spenser, Donne, Crashaw, Vaughan, and Herbert.
7–8. (17th c.) Miltonic vision as a source of inspiration. *Paradise Lost*, books 1 and 2, and illustrations from 1688 to present.
9–10. (18th c.) Life and manners in the eighteenth century. Designs by Hogarth and Rowlandson, accompanying "metrical illustrations"; Fielding's *Joseph Andrews*.
11. Field trip to private collection of rare books.
12–13. (19th c.) Poet-painter-prophet: the illuminated work of Blake. *Visions of the Daughters of Albion*.

14–16. (19th c.) The illustrated novel: a creative partnership. Dickens's *Dombey and Son*, illustrations by Hablot K. Browne.

17–19. (19th c.) The author as artist. Thackeray's *Vanity Fair*.

20–21. (19th c.) Interpretive illustration. Moxon edition (1857) of Tennyson's poetry with illustrations by Holman Hunt, John Millais, and Dante Gabriel Rossetti.

22–23. (19th c.) Imagination and humor: children's literature and *Alice*. Carroll's *Alice's Adventures Underground* and illustrated versions of *Alice in Wonderland*.

24–25. (19th c.) Decorative illustration. Wilde's *Salomé*, Beardsley illustrations.

26. Field trip to library rare-book room.

27–28. (20th c.) the *livre d'artiste* and the private press. Works include Ted Hughes's *Earth-Moon*, Thom Gunn's *Missed Beat*, Denise Levertov's *A Tree Telling of Orpheus* and Mona Van Duyn's *Valentine to the Wide World*.

29–30. Presentation of final papers, projects: ten-minute response to question regarding the definition of illustration and submission of related paper (7-8 pp.) or final project. Possible questions: What kind of literature is best suited to illustration? What are some characteristics of literature that permit illustration? Is an illustrated work created when an author adds text to accompany an already existing visual work? Do different genres require different types of illustration? What are some visual analogues for literary devices that may be used in the illustration of literature?

Literature and the Arts in England: An Introduction
Laura L. Doan
English, State University of New York, Geneseo

Description   Lower-division course and general humanities elective. Offered each term. No prerequisites. Meets three times a week for fifty minutes. Evaluation based on one essay (2-3 pp.) per period, a final examination, and in-class discussion.

Objectives   To introduce students to six periods in English cultural history from the medieval era to modern times; to examine one key literary work (fiction, drama, or poetry) for each period section as a basis for exploring the interrelations among literature, music, painting, sculpture, and architecture; to develop a sense of the cultural framework by viewing literature and the other arts in relation to shifting sources of patronage, the English class system, and ideological and social change.

Schedule
1. Introduction: why examine literature in relation to the other arts?
2. The medieval period. Architecture. Canterbury Cathedral, the pageants and the pilgrimage.
3–5. Poetry. Chaucer, *The Canterbury Tales* (selections); relation to medieval society and the cosmic order.
6–7. Music. The logic of the motet; affinities between the motet and Gothic architecture.
8–9. The Elizabethan period. Painting. Portraiture and the glorification of the individual (Nicholas Hilliard, Isaac Oliver, and George Gower).
10–13. Drama. Shakespeare, *A Midsummer Night's Dream*. Video. Court orders: Elizabeth I, Theseus, Oberon.
14–15. Music. Madrigals: the loss of text in polyphony (Thomas Morley, Thomas Weelkes, John Dowland, and William Byrd).
16–17. The Georgian period. Painting. Hogarth and narrativity, *Marriage à la Mode*.
18–19. Drama. Goldsmith, *She Stoops to Conquer*: theater for the bourgeoisie?
20–21. Music. Handel's oratorio for a middle-class sensibility.
22–23. The Romantic period. Painting and poetry. Blake's vision in visual and poetic imagery. (What happened to English music?)
24–25. Fiction. Brontë, *Jane Eyre*. Women, culture, and society.
26–27. The Victorian period. Poetry and painting. The Pre-Raphaelite brotherhood; a critique of Victorian society.

28–29. Music. Gilbert and Sullivan, *The Mikado*. Video. Music for the empire?

30–32. Drama. Shaw, *Pygmalion*. Video. Middle-class morality.

33–34. The modern period. Painting and sculpture. Wyndham Lewis and the vorticists: the disintegration of the order?

35–36. Fiction. Woolf, *Mrs. Dalloway*. The experiment with form.

37. Music and poetry. Walton and Sitwell, *Façade*. Provocation or playfulness?

38–39. Music and poetry. Benjamin Britten, *War Requiem*, and Basil Spence, Coventry Cathedral: the postwar moment.

40. Conclusion, review, evaluation. The period concept as a way of organizing experience.

Fantasy in Nineteenth-Century Literature and Art
Richard Dellamora
Cultural Studies, Trent University

Description   Taught in alternate years for the past decade. Designed as an elective seminar for students in third and fourth years. No prerequisites, but students usually have already taken or are currently taking at least one course in nineteenth-century English or French literature or in the history of visual arts or a studio arts course. Meets for two one-hour sessions weekly for twenty-four weeks. Students' assignments include a one-thousand-word paper based on careful observation of a relevant work of art they have seen. Some museum field trips.

Objectives   To study the antirealist tradition in nineteenth-century English, Continental, and American literature (fiction, poetry, criticism) and visual arts; to consider key works in the development of aesthetic modernism—including those of Hoffmann, Balzac, Poe, the Pre-Raphaelites, and Baudelaire—in relation to nineteenth-century visual arts and, on occasion, music.

Texts   Lang; Warner and Hough (WH).

Schedule   (by weeks)
1. Introduction: moral, aesthetic, and erotic issues in aestheticism. Wilde's letters in defense of *The Picture of Dorian Gray*.
2. E. T. A. Hoffmann, stories. 2A. Romantic landscape (with slides).
3. Poe, stories and criticism.
4. Balzac, "The Girl with the Golden Eyes." 4A. Poe, criticism.
5–6. Gautier, *Mademoiselle de Maupin*. 5A. Poe, poetry.
7. Carlyle, "The Hero as Poet." 7A. Baudelaire, criticism (WH).
8. Baudelaire, *Les fleurs du mal* and "The Painter of Modern Life" (WH).
9. Baudelaire, poetry. 9A. Ruskin, criticism (WH).
10. Melville, *Typee*. 10A. Ruskin, criticism (WH).
11. Whitman, "Calamus." 11A. J. M. W. Turner (with slides).
12. Dickinson, poetry.
13. D. G. Rossetti, poetry (Lang). 13A. Dante, *La vita nuova* (Rossetti trans.).
14. Dante. C. Rossetti, poetry.
15. Pre-Raphaelite brotherhood. 15A. Burckhardt, *The Renaissance*.
16. Heine, poetry. 16A. Burckhardt, *The Renaissance*.
17. Mallarmé, poetry. 17A. Swinburne, criticism (WH).

18. Wilde, *Salomé*. 18A. Symbolism (with slides).
19–20. Huysmans, *A rebours*. Pater, criticism (WH).
21. Wilde, *Dorian Gray*. Impressionism and postimpressionism (with slides).
22-23. Wilde, *Dorian Gray* and criticism (WH).
24. Exam.

Poetry, Art, and Music (1850-1930)
Ainslie Armstrong McLees
Romance Languages, Randolph-Macon College

Description   One-and-a-half hour lecture each week, followed by an exhibit visit, discussion, and musical presentation. Offered every second semester, organized around a theme (e.g., modernity, experimentation, Romanticism, metaphor). Developed for specialists who wish to explore the relation of their field with the arts. Roundtable discussions, slides.

Objectives   To define and trace the evolution of modern poetry, art, and music; to gain an understanding of interrelations between their aesthetics and those of other fields. Only French literature cited.

Schedule

1. Introduction. Terms: *aesthetics, modern, art, literature, music.* Goldwater and Treves, *Artists on Art*; W. Fleming, *Arts and Ideas*; Shoemaker, *Aesthetic Experience and the Humanities.* Slides: David. Music: Mozart, Beethoven.
2. Toward a modern aesthetic: emerging aesthetics and forms. Hugo, *Préface de Cromwell.* Poetry: Lamartine, Vigny. Slides: Géricault, Delacroix. Music: lied, Chopin, Liszt.
3. Beyond Romanticism: major shifts and continuities. Baudelaire: *Richard Wagner.* Poetry: Baudelaire. Music: Wagner. Slides: Manet.
4. Social issues: reflections in popular culture. Baudelaire: "Heroism of Modern Life" (*Art in Paris*). T. J. Clark, *Image of the People*, chapter 1. Poetry: Baudelaire. Art: Gavarni, Daumier. Music: Popular song.
5. Distortion of form and content: Prose poem, space, harmony and rhythm. Clark, chapter 2. Poetry: Baudelaire, Verlaine, Rimbaud. Music: Debussy. Slides: Courbet, Daumier, Millet.
6. Decadence: the arts and anguish. Satanic themes. Poetry: Baudelaire, Rimbaud. Music: Liszt, Berlioz. Slides: van Gogh, Munch.
7. Artist as visionary. Rimbaud, "Letter to Izambard," "To Paul Demeny." Poetry: Rimbaud. Music: Faustian themes, Paul Winter's *Missa Gaia.* Slides: Pre-Raphaelites, van Gogh.
8. Symbolism. Balakian, *The Symbolist Movement.* Poetry: Verlaine. Music: Fauré, Debussy. Slides: Blake, Gauguin. Discussion: Traditional symbols in religious and secular art. Personal symbolism.
9. Symbolism and impressionism. Balakian; Kronegger, *Literary Impressionism.*

Poetry: Mallarmé. Music: Debussy. Slides: Japanese prints, Monet, Pissarro, Degas, Renoir.

10. Creator as outsider. Baudelaire, "De l'essence du rire" (on mime). Poetry: Laforgue, Verlaine, Michaux, Reverdy. Slides: Renoir, Picasso. Film: *Les enfants du paradis*. Music: Chromatization.

11. The known through word, image, music: conceptualization. Shattuck, *The Banquet Years, The Innocent Eye*. Poetry: Apollinaire. Music: Tonal and atonal. Slides: Rousseau, fauves, cubists.

12. The problem of language. Valéry, *Poet's Notebook*. Poetry: Valéry. Slide: "Le cimetière marin de Sète," by Valéry. Music: Ravel.

13. Dadaism. *Dada Manifesto* (1918). Poetry: Tzara. Music: Satie. Slides: Arp, Ernst, Duchamp. Surrealist games.

14. Surrealism. Breton, *Surrealist Manifesto* (1924 and 1930). Poetry: Eluard, Desnos. Slides: Magritte, De Chirico, Ernst, Tanguy. Music: Stravinsky. Discussion: dreams and the perception of reality.

15. Term paper and roundtable discussion. Topics: evolution of musical, art, and literary forms 1800–1930. Definition of *modern*, applied to music, art, poetry.

Works Cited

Abbruzzese, Margherita. *Goya*. London: Thames, 1967.

Abrams, M. H. *The Mirror and the Lamp: Romantic Theory and the Critical Tradition*. New York: Norton, 1953.

Abse, Dannie, and Joan Abse, eds. *Voices in the Gallery: Poems and Pictures*. London: Tate, 1986.

Addison, Joseph. "The Pleasures of the Imagination." *Spectator* 412 (23 June 1712). *Addison and Steele: Selections from* the Tatler *and* The Spectator. Ed. Robert J. Allen. 2nd ed. New York: Holt, 1970. 397–405.

Agee, James, and Walker Evans. *Let Us Now Praise Famous Men*. Boston: Houghton, 1960.

Aldrich, Virgil C. *Philosophy of Art*. Englewood Cliffs: Prentice, 1963.

Alloula, Malek. *The Colonial Harem*. Trans. Myrna Godzich and Wlad Godzich. Minneapolis: U of Minnesota P, 1986.

Altick, Richard D. *Paintings from Books: Art and Literature in Britain, 1760-1900*. Columbus: Ohio State UP, 1985.

Arakawa, Shusaku. *The Mechanism of Meaning*. New York: Abrams, 1979.

Ardener, Shirley, and Edwin Ardener, eds. *Perceiving Women*. London: Malaby, 1975.

Arnheim, Rudolf. *Art and Visual Perception: A Psychology of the Creative Eye*. 2nd ed. Berkeley: U of California P, 1974.

—. "The Unity of the Arts: Time, Space, and Distance." *Yearbook of Comparative and General Literature* 25 (1976): 7–12.

Aronson, Alex. *Music and the Novel: A Study in Twentieth-Century Fiction*. Totowa: Rowman, 1980.

Babbitt, Irving. *The New Laokoon: An Essay on the Confusion of the Arts*. Boston: Houghton, 1910.

Bachelard, Gaston. *The Poetics of Space*. Trans. Maria Jolas. Boston: Beacon, 1969.

Balakian, Anna. *The Symbolist Movement: A Critical Appraisal*. New York: New York UP, 1967.

Barkan, Leonard. *Nature's Work of Art: The Human Body as Image of the World*. New Haven: Yale UP, 1975.

Barnet, Sylvan. *A Short Guide to Writing about Art*. 2nd ed. Boston: Little, 1985.

Barr, Alfred H. *Cubism and Abstract Art*. 1936. Cambridge: Belknap-Harvard UP, 1986.

Barrell, John. *The Dark Side of the Landscape: The Rural Poor in English Painting, 1730-1840*. Cambridge: Cambridge UP, 1980.

Barricelli, Jean-Pierre. *Melopoiesis: Approaches to the Study of Literature and Music.* New York: New York UP, 1988.

Barricelli, Jean-Pierre, and Joseph Gibaldi, eds. *Interrelations of Literature.* New York: MLA, 1982.

Barthes, Roland. *Camera Lucida: Reflections of Photography.* Trans. Richard Howard. New York: Hill, 1981.

—. *Image, Music, Text.* Trans. Stephen Heath. New York: Hill, 1978.

Barzun, Jacques. *Classic, Romantic, and Modern.* 2nd ed. Boston: Little, 1961.

Basilius, H. A. "Thomas Mann's Use of Musical Structure and Techniques in *Tonio Kröger.*" *Germanic Review* 19 (1944): 284–308.

Baudelaire, Charles. *Art in Paris, 1845–1862.* Trans. Jonathan Mayne. Ithaca: Cornell UP, 1981.

Beaujour, Michel. "Some Paradoxes of Description." *Yale French Studies* 61 (1981): 27–59.

Beaver, Patrick. *The Crystal Palace, 1851–1936: A Portrait of Victorian Enterprise.* London: Evelyn, 1970.

Behrendt, Stephen C. "Art as Deceptive Intruder: Audience Entrapment in Eighteenth-Century Verbal and Visual Art." *Papers on Language and Literature* 19 (1983): 37–52.

—. "Community Relations: The Roles of Artist and Audience in William Carlos Williams' *Pictures from Brueghel.*" *American Poetry* 2.2 (1985): 30–52.

Bell, Clive. *Art.* 1914. New York: Capricorn-Putnam, 1958.

Bennett, Paula. *My Life, a Loaded Gun: Female Creativity and Feminist Poetics.* Boston: Beacon, 1986.

Berger, John. *About Looking.* New York: Pantheon, 1980.

—. *Ways of Seeing.* New York: Viking, 1973.

Berger, Peter L., and Thomas Luckmann. *The Social Construction of Reality: A Treatise in the Sociology of Knowledge.* Garden City: Doubleday, 1966.

Bergman, Pär. *"Modernolatria" et "simultaneità": Recherches sur deux tendances dans l'avant garde littéraire en Italie et en France à la veille de la première guerre mondiale.* Studia Litterarum Upsaliensia 2. Stockholm: Svenska, 1962.

Bernstein, Leonard. *The Unanswered Question: Six Talks at Harvard.* Cambridge: Harvard UP, 1976.

Berthoff, Ann E. *Forming, Thinking, Writing: The Composing Imagination.* Rochelle Park: Hayden, 1978.

Bertrand, Gérard. *L'illustration de la poésie à l'époque du cubisme, 1909–1914.* Paris: Klincksieck, 1971.

Bloom, Harold. *The Anxiety of Influence.* New York: Oxford UP, 1973.

Bloomer, Kent C., and Charles W. Moore. *Body, Memory, and Architecture.* New Haven: Yale UP, 1977.

Bluestone, George. *Novels into Film.* 1957. Berkeley: U of California P, 1973.

Booth, Stephen. King Lear, Macbeth, *Indefinition, and Tragedy.* New Haven: Yale UP, 1983.

Boyum, Joy Gould. *Double Exposure: Fiction into Film.* New York: NAL, 1985.

Braswell, Mary Flowers. "Architectural Portraiture in Chaucer's *House of Fame.*" *Journal of Medieval and Renaissance Studies* 11 (1981): 101–12.

Bremer, Sidney. "Lost Continuities: Alternative Urban Visions in Chicago Novels, 1890–1915." *Soundings* 64 (1981): 29–51.

Breton, André. *Manifestoes of Surrealism.* Trans. Richard Seaver and Helen R. Lane. Ann Arbor: U of Michigan P, 1969.

—. *Poems of André Breton.* Trans. Jean-Pierre Cauvin and Mary Ann Caws. Austin: U of Texas P, 1982.

Brion-Guerry, Liliane, ed. *L'année 1913: Les formes esthétiques de l'oeuvre d'art à la veille de la première guerre mondiale.* 3 vols. Paris: Klincksieck, 1971-73.

Bronson, Bertrand H. "Literature and Music." Thorpe 127–50.

Brook, Barry S. "Sturm und Drang and the Romantic Period in Music." *Studies in Romanticism* 9 (1970): 269–84.

Brooklyn Bridge. 16 mm film. 58 min. Florentine, 1982.

Brown, Calvin S. *Music and Literature: A Comparison of the Arts.* Athens: U of Georgia P, 1948.

—. "The Relations between Music and Literature as a Field of Study." *Comparative Literature* 22 (1970): 97–107.

Brown, Marshall. "Mozart and After: The Revolution in Musical Consciousness." *Critical Inquiry* 7 (1981): 689–706.

Brown, Milton W. *The Story of the Armory Show.* Greenwich: New York Graphic Soc., [1963].

Brownell, Morris R. *Alexander Pope and the Arts of Georgian England.* Oxford: Clarendon, 1978.

Bryson, Norman. *Vision and Painting: The Logic of the Gaze.* New Haven: Yale UP, 1983.

—. *Word and Image: French Painting of the Ancien Régime.* New York: Cambridge UP, 1981.

Bunn, James. "Circle and Sequence in the Conjectural Lyric." *New Literary History* 3 (1972): 511–26.

Burckhardt, Jacob. *The Civilization of the Renaissance in Italy.* Trans. S. G. C. Middlemore. Vol. 1. New York: Harper, 1958.

Burke, Edmund. *A Philosophical Enquiry into the Origin of Our Ideas of the Sublime and Beautiful.* Ed. J. T. Boulton. London: Routledge, 1958.

Burke, Joseph. *English Art, 1714-1800.* Oxford: Clarendon, 1976.

—. "Hogarth, Handel, and Roubiliac." *Eighteenth-Century Studies* 3 (1969): 157–74.

Calinescu, Matei. "Literature and Politics." Barricelli and Gibaldi 123–49.

Calvino, Italo. *Invisible Cities.* Trans. William Weaver. New York: Harcourt, 1974.

Cassill, R. V. *Norton Anthology of Short Fiction.* 2nd ed. New York: Norton, 1982.

Cassirer, Ernst. *An Essay on Man: An Introduction to a Philosophy of Human Culture.* New Haven: Yale UP, 1944.

Cavell, Stanley. *The World Viewed: Reflections on the Ontology of Film.* Rev. ed. Cambridge: Harvard UP, 1979.

Caws, Mary Ann. *The Art of Interference: Stressed Readings in Visual and Verbal Texts.* Princeton: Princeton UP, 1989.

—. *The Eye in the Text: Essays on Perception, Mannerist to Modern.* Princeton: Princeton UP, 1981.

Celan, Paul. "Todesfuge." *Mohn und Gedächtnis.* Stuttgart: Deutsche Verlag-Anstalt, 1952. 37–39.

Cendrars, Blaise. *La prose du Transsibérien et de la petite Jehanne de France—Couleurs simultanées de Mme Delaunay-Terck.* Paris: Edition des Hommes nouveaux, 1913. Text set in standard type as "Prose du Transsibérien et de la petite Jehanne de France" in *Du monde entier. Poésies complètes: 1912-1924.* Paris: Gallimard, 1967, 27–45. 1913 original reproduced in color in Perloff, plates 1A–D.

Clark, Henry F. "Eighteenth-Century Elysiums: The Role of Association in the Landscape Movement." *Journal of the Warburg and Courtauld Institutes* 6 (1943): 165–89.

Clark, Kenneth. *The Gothic Revival: An Essay in the History of Taste.* 3rd ed. New York: Holt, 1962.

—. *The Nude: A Study in Ideal Form.* 1956. Princeton: Princeton UP, 1972.

Clark, T. J. "Clement Greenberg's Theory of Art." *The Politics of Interpretation.* Ed. W. J. T. Mitchell. Chicago: U of Chicago P, 1983. 202–20.

—. *Image of the People: Gustave Courbet and the 1848 Revolution.* Princeton: Princeton UP, 1982.

Cleaver, Dale G., and John M. Eddins. *Art and Music: An Introduction.* New York: Harcourt, 1977.

Clive, Geoffrey. *The Romantic Enlightenment.* New York: Meridian, 1960.

Clüver, Claus. "From Imagism to Concrete Poetry: Breakthrough or Blind Alley?" *Amerikanische Lyrik.* Ed. Rudolf Haas. Berlin: Schmidt, 1987. 113–30.

—. "On Intersemiotic Transposition." *Poetics Today* 10.1 (1989).

—. "Teaching Comparative Arts." *Yearbook of Comparative and General Literature* 23 (1974): 79–92.

Clüver, Claus, Mary Ellen Solt, et al. *Basic Text for C255: Modern Literature and the Other Arts: An Introduction.* Bloomington: Indiana U Comparative Literature Prog., 1986. (Available from Indiana U Bookstore, Indiana Memorial Union, Bloomington, IN 47405.)

Comito, Terry. *The Idea of the Garden in the Renaissance.* New Brunswick: Rutgers UP, 1978.

Cone, Edward T. *The Composer's Voice.* Berkeley: U of California P, 1974.

Cooke, Deryck. *An Introduction to Der Ring des Nibelungen.* Georg Solti, cond. Vienna Philharmonic. London, RDN S-1, 1969.

Coover, Robert. *Pricksongs and Descants.* New York: NAL, 1970.

Copland, Aaron. "How We Listen." Hall and Ulanov 76–82.

—. *What to Listen For in Music.* Rev. ed. New York: NAL, 1957.

Coutts-Smith, Kenneth. *The Dream of Icarus.* New York: Braziller, 1970.

Cowles, Virginia. *1913: The Defiant Swan Song.* London: Weidenfeld, 1967.

Craige, Betty Jean. *Lorca's "Poet in New York": The Fall into Consciousness.* Lexington: UP of Kentucky, 1977.

Crosby, Sumner McKnight. *The Abbey of St.-Denis, 475-1122.* New Haven: Yale UP, 1942.

Culler, Jonathan. "The Linguistic Basis of Structuralism." *Structuralism: An Introduction.* Ed. David Robey. Oxford: Clarendon, 1973. 20–36.

Davidson, Abraham A. *The Story of American Painting.* New York: Abrams, 1974.

Debussy, Claude. *Prelude to "The Afternoon of a Faun."* Ed. William W. Austin. New York: Norton, 1970.

Derrida, Jacques. *The Truth in Painting.* Trans. Geoff Bennington and Ian McLeod. Chicago: U of Chicago P, 1987.

Descartes, René. *Philosophical Writings.* Trans. Elizabeth Anscombe and Peter Thomas Geach. 1954. Indianapolis: Bobbs, 1971.

De Shazar, Mary. *Inspiring Women: Reimagining the Muse.* New York: Pergamon, 1986.

Dewey, John. "The Influence of Darwinism on Philosophy." *The Influence of Darwin on Philosophy.* Bloomington: Indiana UP, 1965. 1–19.

Donington, Robert. "Monteverdi's First Opera." Ed. Denis Arnold and Nigel Fortune, *The Monteverdi Companion.* New York: Norton: 1968. 257–76.

d'Ors, Eugenio. *Lo barroco.* Madrid: Aguilar, 1944.

Dougherty, James. *The Fivesquare City: The City in the Religious Imagination.* Notre Dame: Notre Dame UP, 1980.

Downing, Christine. *The Goddess: Mythological Images of the Feminine.* New York: Crossroad, 1981.

Drachler, Jacob, and Virginia R. Terris. *The Many Worlds of Poetry.* New York: Knopf, 1969.

Eckert, Charles W., ed. *Focus on Shakespearean Films.* Englewood Cliffs: Prentice, 1972.

Eco, Umberto. *The Role of the Reader: Explorations in the Semiotics of Texts.* Bloomington: Indiana UP, 1979.

Ehrenzweig, Anton. *The Hidden Order of Art: A Study in the Psychology of Aesthetic Imagination.* Berkeley: U of California P, 1967.

Eliade, Mircea. *The Myth of the Eternal Return.* Trans. Willard R. Trask. Princeton: Princeton UP, 1954.

Eliot, T. S. "Tradition and the Individual Talent." 1917. *Selected Essays, 1917-1932.* New York: Harcourt, 1964. 3–11.

Ellison, Ralph. Interview. *Writers at Work: The* Paris Review *Interviews.* 2nd ser. Ed. George Plimpton. New York: Viking, 1963. 319–34.

Ellmann, Richard, and Charles Feidelson, Jr., eds. *The Modern Tradition: Backgrounds of Modern Literature.* New York: Oxford UP, 1965.

Emmens, Carol A. *Short Stories on Film and Video.* Littleton: Libraries Unlimited, 1985.

Enser, A. G. S. *Filmed Books and Plays: A List of Books and Plays from which Films Have Been Made, 1928-1974.* Rev. ed. London: Deutsch, 1975.

Ernst, Bruno. *The Magic Mirror of M. C. Escher.* New York: Random, 1976.

Feldman, Edmund Burke. *Thinking about Art.* Englewood Cliffs: Prentice, 1985.

Fine, Elsa. *Women and Art: A History of Women Painters and Sculptors from the Renaissance to the Twentieth Century.* Montclair: Schram, 1978.

Fingesten, Peter. "Topographical and Anatomical Aspects of the Gothic Cathedral." *Journal of Aesthetics and Art Criticism* 20 (1961-62): 3–24.

Finlay, Ian Hamilton, and Ron Costley. *The Wartime Garden.* London: Arts Council, 1977.

Fish, Stanley. "Is There a Text in This Class?" *Is There a Text in This Class? The Authority of Interpretive Communities.* Cambridge: Harvard UP, 1980. 303–21.

—. *The Living Temple: George Herbert and Catechizing.* Berkeley: U of California P, 1978.

Flaherty, Gloria. *Opera in the Development of German Critical Thought.* Princeton: Princeton UP, 1978.

Fleming, John V. The Roman de la Rose: *A Study in Allegory and Iconography.* Princeton: Princeton UP, 1969.

Fleming, Shirley. "Thea Musgrave's Elusive *Ariadne*." *New York Times* 25 Sept. 1977: D19.

Fleming, William. *Arts and Ideas*. 7th ed. New York: Holt, 1986.

Fletcher, Angus. *The Prophetic Moment: An Essay on Spenser*. Chicago: U of Chicago P, 1971.

Foucault, Michel. *Discipline and Punish: The Birth of the Prison*. Trans. Alan Sheridan. New York: Vintage, 1979.

—. *The Order of Things: An Archaeology of the Human Sciences*. Trans. Alan Sheridan. New York: Pantheon, 1973.

Fowler, Alastair. *Kinds of Literature: An Introduction to the Theory of Genres and Modes*. Cambridge: Harvard UP, 1982.

—. "Periodization and Interart Analogies." *New Literary History* 3 (1972): 487–509.

Frank, Ellen Eve. *Literary Architecture: Essays toward a Tradition*. Berkeley: U of California P, 1979.

Frank, Joseph. "Spatial Form in Modern Literature." *Sewanee Review* 53 (1945): 221–40, 433–56, 643–53. *The Widening Gyre: Crisis and Mastery in Modern Literature*. New Brunswick: Rutgers UP, 1963. 3–62.

Fraser-Jenkins, A. D. "Cosimo de' Medici's Patronage of Architecture and the Theory of Magnificence." *Journal of the Warburg and Courtauld Institutes* 33 (1970): 162–70.

Freeman, James. "'The Roof Was Fretted Gold.'" *Comparative Literature* 27 (1975): 254–66.

Freire, Paulo. *Pedagogy of the Oppressed*. Trans. Myra Bergman Ramos. 1970. New York: Continuum, 1981.

Frenz, Horst, and Ulrich Weisstein. "Teaching the Comparative Arts: A Challenge." *College English* 18 (1956): 67–71.

Freud, Sigmund. "Creative Writers and Daydreaming." *The Standard Edition of the Complete Psychological Works of Sigmund Freud*. Ed. James Strachey, with Anna Freud. London: Hogarth, 1959. 143–53.

—. "Fragment of an Analysis of a Case of Hysteria." *Collected Papers*. Trans. Alix Strachey and James Strachey. Vol. 3. New York: Basic, 1959. 13–146.

Fried, Michael. "Art and Objecthood." *Artforum* 5 (Summer 1967): 12–23.

Fry, Edward F. *Cubism*. New York: McGraw, 1966.

Fry, Roger. "The Form-Content Distinction." *Transformations: Critical and Speculative Essays on Art*. New York: Anchor-Doubleday, 1956. 188–99.

Gadamer, Hans-Georg. *Truth and Method*. Trans. and ed. Garrett Barden and John Cumming, London: Sheed, 1975.

Gadol, Joan. *Leon Battista Alberti: Universal Man of the Early Renaissance*. Chicago: U of Chicago P, 1969.

Gardner, Helen. *Art through the Ages*. 6th ed. New York: Harcourt, 1975.

Genette, Gérard. *Figures of Literary Discourse*. Trans. Alan Sheridan. New York: Columbia UP, 1984.

Girdlestone, Cuthbert. *Mozart and His Piano Concertos*. 2nd ed. 1958. New York: Dover, 1964.

Girouard, Mark. *Robert Smythson and the Elizabethan Country House*. New Haven: Yale UP, 1983.

Goldwater, Robert, and Marco Treves, eds. *Artists on Art*. New York: Pantheon, 1958.

Gombrich, E. H. *Art and Illusion: A Study in the Psychology of Pictorial Representation*. 2nd ed. Princeton: Princeton UP, 1961.

—. "Image and Code: Scope and Limits of Conventionalism in Pictorial Representation." *Image and Code*. Ed. Wendy Steiner. Ann Arbor: U of Michigan P, 1981. 11–42.

—. *In Search of Cultural History*. Oxford: Clarendon, 1974.

—. *The Story of Art*. 14th ed. Englewood Cliffs: Prentice, 1985.

Gombrich, E. H., Julian Hochberg, and Max Black. *Art, Perception, and Reality*. Baltimore: Johns Hopkins UP, 1972.

Goodman, Nelson. *The Languages of Art: An Approach to the Theory of Symbols*. 2nd. ed. Indianapolis: Indiana UP, 1976.

Gordon, William J. *The Metaphorical Way of Learning and Knowing*. Cambridge: Porpoise, 1971.

Gorey, Edward. *Amphigorey*. New York: Berkeley, 1972.

Green, Jon D. "Music in Literature: Arthur Schnitzler's *Fräulein Else*." *New York Literary Forum* 10–11 (1983): 141–52.

Greenberg, Clement. "Towards a Newer Laocoön." *Partisan Review* 7 (July-Aug. 1940): 296–310.

Grout, Donald Jay. *The History of Western Music*. 3rd ed. New York: Norton, 1980.

Guitton, Jean. *The Madonna*. New York: Tudor, 1963.

Gutmann, Joseph. *The Temple of Solomon*. Missoula: Scholars, 1976.

Haar, James. "Pythagorean Harmony of the Universe." *Dictionary of the History of Ideas*. Ed. Philip Wiener. Vol. 4. New York: Scribner's, 1973. 38–42.

Haftmann, Werner. *Painting in the Twentieth Century*. 2 vols. New York: Praeger, 1973.

Hagstrum, Jean. *The Sister Arts: The Tradition of Literary Pictorialism in English Poetry from Dryden to Gray*. Chicago: U of Chicago P, 1958.

Hahl-Koch, Jelena, ed. *Schönberg-Kandinsky: Letters, Pictures, and Documents*. Trans. J. C. Crawford. London: Faber, 1984.

Hall, James B., and Barry Ulanov. *Modern Culture and the Arts*. 2nd ed. New York: McGraw, 1972.

Hall, Nor. *The Moon and the Virgin*. New York: Harper, 1980.

Hamon, Philippe. "Rhetorical Status of the Descriptive." *Yale French Studies* 61 (1981): 1–26.

Harding, M. Esther. *Woman's Mysteries, Ancient and Modern*. Rev. ed. New York: Harper, 1971.

Harned, Joseph, and Neil Goodwin, eds. *Art and the Craftsman: The Best of the Yale Literary Review, 1836-1961*. New Haven: Yale Literary Magazine; Carbondale: Southern Illinois UP, 1961.

Harrington, John, ed. *Film and/as Literature*. Englewood Cliffs: Prentice, 1977.

Harris, Ann Sutherland, and Linda Nochlin. *Women Artists, 1550-1950*. Los Angeles: Los Angeles County Museum of Art, 1976.

Hartman, Geoffrey, ed. *Psychoanalysis and the Question of Text*. Baltimore: Johns Hopkins UP, 1978.

Hatzfeld, Helmut. *Literature through Art: A New Approach to French Literature*. New York; Oxford UP, 1952.

Hausser, Elisabeth. *Paris au jour le jour: Les événements vus par la presse, 1900-1919*. Paris: Minuit, 1968.

Heffernan, James A. W., ed. *Space, Time, Image, Sign: Essays on Literature and the Visual Arts*. New York: Lang, 1987.

Hegel, G. W. F. *Hegel on the Arts*. Trans. Henry Paolucci. New York: Ungar, 1979.

Heisenberg, Werner. "The Idea of Nature in Contemporary Physics." *The Physicist's Conception of Nature*. Trans. Arnold J. Pomerans. New York: Harcourt, 1958. 7–31.

Herbert, Robert L., ed. *Modern Artists on Art*. Englewood Cliffs: Prentice, 1964.

Hermeren, Goran. *Influence in Art and Literature*. Princeton: Princeton UP, 1975.

Hersey, George L. *Pythagorean Palaces: Magic and Architecture in the Italian Renaissance*. Chicago: U of Chicago P, 1976.

Hibbard, G. R. "The Country House Poem of the Seventeenth Century." *Journal of the Warburg and Courtauld Institutes* 19 (1956): 159–77.

Hibbard, Howard. *Bernini*. 1965. New York: Penguin, 1984.

Hobbs, Robert Carleton, and Gail Levin. *Abstract Expressionism: The Formative Years*. Ithaca: Cornell UP, 1978.

Hofstadter, Douglas. *Gödel, Escher, Bach: An Eternal Golden Braid*. New York: Basic, 1979.

Hofstadter, Douglas, and Daniel Dennett, eds. *The Mind's I: Fantasies and Reflections on Self and Soul*. New York: Bantam, 1982.

Hollander, John. *The Untuning of the Sky: Ideas of Music in English Poetry, 1500-1700*. Princeton: Princeton UP, 1961.

Holt, Elizabeth G., ed. *A Documentary History of Art*. Vol. 2. Garden City: Anchor-Doubleday, 1958.

Honour, Hugh. *Neo-Classicism*. New York: Penguin, 1968.

Honour, Hugh, and John Fleming. *The Visual Arts: A History*. Englewood Cliffs: Prentice, 1983.

Horton, Andrew S., and Joan Margretta, eds. *Modern European Filmmakers and the Art of Adaptation*. New York: Ungar, 1981.

Hospers, John. *Meaning and Truth in the Arts*. Hamden: Archon, 1964.

Howe, Florence, and Ellen Bass, eds. *No More Masks: An Anthology of Poems by Women*. Garden City: Anchor-Doubleday, 1973.

Hughes, Robert. *The Shock of the New*. New York: Knopf, 1981.

Hughes, Spike. "Beaumarchais: Master of Intrigue." *Opera News* 5 Mar. 1977: 13–15.

Huss, Roy, and Norman Silverstein. *The Film Experience*. New York: Dutton, 1969.

Huysmans, J.-K. *Against Nature*. Trans. Robert Baldick. Baltimore: Penguin, 1968.

Iser, Wolfgang. *The Act of Reading: A Theory of Aesthetic Response*. Baltimore: Johns Hopkins, 1978.

—. *The Implied Reader: Patterns of Communication in Prose Fiction from Bunyan to Beckett*. Baltimore: John Hopkins UP, 1974.

Jakobson, Roman. "Linguistics and Poetics." *Style in Language*. Ed. Thomas A. Sebeok. Cambridge: MIT P, 1960. 350–77.

—. "On the Relation between Visual and Auditory Signs." *Selected Writings*. Vol. 2. Hague: Mouton, 1971. 338–44.

James, Henry. *Letters*. Ed. Leon Edel. Vol. 4. Cambridge: Belknap-Harvard, 1984.

Jameson, Fredric. *Marxism and Form: Twentieth-Century Dialectical Theories of Literature*. Princeton: Princeton UP, 1974.

Janeway, Elizabeth. *Man's World, Woman's Place: A Study in Social Mythology*. New York: Morrow, 1971.

Janson, H. W. *History of Art*. 3rd ed. New York: Abrams, 1986.

Janson, H. W., and Joseph Kerman. *History of Art and Music.* Englewood Cliffs: Prentice, 1969.

Jauss, Hans Robert. *Towards an Aesthetic of Response.* Trans. Timothy Bahti. Minneapolis: U of Minnesota P, 1982.

Jensen, H. James. *The Muses' Concord: Literature, Music, and the Visual Arts in the Baroque Age.* Bloomington: Indiana UP, 1976.

Johnson, J. Theodore, Jr. "Orpheus and the Orphic Mode in Literature and the Fine Arts." *Register of the Spencer Museum of Art* 5.9 (1981): 66–87.

Jones, Peter, ed. *Imagist Poetry.* London: Penguin, 1972.

Jorgens, Jack J. *Shakespeare on Film.* Bloomington: Indiana UP, 1976.

Jung, C. G. "Psychology and Literature." *Modern Man in Search of a Soul.* Trans. W. S. Dell and C. F. Baynes. New York: Harcourt, 1933. 152–72.

Kagan, Andrew. *Paul Klee: Art and Music.* Ithaca: Cornell UP, 1983.

Kandinsky, Wassily. *Complete Writings on Art.* Ed. Kenneth C. Lindsay and Peter Vergo. 2 vols. Boston: Hall, 1982.

Kasulis, Thomas P. "Questioning." *The Art and Craft of Teaching.* ed. Margaret M. Gullette. Cambridge: Harvard–Danforth Center for Teaching and Learning, 1982. 38–48.

Kaufmann, U. Milo. *The Pilgrim's Progress and the Traditions in Puritan Meditation.* New Haven: Yale UP, 1966.

Kazin, Alfred. *The Writer and the City.* 16 mm film. 29 min. University-at-Large, 1970.

Kendrick, Laura. "Chaucer's *House of Fame* and the French Palais de Justice." *Studies in the Age of Chaucer* 6 (1984): 121–33.

Kennedy, X. J. *An Introduction to Poetry.* 5th ed. Boston: Little, 1982.

Kerman, Joseph. *Listen.* 3rd ed. New York: Worth, 1980.

—. *Opera as Drama.* New York: Vintage-Knopf, 1956.

Kestner, Joseph. "A World Apart: . . . A Subculture That Inspired Such Romantic Artists as Dumas and Verdi." *Opera News* 28 Mar. 1981: 13–14, 26–28.

—. "Woe to the Vanquished: The Characters Inhabiting Murger's *Vie de Bohème* and How They Emerged in Puccini's Opera." *Opera News* 19 Mar. 1977: 15 17.

Keyshian, Harry. *Medieval and Renaissance Plays (Excluding Shakespeare) on Record, Film, and Television Tape.* Madison: H. Keyshian [English, Fairleigh Dickinson U, Madison], 1972.

Klein, Michael, and Gillian Parker, eds. *The English Novel and the Movies.* New York: Ungar, 1981.

Koestler, Arthur. "Humour and Wit." *Janus: A Summing Up.* London: Hutchinson, 1978. 109–21.

Kozintsev, Grigorii. *King Lear, the Space of Tragedy: The Diary of a Film Director.* Berkeley: U of California P, 1977.

Kramer, Lawrence. *Music and Poetry: The Nineteenth Century and After.* Berkeley: U of California P, 1984.

Krauss, Rosalind. *The Originality of the Avant-Garde and Other Modernist Myths.* Cambridge: MIT P, 1985.

Krauss, Rosalind, et al. *L'Amour Fou: Photography and Surrealism.* New York: Abbeville, 1985.

Krieger, Murray. "The Ekphrastic Principle and the Still Movement of Poetry: Or, *Laokoön* Revisited." *The Play and Place of Criticism.* Baltimore: Johns Hopkins UP, 1967. 105–28.

Krinsky, Carol Herselle. "Representations of the Temple of Solomon before 1500." *Journal of the Warburg and Courtauld Institutes* 33 (1970): 1–19.

Kronegger, Maria Elizabeth. *Literary Impressionism.* New Haven: New Coll. and Univ. P, 1973.

Kuhns, Richard. *Psychoanalytic Theory of Art: A Philosophy of Art on Developmental Principles.* New York: Columbia UP, 1983.

Lacan, Jacques. *The Four Fundamental Concepts of Psychoanalysis.* Trans. Alan Sheridan-Smith. New York: Norton, 1981.

Landy, Alice, ed. *The Heath Introduction to Literature.* Lexington: Heath, 1980.

Lang, Cecil Y., ed. *The Pre-Raphaelites and Their Circle.* 2nd ed. Chicago: U of Chicago P, 1975.

Langer, Susanne K. "Deceptive Analogies: Specious and Real Relationships among the Arts." Hall and Ulanov 22–31.

—. *Feeling and Form.* New York: Scribner's, 1953.

—. *Mind: An Essay on Human Feeling.* Vol. 1. Baltimore: Johns Hopkins UP, 1967.

—. *Philosophy in a New Key.* 3rd ed. Cambridge: Harvard UP, 1960.

Laude, Jean. "On the Analysis of Poems and Paintings." *New Literary History* 3 (1972): 471–86.

Lauritzen, Monica. *Jane Austen's* Emma *on Television: A Study of a BBC Classic Serial.* Goteborg: Acta Universitatis Gothoburgensis, 1981.

Lauter, Estella. *Women as Mythmakers: Poetry and Visual Art by Twentieth-Century Women.* Bloomington; Indiana UP, 1984.

Lauter, Estella, and Carol S. Rupprecht, eds. *Feminist Archetypal Theory.* Knoxville: U of Tennessee P, 1985.

Lawrence, Mary. *Mother and Child.* New York: Crowell, 1975.

Lee, Rensselaer W. *Names on Trees: Ariosto into Art.* Princeton: Princeton UP, 1976.

—. *Ut Pictura Poesis: The Humanistic Theory of Painting.* New York: Norton, 1967.

Lees-Milne, James. *Baroque in Italy.* London: Batsford, 1959.

Lehmann, Karl. "The Dome of Heaven." *Modern Perspectives in Western Art History.* Ed. W. Eugene Kleinbauer. New York: Holt, 1971. 227–70.

Leichtentritt, Hugo. *Music, History, Ideas.* Cambridge: Harvard UP, 1958.

Leonard, William T. *Theatre: Stage to Screen to Television.* Metuchen: Scarecrow, 1981.

Lessing, Gotthold Ephraim. *Laocoön: An Essay on the Limits of Painting and Poetry.* Trans. Edward A. McCormick. 1962. Baltimore: Johns Hopkins UP, 1984.

Lockspeiser, Edward. *Music and Painting: A Study in Comparative Ideas from Turner to Schönberg.* London: Cassell, 1973.

Lorenz, Konrad, Lewis Mumford, and Aaron Copland, *The City.* 16 mm film. 44 min. Pyramid Films, 1939.

Machlis, Joseph. *The Enjoyment of Music.* 3rd ed. New York: Norton, 1970.

Mack, Maynard. *The Garden and the City: Retirement and Politics in the Late Poetry of Pope, 1731-1743.* Toronto: U of Toronto P, 1969.

—, gen. ed. *The Norton Anthology of World Masterpieces,* 5th ed. 2 vols. New York: Norton, 1985.

Magill, Frank N., ed. *Cinema: The Novel into Film.* Pasadena: Salem, 1980.

Manvell, Roger. *Shakespeare and the Film.* London: Dent, 1971.

—. *Theater and Film: A Comparative Study of the Two Forms of Dramatic Art, and of the Problems of Adaptation of Stage Plays into Films.* Rutherford: Fairleigh Dickinson UP, 1979.

Maravall, José Antonio. *Culture of the Baroque: Analysis of a Historical Structure.* Trans. Terry Cochran. Minneapolis: U of Minnesota P, 1986.

Marcus, Fred H. *Film and Literature: Contrasts in Media.* New York: Intext, 1971.

—. *Short Story/Short Film.* Englewood Cliffs: Prentice, 1977.

Marin, Louis. "Toward a Theory of Reading in the Visual Arts: Poussin's *The Arcadian Shepherds.*" Suleiman and Crosman 292–304.

Marino, Giambattista. *Opere scelte.* Ed. Giovanni Getto. 2nd ed. Vol. 1. Torino: UTET, 1962.

Martin, John Rupert. *Baroque.* New York: Harper, 1977.

Martin, Marianne W. *Futurist Art and Theory, 1909–1915.* Oxford: Clarendon, 1968.

Martz, Louis L. *The Wit of Love: Donne, Carew, Crashaw, Marvell.* Notre Dame: U of Notre Dame P, 1969.

Mast, Gerald. "Literature and Film." Barricelli and Gibaldi 278–306.

Mast, Gerald, and Marshall Cohen, eds. *Film Theory and Criticism.* 3rd ed. New York: Oxford UP, 1985.

McClung, William Alexander. *The Architecture of Paradise: Survivals of Eden and Jerusalem.* Berkeley: U of California P, 1983.

—. *The Country House in English Renaissance Poetry.* Berkeley: U of California P, 1977.

McDougal, Stuart Y. *Made into Movies: From Literature to Film.* New York: Holt, 1985.

McFarland, Thomas. "Literature and Philosophy." Barricelli and Gibaldi 25–46.

McMillan, Douglas J., ed. *Approaches to Teaching Goethe's Faust.* New York: MLA, 1987.

Meltzer, Françoise. *Salome and the Dance of Writing: Portraits of Mimesis in Literature.* Chicago: U of Chicago P, 1987.

Merriman, James D. "The Parallel of the Arts: Some Misgivings and a Faint Affirmation." *Journal of Aesthetics and Art Criticism* 31 (1972-73): 153–64, 309–21.

Miller, Gabriel. *Screening the Novel: Rediscovered American Fiction in Film.* New York: Ungar, 1980.

Miller, Nancy K., ed. *The Poetics of Gender.* New York: Columbia UP, 1986.

Mirollo, James V. *Mannerism and Renaissance Poetry: Concept, Mode, Inner Design.* New Haven: Yale UP, 1984.

—. *The Poet of the Marvelous: Giambattista Marino.* New York: Columbia UP, 1963.

Mitchell, W. J. T. *Blake's Composite Art: A Study of the Illuminated Poetry.* Princeton: Princeton UP, 1977.

—. *Iconology: Image, Text, Ideology.* Chicago: U of Chicago P, 1986.

—. "Visible Language: Blake's Wond'rous Art of Writing." *Romanticism and Contemporary Criticism.* Ed. Morris Eaves and Michael Fischer. Ithaca: Cornell UP, 1986. 46–95.

Mohr, Jean, and Edward Said. *After the Last Sky: Palestinian Lives.* New York: Pantheon, 1986.

Moore, Honor. *The New Women's Theater: Ten Plays by Contemporary Women.* New York: Vintage, 1977.

Mulvey, Laura. "Visual Pleasure and Narrative Cinema." Mast and Cohen 803–16.

Munro, Eleanor. *Originals: American Women Artists.* New York: Simon, 1979.

Munro, Thomas. *The Arts and Their Interrelations.* Rev. ed. Cleveland: Case Western Reserve UP, 1967.

Neihardt, John G. *Black Elk Speaks*. Lincoln: U of Nebraska P, 1979.

Nelson, Robert J. *Play within a Play: The Dramatist's Conception of His Art: Shakespeare to Anouilh*. 1958. New York: Da Capo, 1971.

Nemser, Cindy. *Art Talk: Conversations with Twelve Women Artists*. New York: Scribner's, 1975.

Neubauer, John. *The Emancipation of Music from Language: Departure from Mimesis in Eighteenth-Century Aesthetics*. New Haven: Yale UP, 1986.

Neumann, Erich. *The Great Mother*. Princeton; Princeton UP, 1955.

Nietzsche, Friedrich. *The Gay Science*. Trans. Walter Kaufmann. New York: Random, 1974.

1913. Paris: Bibliothèque Nationale, 1983. Exhibition catalog.

Oates, Joyce Carol. "Imaginary Cities: America." *Literature and the Urban Experience*. Ed. Michael Jaye and Ann Chalmers Watts. New Brunswick: Rutgers UP, 1981. 11–33.

Panofsky, Erwin. *Abbot Suger on the Abbey Church of St.-Denis and Its Art Treasures*. 2nd ed. Princeton: Princeton UP, 1979.

—. "Et in Arcadia Ego: Poussin and the Elegiac Tradition." *Meaning in the Visual Arts* 295–320.

—. *Gothic Architecture and Scholasticism*. 1951. New York: NAL, 1957.

—. "The History of Art as a Humanistic Discipline." *Meaning in the Visual Arts* 1–25.

—. *Meaning in the Visual Arts*. Garden City: Anchor-Doubleday, 1955.

—. "Style and Medium in the Motion Pictures." Mast and Cohen 215–33.

Park, Roy. "'Ut Pictura Poesis': The Nineteenth-Century Aftermath." *Journal of Aesthetics and Art Criticism* 28 (1978-79): 155–64.

Pascal, Roy. "Narrative Fictions and Reality." *Novel* 11 (1977): 40–50.

Pater, Walter. *The Renaissance: Studies in Art and Poetry*. New York: Macmillan, 1904.

Peary, Gerald, and Roger Shatzkin, eds. *The Modern American Novel and the Movies*. New York: Ungar, 1978.

—. *The Classic American Novel and the Movies*. New York: Ungar, 1978.

Peirce, C. S. *Collected Papers*. Vols. 2 and 4. 1932. Cambridge: Harvard UP, 1977.

Perez-Gomez, Alberto. *Architecture and the Crisis of Modern Science*. Cambridge: MIT P, 1983.

Perloff, Marjorie. *The Futurist Moment: Avant-Garde, Avant Guerre, and the Language of Rupture*. Chicago: U of Chicago P, 1986.

Petersen, Karen, and Mary Stofflet. *American Women Artists: Twentieth Century*. Slide program. New York: Harper, 1981.

—. *Women Artists: Photography*. Slide program. New York: Harper, 1981.

—. *Women Artists: Sculpture*. Slide program. New York: Harper, 1981.

Petersen, Karen, and J. J. Wilson. *Women Artists: Images, Themes, and Dreams*. Slide Program. New York: Harper, 1975.

—. *Women Artists: Third World*. Slide program. New York: Harper, 1975.

—. *Women Artists: Twentieth Century*. Slide program. New York: Harper, 1975.

Petersson, Robert T. *The Art of Ecstasy: Teresa, Bernini, and Crashaw*. New York: Atheneum, 1970.

Pevsner, Nikolaus. *High Victorian Design: A Study of the Exhibits of 1851*. London: Architectural P, 1951.

Pickering, James, ed. *The City in American Literature*. New York: Harper, 1977.

Potter, John, and Suzanne Potter. "The Tempest Within: Love and Glory Create the Stormy Psychological Weather of Shakespeare's *Othello.*" *Opera News* 4 Feb. 1978: 9–11.

Pratt, Kenneth J. "Rome as Eternal City." *Journal of the History of Ideas* 26 (1965): 25–44.

Praz, Mario. *The Flaming Heart.* New York: Anchor-Doubleday, 1958.

—. *Mnemosyne: The Parallel between Literature and the Visual Arts.* Princeton: Princeton UP, 1970.

Queneau, Raymond. *Exercises in Style.* Trans. Barbara Wright. New York: New Directions, 1981.

Reynolds, Graham. *Turner.* London: Thames, 1969.

Richardson, Robert. *Fiction and the Camera Eye: Visual Consciousness in Film and the Modern Novel.* Charlottesville: UP of Virginia, 1976.

Riffaterre, Michael. "Descriptive Imagery." *Yale French Studies* 61 (1981): 107–25.

Rimbaud, Arthur. *Complete Works.* Trans. Paul Schmidt. New York: Harper, 1976.

Rolland, Romain. *Beethoven the Creator.* Trans. Ernest Newman. New York: Dover, 1964.

Rose, Jacqueline. *Sexuality in the Field of Vision.* London: Verso, 1986.

Rosen, Charles. *The Classical Style.* New York: Norton, 1972.

Rosenau, Helen. *Boullée and Visionary Architecture.* London: Academy, 1976.

—. *Visions of the Temple: The Image of the Temple of Jerusalem in Judaism and Christianity.* London: Oresko, 1979.

Rosenberg, Harold. "Action Painting: Crisis and Distortion." *The Anxious Object: Art Today and Its Audience.* New York: Collier, 1964. 39–47.

Rosenblum, Robert. *Transformations in Late Eighteenth-Century Art.* Princeton: Princeton UP, 1969.

Rubenstein, Charlotte Streifer. *American Women Artists from Early Indian Times to the Present.* Boston: Avon, 1982.

Russell, Jeffrey Burton. *The Devil: Perceptions of Evil from Antiquity to Primitive Christianity.* Ithaca: Cornell UP, 1977.

—. *Lucifer: The Devil in the Middle Ages.* Ithaca: Cornell UP, 1984.

—. *Mephistopheles: The Devil in the Modern World.* Ithaca: Cornell UP, 1986.

—. *Satan: The Early Christian Tradition.* Ithaca: Cornell UP, 1981.

Rykwert, Joseph. *The First Moderns: The Architects of the Eighteenth Century.* Cambridge: MIT P, 1980.

—. *On Adam's House in Paradise: The Primitive Hut in Architectural History.* Cambridge: MIT P, 1972.

Sartre, Jean-Paul. "Existentialism." *Existentialism and Human Emotions.* Trans. Bernard Frechtman. New York: Philosophical Library, 1957. 9–51.

Schapiro, Meyer. *Modern Art: Nineteenth and Twentieth Centuries.* New York: Braziller, 1978.

—. "On Some Problems in the Semiotics of Visual Art: Field and Vehicle in Image-Signs." *Semiotica* 1 (1969): 223–42

Scher, Steven Paul. "How Meaningful is 'Musical' in Literary Criticism?" *Yearbook of Comparative and General Literature* 21 (1972): 52–56.

—. "Literature and Music." Barricelli and Gibaldi 225–50.

—. "Thomas Mann's 'Verbal Score': Adrian Leverkühn's Symbolic Confession." *MLN* 82 (1967): 403–20.

—. *Verbal Music in German Literature.* New Haven: Yale UP, 1968.

Schmidgall, Gary. *Literature as Opera.* New York: Oxford UP, 1977.

Schwartz, Murray M., and David Willbern. "Literature and Psychology." Barricelli and Gibaldi 205–24.

Schor, Naomi. *Reading in Detail: Aesthetics and the Feminine.* New York: Methuen, 1987.

Shattuck Roger. *The Banquet Years: The Origins of the Avant Garde in France, 1885 to World War I.* Rev. ed. New York: Vintage, 1968.

—. *The Innocent Eye: On Modern Literature and the Arts.* New York: Farrar, 1984.

—, ed. and trans. *Selected Writings of Guillaume Apollinaire.* New York: New Directions, 1971.

Shoemaker, F. *Aesthetic Experience and the Humanities.* 1943. New York: AMS, 1986.

Simson, Otto von. *The Gothic Cathedral: The Origins of Gothic Architecture and the Medieval Concept of Order.* Rev. ed. Princeton: Princeton UP, 1962.

Sinyard, Neil. *Filming Literature: The Art of Screen Adaptation.* London: Croom, 1986.

Slatkin, Wendy. *Women Artists in History.* Englewood Cliffs: Prentice, 1985.

Smarr, Janet L., ed. *Italian Renaissance Tales.* Rochester: Solaris, 1983.

Solt, Mary Ellen, ed. *Concrete Poetry: A World View.* Bloomington: Indiana UP, 1968.

Sontag, Susan. *Against Interpretation.* 1966. New York: Farrar, 1986.

Spaethling, Robert. *Music and Mozart in the Life of Goethe.* Columbia, SC: Camden, 1987.

Stein, Jack M. *Poem and Music in the German Lied from Gluck to Hugo Wolf.* Cambridge: Harvard UP, 1971.

—. *Richard Wagner and the Synthesis of the Arts.* Detroit: Wayne State UP, 1960.

Steinberg, Leo. *Other Criteria: Confrontations with Twentieth-Century Art.* New York: Oxford UP, 1972.

Steiner, Wendy. *The Colors of Rhetoric: Problems in the Relation between Modern Literature and Painting.* Chicago: U of Chicago P, 1982.

—. *Exact Resemblance to Exact Resemblance: The Literary Portraiture of Gertrude Stein.* New Haven: Yale UP, 1978.

Stern, Kenneth. "*Norma*'s Gallic Roots: Bellini's Bel Canto Tragedy Grew from a Drama by Alexandre Soumet." *Opera News* 17 Mar. 1979: 13–15, 34.

Stevens, Wallace. "The Relations between Poetry and Painting." Hall and Ulanov 274–85.

Stewart, Stanley. *The Enclosed Garden: The Tradition and the Image in Seventeenth-Century Poetry.* Madison: U of Wisconsin P, 1966.

Stokes, Adrian. *The Invitation in Art.* London: Tavistock, 1965.

Stonewater, Jerry K. "Strategies for Problem Solving." *New Directions for Teaching and Learning* 3 (1980): 33–57.

Street, Douglas, ed. *Children's Novels and the Movies.* New York: Ungar, 1983.

Strunk, Oliver, ed. *Source Readings in Music History: From Classical Antiquity through the Romantic Era.* New York: Norton, 1950.

Suleiman, Susan, ed. *The Female Body in Western Culture: Contemporary Perspectives.* Cambridge: Harvard UP, 1985.

Suleiman, Susan, and Inge Crosman, eds. *The Reader in the Text.* Princeton: Princeton UP, 1980.

Sullivan, Victoria, and James Hatch, eds. *Plays by and about Women: An Anthology.* New York: Vintage, 1973.

Swift, Jonathan. *The Writings of Jonathan Swift*. Ed. Robert A. Greenberg and William B. Piper. New York: Norton, 1973.

Sypher, Wylie, ed. *Art History: An Anthology of Modern Criticism*. New York: Vintage, 1963.

—. *Four Stages of Renaissance Style: Transformations in Art and Literature, 1400–1700*. Anchor-Doubleday, 1955.

—. *Rococo to Cubism in Art and Literature: Transformations in Style in Art and Literature from the Eighteenth to the Twentieth Century*. New York: Vintage, 1963.

Talon, Henri. "Space and the Hero in *The Pilgrim's Progress*: A Study in the Meaning of an Allegorical Universe." *Etudes Anglaises* 14 (1961): 124–30.

Taylor, René. "Hermeticism and Mystical Architecture in the Society of Jesus." *Baroque Art: The Jesuit Contribution*. Ed. Rudolf Wittkower and Irma B. Jaffe. New York: Fordham UP, 1972. 63–94.

Thomas, Dylan. "Notes on the Art of Poetry." Hall and Ulanov 267–73.

Thorpe, James, ed. *Relations of Literary Study: Essays on Interdisciplinary Contributions*. New York: MLA, 1967.

Todorov, Tzvetan. *Mikhail Bakhtin: The Dialogic Principle*. Minneapolis: Minnesota UP, 1984.

Trachtenberg, Alan. *Brooklyn Bridge: Fact and Symbol*. New York: Oxford UP, 1965.

Tuchman, Barbara. *The Proud Tower: A Portrait of the World before the War, 1890–1914*. New York: Macmillan, 1966.

Uspenskij, Boris. *A Poetics of Composition: The Structure of the Artistic Text and Typology of Compositional Form*. Trans. Valentina Zavarin and Susan Wittig. Berkeley: U of California P, 1973.

Varriano, John. *Italian Baroque and Rococo Architecture*. New York: Oxford UP, 1986.

Vickery, John B. "Literature and Myth." Barricelli and Gibaldi 67–89.

Vitruvius. *De architectura*. Ed. and trans. Frank Granger. Loeb Classical Library. London: Heinemann; New York: Putnam's, 1931.

—. *The Ten Books of Architecture*. Trans. Morris Hicky Morgan. 1914. New York: Dover, 1960.

Vitz, Paul C., and Arnold B. Glimcher. *Modern Art and Modern Science: The Parallel Analysis of Vision*. New York: Praeger, 1984.

Wagner, Geoffrey. *The Novel and the Cinema*. Rutherford: Fairleigh Dickinson UP, 1975.

Wallace, Robert K. *Emily Brontë and Beethoven: Romantic Equilibrium in Fiction and Music*. Athens: U of Georgia P, 1986.

—. *Jane Austen and Mozart: Classical Equilibrium in Fiction and Music*. Athens: U of Georgia P, 1983.

—. "Teaching *Moby-Dick* in the Light of Turner." *Approaches to Teaching Melville's Moby-Dick*. Ed. Martin Bickman. New York: MLA, 1985. 135–39.

Warner, Eric, and Graham Hough, eds. *Strangeness and Beauty: An Anthology of Aesthetic Criticism, 1840–1910*. 2 vols. Cambridge: Cambridge UP, 1983.

Warnke, Frank J., ed. *European Metaphysical Poetry*. New Haven: Yale UP, 1961.

Washington, Mary Helen. *Black-Eyed Susans*. Garden City: Anchor-Doubleday, 1975.

Wayne, Don E. *Penshurst: The Semiotics of Place and the Poetics of History*. Madison: U of Wisconsin P, 1984.

Wees, William. *Vorticism and the English Avant-Garde*. Toronto: U of Toronto P, 1972.

Weisstein, Ulrich. "Literature and the Visual Arts." Barricelli and Gibaldi 251–77.

—. *Comparative Literature and Literary Theory: Survey and Introduction.* Trans. William Riggan. Bloomington: Indiana UP, 1973.

Weisstein, Ulrich, et al. "Comparing the Arts." *Yearbook of Comparative and General Literature* 25 (1976): 5–30.

Welch, Jeffrey E. *Literature and Film: An Annotated Bibliography, 1900–1977.* New York: Garland, 1981.

Wellek, René. "The Concept of Baroque in Literary Scholarship." *Concepts of Criticism.* Ed. Stephen G. Nichols, Jr. New Haven: Yale UP, 1963. 69–127.

—. "The Parallelism between Literature and the Arts." *English Institute Annual 1941.* New York: Columbia UP, 1942. 29–63.

Wellek, René, and Austin Warren. *Theory of Literature.* 3rd ed. New York: Harcourt, 1962.

West, Nathanael. Miss Lonelyhearts *and* The Day of the Locust. New York: New Directions, 1962.

Wheeler, Monroe. *Soutine.* New York: Mus. of Modern Art, 1950.

Whitman, Cedric H. *Homer and the Heroic Tradition.* Cambridge: Harvard UP, 1958.

Wilson, Donald. "*Anna Karenina*: Novel into Drama." *New York Times* 5 Feb. 1978: D29.

Winn, James A. *Unsuspected Eloquence: A History of the Relations between Poetry and Music.* New Haven: Yale UP, 1981.

Wittgenstein, Ludwig. *Philosophical Investigations.* Trans. G. E. M. Anscombe. New York: Macmillan, 1953.

Wittkower, Rudolf. *Architectural Principles in the Age of Humanism.* 1952. New York: Norton, 1971.

—. *Palladio and English Palladianism.* London: Thames, 1974.

Wolfe, Tom. *The Painted Word.* New York: Bantam, 1976.

Wolff, Toni. *Structural Forms of the Feminine Psyche.* Zurich: Jung Inst., 1956.

Wölfflin, Heinrich. *Renaissance and Baroque.* Trans. Kathrin Simon. Ithaca: Cornell UP, 1967. Trans. of *Renaissance und Barock.* 1888.

Worth, Sol. "Pictures Can't Say Ain't." *Versus* 12 (1975): 85–108.

Yates, Frances A. *The Art of Memory.* Chicago: U of Chicago P, 1966.

Yinger, Robert J. "Can We Really Teach Them to Think?" *New Directions for Teaching and Learning* 3 (1980): 11–31.

Index